ALSO BY LISA HEFFERNAN
(writing as Lisa Endlich)

*Be the Change: Candid Conversations
with the World's Most Successful Philanthropists*

Optical Illusions: Lucent and the Crash of Telecom

Goldman Sachs: The Culture of Success

Praise for *Grown and Flown*

"Heffernan and Harrington deliver the book we've all been waiting for: a wise, researched, and *essential* handbook on raising late adolescents and young adults. At once practical and profound, *Grown and Flown* brims with sensible advice *and* describes how we can support older children while fostering their independence."

—Lisa Damour, Ph.D., author of the *New York Times* bestsellers *Under Pressure* and *Untangled*

"Lisa Heffernan and Mary Dell Harrington have created an extraordinary digital community of parents and caregivers. With this new book, they expand their reach, providing a dynamic melding of knowledge sourced from experts with that of members in the parenting community speaking from experience. Together, they provide the fodder for starting those ever-important 'digital watercooler' conversations about raising teens. And they offer forward-looking ideas in helping families with teens to build not only independence in them today but the healthy *inter*dependence we all seek far into the future with our children as they transition into adult lives."

—Ken Ginsburg, M.D., MSEd, cofounder of the Center for Parent and Teen Communication and adolescent medicine specialist at the Children's Hospital of Philadelphia

"Children often give you greater purpose and provide a cadence to your daily life. Even though I always told myself 'roots and wings,' when I became an empty nester, it was tough. I highly recommend *Grown and Flown* to every parent to help with this challenging transition!"

—Katie Couric

"*Grown and Flown* is chock-full of grounded, expert advice on how to support your teen in their transition to young adulthood. There's something for every parent in this smart, accessible guide."

—Lori Gottlieb, author of the *New York Times* bestseller *Maybe You Should Talk to Someone*

"There is no better company in this gnarly, possibly fantastic transition than *Grown and Flown*. The perspective in these pages has been invaluable to me." —Kelly Corrigan, author of the *New York Times* bestseller *Tell Me More*

"This book will be my treasured handbook for years to come as I cope with my kids getting older and (perhaps?) fleeing the coop. I'm so grateful for Lisa and Mary Dell for their research, insights and advice that will help so many other moms and me as we navigate uncertain times ahead." —Zibby Owens, founder of Moms Don't Have Time to Read Books

"This book is for any parent who wants to build the strong, healthy, flexible relationships you need to help your teenager navigate the complexity of modern life and emerge at the other end ready to launch successfully. As a college president, I hope every parent will read this book and use it as a guide for interacting with and guiding their children." —Dr. Adam Weinberg, president of Denison University

"This book is even better than a sage on speed-dial. Lisa Heffernan and Mary Dell Harrington intuited a vast need when they cofounded an online parent community. Consider *Grown and Flown* an indispensable, non-judgmental lifeline to answer endless questions, even if your baby is fifteen—or twenty-five." —Sally Koslow, author of *Slouching Toward Adulthood* and *Another Side of Paradise*

"I'm constantly treading the line between letting my kids know that they can count on me for everything . . . and figuring out a way to let them fail. *Grown and Flown* is such a great resource for this—among a million other things, it teaches me how and when to get out of their way." —Jenny Rosenstrach, *New York Times* bestselling author of *How to Celebrate Everything*

GROWN

and

FLOWN

How to Support Your Teen,
Stay Close as a Family, and
Raise Independent Adults

LISA HEFFERNAN *and*
MARY DELL HARRINGTON

FLATIRON
BOOKS
NEW YORK

To Mel, Walker, and Annie
To Mark, Sam, Tommy, and Harry
You are everything.

GROWN AND FLOWN. Copyright © 2019 by Lisa Heffernan and Mary Dell Harrington. All rights reserved. Printed in the United States of America. For information, address Flatiron Books, 120 Broadway, New York, NY 10271.

www.flatironbooks.com

Grown and Flown® and Grown & Flown® are registered trademarks of Grown and Flown LLC.

Library of Congress Cataloging-in-Publication Data

Names: Heffernan, Lisa, 1959– author. | Harrington, Mary Dell, author.
Title: Grown and flown : how to support your teen, stay close as a family, and raise independent adults / Lisa Heffernan and Mary Dell Harrington.
Description: First edition. | New York : Flatiron Books, [2019] |
Identifiers: LCCN 2019016761 | ISBN 9781250188946 (hardcover) | ISBN 9781250188953 (ebook)
Subjects: LCSH: Parent and teenager. | Parenting. | Teenagers—Social conditions.
Classification: LCC HQ799.15 .H445 2019 | DDC 306.874—dc23
LC record available at https://lccn.loc.gov/2019016761

ISBN 978-1-250-75137-9 (trade paperback)

Our books may be purchased in bulk for promotional, educational, or business use. Please contact your local bookseller or the Macmillan Corporate and Premium Sales Department at 1-800-221-7945, extension 5442, or by email at MacmillanSpecialMarkets@macmillan.com.

First Flatiron Books Paperback Edition: 2020

10 9 8 7 6 5 4 3 2 1

Contents

Grown and Flown

Life gave them to me. I'm preparing myself, as best I can, to give them back to life.

—CHARLES M. BLOW

We had a little bit of Mom Swagger going on. We had overparented each of our oldest sons straight into college, and our younger kids seemed to be making progress through high school. We had started a website that focused on the Grown and Flown years of parenting—the period when our offspring are moving through ages fifteen to twenty-five—and our roles as parents are changing. We had gathered other writers whose work we admired and published them on the site. We had cultivated a small audience, established an online community, and just for a moment, we thought we knew what we were doing.

Then came the email.

The writer of the email, Janet, said she had been following us on social media, reading our site, and had gleaned a few useful things along the way. Flattery is a powerful force. Given that this was our first fan letter, Swagger might have just tilted over into Smugness, but we read on.

> My daughter Kate is starting college in September
> and my husband was just diagnosed with stage 4
> cancer. Financially, thankfully, we should be okay.
> My concern is my daughter and getting her off to

a good and mentally sound start. I couldn't find
anything online—then I thought of you.

I want her to go and be excited and happy about
her new start, without having to worry about her
father. Pipe dream, I know, but I'm hoping to get
her as close to that as possible. My first thought
is to reach out to the college to find a person—
the person—to be a contact. I don't want to have to
call and explain everything five times before I
can get her some support.

Any advice, suggestions, or resources you could
provide would be most welcome.

To say that we had not one useful piece of advice to offer our first
fan would be an understatement. We, who had effortlessly poured
ourselves onto the digital page up to this point, were at a loss for
words. We could not, dared not, fob her off with some sort of parenting platitude that would make us sound knowledgeable. We offered
our sorrow and our support and told her we were thinking about her.

And then we did what parents have always done, something
that would help us to become better parents and hopefully help the
millions of readers who would later find Grown and Flown to become better parents. We admitted that we had absolutely no idea
what to do. We fessed up to having little insight to give her.

Instead, we offered the one thing we could and said we would
ask other parents, our larger community, what they would do in
her situation. We acknowledged to her and our readers that with
only five data points—the kids in our two families—we didn't
know much outside of our own experiences. Alongside her, we had
much to learn from others.

We reached out through social media to our readers, some of

whom might have walked in her shoes and some of whom, we hoped, had helped in situations similar to this in their professional work with teens or college students. It was all that we had to give.

The response was overwhelming and heartening. After posting Janet's question anonymously, we stepped back and let the community lift and guide her. And we turned a crucial page in our outlook toward parenting. Experts are essential, and they draw from their experience as they show us what science and research have to offer us. But a parent community can be an invaluable asset, offering support, insight, and all the lessons they have learned while raising their kids. This we could provide.

This reader, our reader, gave Grown and Flown purpose. We would no longer just chitchat about being parents and share our latest off-the-cuff idea or weekly story from our families, hoping it might resonate with our readers. We had to do more.

Beyond the tragedy unfolding in Janet's life, her problems in finding guidance to help her daughter were manifold. She had reached that stage of parenthood where our experts abandon us. When our children reach their late teen years, we no longer go in to see the pediatrician with them. Rarely do we interact with their teachers, and we are not supposed to talk to their coaches or advisers. That is up to them to do.

Our community disbands as well. Long gone are pickups and drop-offs of teens, who have now learned to drive. There is no more lingering at the door of a friend's house while we catch up with fellow parents. No more parking-lot or bus-stop chats as we ferry our kids to school.

When our parenting challenges were toilet training or quelling tantrums, it was easy to discuss them with a friend or neighbor. With the appearance of teen anxiety or depression, and our children bearing ever more of a resemblance to adults, their privacy becomes paramount. Their issues are not so easily discussed when we run into friends in the grocery store. And even when we are happy to divulge their stories in the name of finding some real help, we might not know someone whose kid had been cited for academic dishonesty or a DUI. In the tiny orbit of people we know in real life, it becomes harder, or even impossible, to find someone who has experienced the same pain or joy we are living through.

Finally, this stage of parenting often feels as though it goes unnoticed. The internet is full of smart, funny, insightful, inspiring websites dedicated to raising kids *until* they are teens. But then the high school years seem to be overlooked. And there is barely a word written about being the parent of a college student. It is as if our kids turn thirteen and someone says, "You got this," leaving us to apply the lessons we have learned in the first dozen years to the next couple of easy, glide-path years preceding launch. You've done the hard work, you've created and then shaped a human being, and now your work is largely done.

Only that is entirely wrong.

We founded Grown and Flown without a clear idea of what it would become. We had only the notion that, with each of our youngest being fifteen years old and our oldest sons ages nineteen and twenty, we were in the midst of the most confusing, challenging, and consequential years of parenting—and we were doing it with less community, fewer experts, and no help online.

So Lisa called Mary Dell one day and said she thought we needed a blog. We needed a website and maybe a Facebook page where we could ignite a conversation among parents of teens. We needed a digital watercooler, a place where parents would linger and chat while giving each other the support that was often missing in our real lives. At the time, the Motherlode column in *The New York Times* would occasionally have wonderful writing about being the parent of a high school student. But if you searched around beyond that, there wasn't much more.

Mary Dell said yes before even hearing half of the half-baked idea. She was immediately on board with starting a new site, trialing a new concept, and establishing a new business, while readily acknowledging that neither Mary Dell nor Lisa had any idea what that would entail, or even what it would look like. Mary Dell had confidence, even though it was not clear there was anything to have confidence in.

Here was the plan to start: We would write about how lost and challenged we felt as parents of teens and twentysomethings. We would examine what had worked and where we had failed. We would talk to other parents about how raising a son and a daughter (Mary Dell) or three sons (Lisa) left us feeling out of our depth every day. But who would we talk to? We couldn't say. What would we tell them? More questions. Would anyone even be interested? Time, as it usually does, would tell. But we felt certain that if we could gather others around for the conversation, we would all emerge better parents.

Our understanding of the internet and its possibilities was so limited that we thought we would just use our first names, no photos of ourselves or our families, and that no one would know, or care, who the women were behind the website. We wanted to be out in the world igniting a big important conversation about the challenges and joys of raising teens. We wanted to help parents rethink the paradigm of how our families would alter over the years as our kids left home. But we were so internet-shy that we wanted to remain entirely anonymous.

Having our kids in the nineties was just an utter stroke of genius for the tech support we would need twenty years hence. So, one of Lisa's sons sat us down on a cold, bright January morning in her kitchen. He hovered his hands over the keyboard and said, "I am going back to school tomorrow, give me a name and a domain, and you will be online before I get back to campus. If you don't tell me now, I will be back in May." After years of pushing our kids, one of them was pushing us.

We were paralyzed. It was like naming a baby, and we felt compelled to examine every option we could imagine. Lisa's son reminded us that unlike our newborns, we could effortlessly rename a website if we got it wrong, and the ethos in any tech business was to move quickly. Still, we stalled. We wanted the site to touch on the painful frustrating moments of raising teens. We wanted it to capture the love and closeness in our families that we were desperate to retain. We wanted it to encapsulate the pride we feel as parents when our kids go off to college or work or the military knowing that they are ready for this next step. And, we wanted it to say all of that in four words or less.

After many poorly conceived starts, we came upon Grown and Flown. Grown and Flown is what British parents call their kids who have left home. Lisa had lived in England for a dozen years and had always liked, if dreaded, the term. When we googled "Grown and Flown," the hits were all about a Christina Rossetti poem of lost love. And we were certainly feeling lost love, but not the kind of which the pre-Raphaelite spoke.

From the start, we had misjudged the content of the site entirely. We thought parents of high school and college kids would want to read and talk about what their lives would be like as their families dispersed, about a time when parenting would matter less. It turns out that time never comes. We have since learned from our own lives and by listening to tens of thousands of parents that parenting never ends. What parents want to know boils down to this: How does my family stay close as we move apart? How do we hold on to the essence of the life we have had? How do we maintain one of the most important relationships any of us will ever have while simultaneously nourishing our kid's independence?

Grown and Flown started slowly and then built up steam. We

would love nothing more than to take total credit for the site's growing popularity, but we had the wind in our sails. First, we were talking to parents about the one thing they cared about more than anything else, so it wasn't hard to get their attention. Second, as we soon found out, we had discovered a bit of white space on the internet, and had surprisingly little competition around this topic. Third, we were just entering the era of the digital parent. These were parents whose children had been born in the twenty-first century. While not technically digital natives, this generation of parents had sought out digital resources in raising their kids from the start, and they would seek us out now that their house was full of teens. Finally, there has been a seismic change in some of the most important aspects in the relationship between parents and their teens and young adults. This has left many parents feeling bewildered and unable to look to their own teen years as a guide to raising their kids. We saw it, heard about it, and were living it every day, but now we were going to explore it with our readers, our community, and in this book.

At the beginning, Lisa wrote and wrote, mining her only marginally interesting life for content. Mary Dell wrote, edited, and published. Lisa managed the tech, with frantic calls to her offspring, and Mary Dell figured out ways to make some money so that we could pay others to write for the site as well. It soon became clear that the tales of five teenage kids in suburban New York were simply not enough material and didn't speak to a broad enough slice of the panorama of parenting to capture everything we hoped to say. So we gathered other writers who could speak from professional expertise or from experience and cover the many aspects of parenting that were unknown to us. We shared their writing and our own on any form of social media we felt able to tackle (Snapchat was simply a bridge too far). Most important, we started a Facebook group to continue the discussion.

Our expectations for this Facebook group—Grown and Flown Parents—were modest. We assumed it would be the two of us talking a few times a week with our writers and friends we knew in real life. We knew that parenting teens and college kids was changing in some very fundamental ways, and we wanted to understand this better for our readers and ourselves. To our amazement, the group has become a destination for more than one hundred thousand parents, the majority of whom visit and interact daily. It is the place where we learn what parents hold most dear and what keeps them up at night. We know what questions they have, from where to buy the most durable twin XL sheets to how to find a therapist for their college teen. It is the place where parents who come from all corners of this country and every political perspective can discuss and share ideas about the thing that matters the most to them—their children and the earnest desire to be a better parent. This group has become the heartbeat of Grown and Flown.

In early 2013, the AARP published a survey that shed a blinding light on the paradigm shift in parenting we were hearing about from readers daily. They asked young adults and their parents how they felt about each other and compared that to how those same parents remember feeling about their parents when they were in their early twenties. What the survey found echoed what we were seeing all around us. Our kids' generation communicates with us more. The survey showed that 62 percent of today's young adults communicated with their parents at least once a day, compared to 41 percent of their parents when they were the same age. Sure, it is cheaper to call than it was thirty years ago, but the rest of the survey suggested that new technology and reduced calling rates were not what caused this shift in behavior. A 2019 survey for *The New York Times* showed that parents at every income level were involved in their adult children's daily lives, with fully 80 percent saying they were "always" or "often" in text message communication. The AARP survey found that our kids socialize with us more: 60 percent of the twentysomethings saw their parents socially once a week versus 42 percent of their parents who had seen their parents at that age. And perhaps even more important, our young adults are also more comfortable discussing their career, financial life, and social life with us. When we were young adults, daughters were more likely to talk openly with their parents, but in our kids' generation this difference between genders has disappeared, and sons are equally comfortable discussing these personal matters with their parents. Marry this with the fact that we have a tool for constant contact always in the palm of our hands, and it becomes clear that our relationship with our teens and young adults is closer, more connected, and a bigger part of both of our lives.

The Grown and Flown years begin the day your oldest secures a driving permit and end when your youngest moves into their first real apartment. Not that grungy place they moved into with a gang of college sophomores, with a bathroom so filthy that you swear you will never cross the threshold, but the one where they are paying the rent. During those intervening years, which for some families can span fifteen years or more, your family is in transition, your kids are in varying states of independence, and nothing is the way it was or will be.

We would argue, and the research confirms, that the role we play in our kids' lives as they move from the final days of childhood over the threshold of adulthood is as important as any other time in their lives. These are the defining years, the years when our children make some of the most consequential decisions of their lives. This is when our teens discover who they are. This is when they learn about risk. For better or worse, our influence on our teens and then later young adults is far greater and lasts much longer than we ever imagined. Our role in their lives and the attachment we have formed will impact everything, from their potential drinking, drug use, and sexual behavior to their mental health and more. A study of first-semester freshmen, which monitored communication between parents and their new college students and the drinking patterns of those students, found that "increased parent communication is associated with less drinking among first-year college students." Students ingested less alcohol on the days they spoke with their parents. The popular press overflows with studies suggesting the negative impact of the close connection between the generations, but research may show otherwise.

The oft-cited argument for backing away from our involvement in our teens and college students' lives is that "We only spoke to our parents once a week, and we were fine." But were we? Was minimal guidance during our young adult lives truly a good thing? Instead of relying on those older than us for advice, we often leaned on our peers, who knew no more than we did. During our high school years, our parents often had no idea where we were, and by college we were almost totally independent. Yet, looking at the data on drug use, drinking, and teen pregnancy for our generation, it is not clear that this was ideal either. Many experts urge parents to diminish their involvement in their teens' and college students' lives. They suggest parents return to the ways that we were parented, with a more hands-off approach in order to make certain our kids learn to be independent. But we would argue that not only is there no returning to an earlier time but that the relationship between the generations today is vastly improved. It has been fundamentally altered, and the question is not how we go back but rather how we go forward—and how, within the new paradigm of a more intertwined relationship, we ensure that our sons and daughters take full responsibility for their adult lives.

As our own kids wound their way through high school and college, we struggled, like all other parents, with finding the right balance between urging their independence, helping them when they needed us, and staying close. They often called or texted at the point of making a decision, from the minor "Do I put more air in the tires when that light goes on?" to the major "One of the kids here is in bad shape, what does drunk enough to go to the hospital look like?" Were they too enmeshed, a clingy generation who could not figure out things on their own? Or was technology and a new approach to parenting allowing us to continue to teach and advise at moments large and small?

There was never a time when we felt like we had this balance just right. Over the last couple of years, we have listened to tens of thousands of parents who echoed similar concerns and questions, and we have learned just how pervasive this struggle is. The fear of becoming a "helicopter parent" was impacting the behavior of a generation of parents. We were told our kids had to separate, stand on their own, and that by remaining as a highly influential force in their lives we endangered their ability to establish autonomy. But this seemed like a false and flawed dichotomy. Being close to your teen is *not* the same as doing things for them or clearing their path and disabling them. That is conflating two issues, and we often see this done. You can be close to your young adults, talk to them regularly, share dinners and group texts with the family, and still let them find their own way and solve their own problems. Listening to your teen and keeping a wide-open channel of communication is not that same as, and should not be confused with, hovering over their lives.

Generations of humanity have lived and thrived in close proximity with the older generations highly involved in the lives of the younger generations. And most everyone successfully reached adulthood. It seemed that the paradigm of the latter half of the twentieth century had become *the* paradigm, and if we only looked back a bit further, to the sweep of human existence, we would see a very different picture.

Dr. Karen Fingerman, professor of human development and family sciences at the University of Texas at Austin, interviewed thirty-five hundred parents over the course of two decades of studying family relationships and found that, across all socioeconomic groups, grown children do better in life when their parents are highly involved. Crucially, she points out that the way parents and their teens separated in the 1960s, '70s, and '80s was a historical outlier. "Most cultures have maintained closeness between parents and children," she observes. "In America, the middle twentieth century was an anomaly—in some way the baby boomers are the odd ones."

Other than this anomalous period in time, it would be hard to point to another era in human history where eighteen-year-olds connected with their families only a few times a month (the exception to this would be draftees, but they had almost none of their own agency). The more constant connection that parents now have with their teens, college students, or young adults may be akin to the more regular interaction that families have had for all of time.

When Janet reached out to us for advice about her daughter, she helped form Grown and Flown and helped us develop as parents. She taught us that even as our real-world community and expert guidance has faded, we needed to discover new sources as we face these most important parenting years. As the relationship between parents and their teens and young adults has evolved at lightning speed, we have much understanding to gain from each other.

We also learned that the line between autonomy and connectedness is different in every family. There are no right answers, and there never were. Supporting our teens as they move toward independence is essential, of course, but we would argue that it's perhaps only one of the two most important things we need to do as parents. Dr. Kenneth Ginsburg, a pediatrician specializing in adolescent medicine at the Children's Hospital of Philadelphia and a professor of pediatrics at the Perelman School of Medicine at the University of Pennsylvania, explains:

> Our overemphasis on independence may undermine what has allowed us to thrive throughout the millennia. We thrive best, and indeed survive, when we remain connected. Although we raise our children to be able to fly on their own, we must also prepare them to understand connection is the most important force in their lives. We do this neither by blanketing them with overprotection nor by demanding their full attention. We do this by taking care not to install the control buttons from which they must flee. We do this by noticing their growing wisdom and development . . . and honoring their increasing independence. We do this by recognizing them as the experts in their own lives, and by sharing our own experience when needed. We do this by backing away from believing every moment with our children must be productive and by returning to what has always worked—being together. Just being. Yes, they will fly away and the launching may even have its painful moments. But ultimately, we want to raise children who choose interdependence, knowing that nothing is more meaningful or makes us more successful than being surrounded by those we love.

Why would we start a book offering parenting advice with the admission that we know so much less than we thought we did?

Because this is not just a book of our parenting reflections but rather a collection of some of the best, smartest, most sincere, and most insightful thoughts other parents have to offer about how to navigate the teen and college years. It is full of wisdom from nationally known experts who have studied families for years as professors, researchers, psychologists, and educators. It is the book we wish we had as our families entered the Grown and Flown years.

In the pages that follow we will walk through some of the most important milestones and changes families go through as our teens move toward adulthood. A few of these stories are our own; most are not. We have five kids between our two families, and that is just not enough input on which to draw conclusions. We are also too keenly aware of the many missteps we made along the way. What we offer of our family's lives comes largely from this hard-won knowledge, as the following two anecdotes will show.

MARY DELL

First children are our guinea pig kids and it is their birth-order fate in life to present us with a disproportionate number of firsts—both the sublime kind (first steps! first days of school!) and the not-so-wonderful ones (first traffic ticket; first broken heart). I have one sister and no brothers, so our son presented even more newness for me than if his sister had arrived first. That is one explanation I cling to for the abundance of mom-fails that more frequently involved *him* over *her*.

One blunder I wish I could get a do-over for happened at dinnertime, just before the beginning of our son's junior year of high school. Cooking on a typical weeknight for my family meant keeping broccoli from getting too mushy or rice from sticking to the bottom of the pan while placating my daughter's complaints of *starvation* all while estimating the ETA for our son. My husband typically joined dinners in progress after his commute home from the city, missing the nightly dinner pregame.

This year, for the first time, our son was driving himself to and from school for football practice. His route took him on a busy interstate during rush hour, so I always had an eye on the clock when I knew he was on the road. I heard the garage door open and then shut, and in strolled our son, joining his sister at the table. He was surprisingly energized that night (red flag) compared to the exhausted boy who usually dragged himself into the house at 7:00 p.m. after another grueling, two-a-day workout.

He wore a too-broad grin and an unfamiliar baseball cap—clues that I completely missed. Had I only said, "Care for some chicken, dear?" instead of screaming a loud "*What?*" when he revealed a shaved head with only a strip of hair running down the middle, I would have taken a few breaths and reminded myself that it was just hair, truly.

Giving him not one moment to explain the football team-building haircut, I delivered my lecture about respect and school rules and how an unconventional haircut would be received at his school, which had strict dress- and hair-code rules.

Where he saw a fun prank, I saw a torpedo crashing into the relationships he had built with his coaches and teachers, relationships that mattered to him and that would sustain him during the tough junior year ahead.

The next day the team shaved their heads and I felt like a terrible mom.

There is a reason why this vignette of my son's teen life sticks with me, and there are lessons I have tried to take from it. First is that listening may be the most underrated parenting skill of all, and had I only listened to my son rather than starting a mom-lecture, I would have learned all I needed to know about the short-lived team-hair stunt.

Second is that our teens are supposed to push on boundaries even if that pushing causes us temporary emotional bruising. It is how they learn to differentiate themselves from us, a crucial life experience.

I also learned that I needed to respect the team and their efforts to build trust and brotherhood. The bonding over silly things like haircuts or pregame routines or team dinners or what words they would end each huddle with were sacred to these young men who were learning to put the good of the group above themselves.

I knew that my overreaction reflected a highly elevated stress level, stress that came from watching our son drive to school every day. I was also anxious about the school year ahead. Junior year was spoken about by moms of older kids as the *hardest year*, and veteran parents warned us about what was to come with vivid stories of late-night studies, SAT prep, college applications, and exhausted kids.

Of course, hair grows back, but words can last forever. The next day, I apologized to my son, and I hoped he would forgive me for talking too much and listening too little. I also apologized to our daughter, who was an innocent bystander that night when her mom went a little nuts.

Had Lisa and I only started Grown and Flown a few years earlier, I would have known more about the teen brain and adolescent behavior from experts like Dr. Frances Jensen, Dr. Jess Shatkin, or Dr. Ken Ginsburg. These are all amazing doctors and parents whom we have had the pleasure of interviewing for this book.

I also would have had the benefit of the digital tribe of parents who are at the heart of Grown and Flown. We see how this community shares and teaches every day in myriad ways as they chat and comment about their teens and young adult children. Maybe, just maybe, my haircut mistake might not have ever happened with this resource to turn to.

LISA

I have lived all my life in boy world. I have only sons, only brothers, married a man, and for many years worked in a male-dominated field. I felt as prepared as any mother can to live among the Y chromosomes. When I had my third son, it all felt right. Except that my boys fought. They hit and bit and wrestled until they made each other bleed. They did this at home and in public places, and at no point did I ever learn how to alter their behavior. I often felt so out of control that I would mumble to myself the constant refrain "You are the adult; they are the children."

I feared they would hurt each other. And, they did. I feared they would hate each other. And, thankfully, they did not. I thought it was my job to get this under control, and even now, I don't know if it was. I often wondered how much of this went on in other families, and I never knew. And I hoped, mistakenly, that as we entered the teen years, all of this would end.

At home I alternated between breaking them up and screaming in frustration that I wasn't going to break them up and they needed to work it out themselves. I would send them to separate rooms or shut the door so that I could no longer hear them and just let them go at it. Natural consequences, I told myself. I once stood at a check-in line at an airport only to have the ticket agent signal to look behind me at the bloody nose one son had just given the other. Did I need a Kleenex with the boarding passes for the blood that was running down his face?

Other families did not seem to have this level of conflict embedded in their lives. Or maybe, I thought, they kept it behind closed doors.

One evening, we took the two who fought the most out for dinner to a local burger place when their brother was away. We ordered our meals and while we ate, they argued. We were sitting at a small table with a pedestal base, not the four strong legs that were needed to support us. I was having the all-too-familiar internal monologue: "I love my family," I reminded myself. "I love spending quality time together. This is how families bond, enjoying meals together. I am going to kill these two. I cannot stand one more meal with them. I am never going out with them again. What about this is fun?"

At one point, one of them had wound the other up so badly that he stood up, reached right across the table, and tried to smack his brother's head. As he did so, he took the *entire* table with him. Four meals. Four sets of dishes and glasses. Four sets of cutlery and one centerpiece. It all crashed to the floor in a pile. There was a heap of shattered glass and dish shards. The table lay on its side. Water went everywhere and our uneaten burgers lay among the ruins.

I wanted to tell the waitress that my kids were never like this, that I couldn't believe what had happened, that I was as shocked as she was. But even I could not stretch the truth that far. My husband did the sensible thing and asked me how much cash I had in my bag. We grabbed the boys by the scruffs of their collars, like mother cats lifting their kittens, even though they were both taller than I. We tried to pick up the pile of debris, but the staff assumed, with more than a little evidence, that we were trouble and just wanted us out of their restaurant. My husband signed the check and gathered up every dollar we had in our possession and handed it to the waiter as recompense for the debris.

We were furious, humiliated, and had just lost our favorite local. I didn't know whether to punish them or whether the looks on our faces were their punishment. I could make them work off the cost of the breakage, I could lecture, I could refuse to leave home with them, or I could beg them once again to grow up. I never stopped them or changed their behavior, and maybe I never could. I struggled with these questions alone. But I know now that a community of parents and access to experts would have allowed me to reflect on my actions and directions in a far more thoughtful way.

These pages do not walk you through your kids' lives the way you are experiencing them. We don't wind from middle school through high school and then on to college or real life, exactly. Instead, we have tried to take a measured look at many of the aspects of our life with teens and young adults and reflect on them, whether your offspring is fifteen or twenty-three. We start with what we feel matters most—a look at family life. Then we wind our way through happiness, health, mental health, academics, and separation as their lives move on.

We now have twentysomethings who are working or are back at school. As the data suggests, we see the ones who live near us practically every week and communicate with the ones who live near and far many times a week. They send photos of what they eat or things they have seen and still seem willing to share the details of their lives. They call and ask questions that Google can answer, and we remain grateful for that. It is much too early to call this a success, but our goal for our families was just this: to let our kids fly, to watch them explore the world on their own, and at the same time to remain close.

When we first envisaged Grown and Flown, we thought the website and community would be all about letting go, about life after kids and about the empty nest. We were wrong. What parents of teens and college kids want to know is how we keep our families close as we move apart. They want to know how to give their teens independence while holding on to the family intimacy that is essential for them and us. In our many thousands of conversations with parents, if we have learned only one thing, it is that every parent and every family has the exact same goal, and each will reach it in an entirely different way. What follows are some of those ways.

CHAPTER ONE
Family Life

From the very beginning, family drew us in and consumed us. It's better than you ever imagined it could be, right?

In our days as single workingwomen, we could never have predicted the irresistible pull of a tiny baby to love and hold. Who knew that three-year-olds are the most adorable beings on the planet, or that ten-year-olds can be not only funny but also insightful? And yes, teens do live up to their terrible press at times, but who knew that watching a being teetering on the edge of adulthood could be a blessing beyond words?

If you are reading these words, of course you know.

You know that despite its dizzying ups and downs, family life is the greatest joy of your existence. You know that, each in their own way, your kids are more amazing than you ever dreamed. You have known love so fierce and protective that you would do anything for another person. You know that listening to every seemingly insignificant detail of your teen's life, all the way down to what they had for lunch, can be fascinating. And you know that as your family travels through the high school years, much of this is about to change.

As it is for most families, the transition through the high school years and on into college was an upheaval in our homes.

Our kids wanted to spend less time with us and more with their friends. They shut down or poured forth in conversation, and we never knew why or when they would be in either of these states. They could be terrible to their siblings and mouthy with us as they pushed us and their fathers away. Mostly that felt like they were obeying the natural order of the universe, even if it was sometimes painful. On some days it was easy to feel as though nothing about our parenting was working. Yet on other days, when we saw glimpses of the adult emerging from the teen, they took our breath away. Occasionally we could feel both those things in the same day.

Two words: "all normal."

This roller coaster was driven in part by the fear of how our families, nurtured with the very best that was in us, were facing both inevitable and cataclysmic change.

Our fear as their lives moved on was simply losing the closeness of our families as our contact with our kids diminished. Sure, we were worried about our children's safety and their ability to make friends and find paths to their adult lives. We hoped they would be able to handle the academic load of college, to use good judgment, to be at least friendly with their roommates, if not friends. But we harbored larger concerns as well. We were worried that the kids who were barely home, the ones who had seemed to fly in through the door and then right back out again ever since the summer after tenth grade, would go off to college and we would barely hear from them again.

Some of this fear was based on the one-word answers we were getting all through high school, and some of it was based on our now-faded memories of barely communicating with our own parents in high school. We worried that the close contact we had with them at home was only because we were literally in their face and once they were gone it would simply slip away. Most parents tell us this turns out not to be the case and that many kids reach out far more in their college years than they did during their sullen high school years—because of maturation, and because they have new experiences to share (and more than a small measure of homesickness). Studies show that twentysomethings want to communicate and remain close with their parents to a far greater degree than previous generations, and so our own experience of being teens, now decades old, should not be seen as a guide.

We also feared growing apart. Every family has its own unique dynamic, and as our kids went off to college, we despaired at losing the rich interactions. This family zeitgeist had developed over decades, and the thought of losing it seemed painful. We feared that our families would never be the same again.

A source of relief came from reminding ourselves of the seamless transition all of our families can now make from the real dinner table to the digital one. Thanks to GroupMe or WhatsApp or any texting app installed on all our phones, we gather virtually to tease, laugh, and argue; to share and send photos; to inflict idiotic videos and random thoughts on one another. At the digital dinner table, our family makes plans to meet, and we share what we are doing when we are apart. It allows us to do everything but eat off each other's plates.

We were both unsure about how our family roles—be they parent and child or sibling to sibling—would be redefined. It is hard not to wonder what kind of a parent you are to a teen who doesn't live in your home. Or what kind of parent you are to a teen who lives at home but is technically an adult and no longer under your control. Are we a lesser parent? What is our role, our authority? If our job is to protect and care for our kids, how can we do this job if our kids are not even there? What roles will we play in the lives of our newly independent kids, and what roles will they play in each other's lives?

SIBLINGS UNRIVALED

Growing up, as in most families, our kids were constantly thrust together with their siblings. They rode the school bus twice a day. They were cooped up in our cars together on family vacations. They gathered at the dinner table together all their lives. They followed each other through the same schools with many of the same teachers. But what, we wondered, would happen when they were off at different colleges or on different paths? Would they remain close later when they worked in different cities? Lisa was obsessed over the relationship between her sons, while not fully understanding until her boys were nearly grown why it was so important to her. Here she explains:

> There is one aspect of parenting I feel more strongly about than most others. I want my sons to be close—best-friend, always-there-for-each-other close. I want them to have the kind of intimacy that comes from having spent a lifetime together, and I desperately want it to last. But why I feel this so passionately, why it ranks near the top of the list of things I wish for my family, I would struggle to say.
>
> Maybe it's because I believe so strongly that siblings are monumental in our lives. And when I came across this passage by Jeffrey Kluger in *The Sibling Effect: What the Bonds Among Brothers and Sisters Reveal About Us*, I had evidence to support that conclusion:
>
> "From the time they are born, our brothers and sisters are our collaborators and co-conspirators, our role models and cautionary tales. They are our scolds, protectors, goads, tormentors, playmates, counselors, sources of envy, objects of pride. They teach us how to resolve conflicts and

how not to; how to conduct friendships and when to walk away from them."

By the time a child is eleven, she has typically spent one-third of her free time with her siblings, more than is spent with any other person. As Kluger reminds us, the sibling relationship is often the longest-lasting one in our lives.

Siblings socialize each other. My three boys shared a single bedroom and bathroom growing up. Everything they learned about taking turns, respecting personal space, and accommodating the needs and desires of others they learned from one another in those two rooms. (Lest I paint too rosy a picture, everything they learned about hitting, biting, headlocks, and getting in the last shot, verbal or physical, they likewise learned there.) I often feel that they prepared each other for the outside world, perhaps more so than I was able to. Kluger describes himself and his three brothers as forming "a loud, messy, brawling, loyal, loving, lasting unit." And that sounds just about right to me.

Could it be that I want my sons to remain close because I believe that in no small measure they created each other? Psychologists call this "de-identification," but we parents know the phenomenon in its more familiar guise: our kids worked really hard not to be like each other. How many families do we know where the younger siblings are less cautious, either because they don't want to emulate the oldest or because—as I suspect with my kids—they know whatever the problem, the oldest has got it covered? Siblings broaden our world by bringing their interests and friends right through our front door. If they are older, they can be an example, either good or bad, or a road map. If they are younger, they provide a challenge, a different way to do things, a cause for reflection.

My desire for closeness among my children started when they were tiny. Our three boys were born in four years. And while, perhaps, I had a fantasy of built-in playdates and their ability to amuse themselves without parental intervention, the reality was often very different. They surely loved each other, and when each of them entered our home, from school, soccer, or a playdate, the first question was about the location of their brothers. Yet they fought with a physical ferocity that at times left me staggering. A game would begin, there would be a break where they seemingly tried to kill each other, and then their play would resume—as if random outbreaks of violence were to be expected.

My kids shared nicknames and inside jokes that conveyed both endearment and ridicule, and more than once, okay, more than a hundred times, my husband had to reassure me that brothers say terrible things to each other as a sign of affection. He would remind me that it did not mean they hated each other; the cruel quips that they hurled at each other were a symbol of their love and nothing to worry about.

"The traditional view is that having a brother or sister leads to a lot of competition for parents' attention and love," writes Dr. Claire Hughes in her book *Social Understanding and Social Lives*. "In fact, the balance of our evidence suggests that children's social understanding may be accelerated by their interaction with siblings."

Maybe my hopes that my kids will stay close stem from my fondness for my own brothers—two of the kindest and most loving men I have ever known. They were playmates and confederates for me, and they have been wonderful uncles to my boys from day one. At no point in my life did they ever let me down when I needed them. So, it's possible

I may be "projecting" a little bit here: I want my children to enjoy the same strain of loyalty my brothers and I have been able to draw on.

As my sons began to go their separate ways to college, I started to panic. Had their emotional closeness been purely a function of their physical proximity? Like so many siblings, they are very different personalities with wildly divergent interests. Had their daily interactions formed the glue bonding them together? Without driving to school together, without sitting side by side at the dinner table—would it all simply evaporate?

Thus far, it appears, I needn't have worried: they text and video-chat and send an endless string of messages. Still, the nagging question remains: Why do I care so much?

After I finished examining my better motives for their enduring friendship, I took a hard look at myself, for as Kluger pointedly says, "Reproducing is a genetically narcissistic act." Maybe, this was just about me.

My sons, husband, and I—the five of us—were a period in time, a two-decade-long loving embrace, that in truth can never be the same again. For now there will be partners and studies, later, spouses, grandchildren, and careers, and those magical decades will exist only in our hearts. But, if they have each other, they will always have the five of us together.

For as long as they are bound together, in the decades when their father and I are here with them, and for the many in which we will not be, my sons can at any moment conjure up our regular Sunday-night dinners, with roast chicken, carrots, onions, and baked potatoes. They can be whisked back to a summer at the beach with our closest friends. They can remember moving houses and countries together, and the schools and teachers they shared over many years. For as long as the three of them are close, all five of us are close, be it a year from now or fifty years from now. Their love for each other re-creates what my husband and I created.

They hold each other's childhood, and with a word or a phrase the five of us are back together again. I told them that I wanted them to be close forever because in the end they would always have each other, because it is truly a blessing in life if there is someone who can be counted on at any time. But I now realize I was being far more selfish, because as long as they are there for each other, they will always have us.

IN SIBLING SPATS, WHAT IS OUR ROLE?

When you're down in the trenches of child-rearing, the constant bickering and unending rivalry among the kids is wearying beyond words. Our teens come home and create a poisonous atmosphere, hurling snark and attitude, most of it aimed squarely at their siblings from the moment they enter the house. We asked psychologist Dr. Lisa Damour, who directs the Laurel School's Center for Research on Girls and wrote the *New York Times* bestsellers *Untangled: Guiding Teenage Girls Through the Seven Transitions Into Adulthood* and *Under Pressure: Confronting the Epidemic of Stress and Anxiety in Girls*, and is the mother of two, to help us deconstruct what's going on and how to defuse it.

She explains:

It's easy to picture the scene. A fifth grader sits at the kitchen table doing her homework while she eagerly waits for her tenth-grade sister to come home from school. But when the door opens, the atmosphere shifts abruptly. From the way she enters the house, it's immediately clear that the teenager had a terrible day.

Before anyone can say a word, the teenager turns to her younger sister and snaps, "Did you go into my bag this morning? You know you're not allowed to, and I didn't have the highlighter I needed for class." She adds harshly, "Also, please tell me that you didn't walk around with your hair like that all day. You look so stupid."

The teenager then stalks off to her room and leaves one badly bruised sister and one shocked and furious parent in her wake.

What just happened?

What should happen now?

And how do we avoid a repeat performance?

Here's what happened. The teenage girl wielded an ancient and ugly psychological defense called "turning passive into active." People who use this defense get psychological relief at someone else's expense by turning the tables when they are suffering. In our scenario, the adolescent may have felt that she was sorely mistreated all day. This is, of course, highly unlikely, but we know that teenagers' emotions can run high and perspective can be lost.

Feeling that she's been on the receiving end of mistreatment, the teenager seeks relief by becoming the one dishing out the abuse. Unfortunately, the younger sister found herself in the wrong place at the wrong time.

What should happen now? Ideally, the parent in this scenario would try to stick up for the younger sibling, even as the teenager storms away. It may be sufficient for the parent to say (or shout), "Hey, wait a minute. No one around here treats you that way—you should not treat your sister that way." Next, the parent might look to give the little sister some support and some context by consoling her along these lines: "You didn't have that coming, and I'm sorry she went after you. Her days are long and she's probably stressed, but she has no right to act like that."

How do we avoid a repeat performance? After some cooling off, the parent might find a moment to touch base with the teenager about what happened. Without expecting agreement, or even a response, the parent could gently say, "Your little sister adores you, and when you're hard on her, it cuts deep. It would mean a lot to her, and to me, if you'd go out of your way to be kind to her when you're ready." In another moment, the parent might add, "I know that your days are hard and that you come home pretty cooked. Got any ideas for how you might blow off some of that steam in a way you won't feel bad about later on?"

Here's the bottom line: most teenagers are well aware when they've hurt their sibling and don't feel good about it. When dealing with the aftermath of these moments, we should work with the understanding that teens have powerful emotional impulses that sometimes get the better of them. All the same, adolescents almost always want to make things right and are looking for our help in doing so.

As the parents of teens, one of the most important things we had to learn was not to rise to the bait, to step back from provocation, and to find those quiet moments to seek out real and lasting solutions to family conflict, as Damour suggests. Sometimes this meant letting misbehavior pass, like a physical or verbal swipe at a sibling, and dealing with it once emotions are off the boil. Easy? Nope. But when we achieve this we not only teach our kids how to get along with family in the moment but also, and perhaps even more important, we model ways they can resolve conflict with those they love now and over the course of their lives.

FAMILY FEELING

The sibling relationship is essential to both family closeness and peaceful family life, and so is the parent-kid relationship. Susan Bonifant, a contributor to *The Washington Post* and the mother of four young adults, offers a way to frame our relationship with our young adults and preserve the closeness we have spent decades trying to build. Susan explains:

> A while back, I wrote an essay for *The Washington Post* about staying close to older kids as they transition into adulthood. In the piece, I shared a closeness strategy that I used with my own children, which I called "being the neighbor."
>
> Using the neighbor lens, I learned to view my older children the way an objective stranger might: without bias or assumptions, without a personal stake in their choices and issues, but with interest in who they are, what they know, what they think about, hope for, and want in their lives.
>
> As the "neighbor parent," I lost the inclination to judge and learned to ask more than assume. More important, I learned that my children's personal stakes in the decisions they make are the only ones that matter. This changes everything.
>
> *Washington Post* readers liked this idea of establishing distance and objectivity to stay close, but the truth is, while

mindful distance is required to protect our close relationships, much heavy lifting is required to create close relationships from the beginning.

What makes families close? And most interesting to me, how do we stay that way as our children transition out of our nest and into their own?

I brought these questions to Brenda Quinn, a valued psychotherapist in our community who has spent two decades helping families remain close despite the demands of a busy world—our work, their studies and sports, and the constant distraction of social media.

"Family closeness is dependent on a culture of love with limits," says Quinn. "When I think of family closeness, I think of healthy attachment characterized by consistent communication, clear expectations, a focus on character . . . all steeped in a culture of love and respect.

"In early years, focus needs to be on the formation of 'roots,'" added Quinn. "Roots are deepened as children feel loved and liked within the clear scaffolding of limits."

To explore this idea of "roots" and scaffolding, I talked to four friends I have known since we met on the playground with toddlers in tow, two decades ago. Each of us has four children who now range in age from seventeen to thirty-four.

By typical measures, our kids are successful. The ones who are in college are doing well, and the ones who are living independently are paying their own bills. All of them love "coming home," even if their actual home is elsewhere.

I asked each friend what they did to be close as a family and how they stayed close through transitions, and Quinn's predictors of family attachment were heavily involved in their reflections.

Dennie and her husband wanted to raise children with a solid attachment to family and a strong work ethic. Family time was firmly established, and no one opted out. When they were old enough, the kids were encouraged to work. "We taught our kids the smartest one isn't always the most successful but the hardest-working kid is always successful," said Dennie.

Jane and her husband wanted their children to develop personal accountability and a healthy respect for community. All kids were required to attend church and give back through volunteering and fund-raising. All were taught to deal with the "logical consequences" of their choices. "My son told me that on my tombstone, it's going to say 'logical consequences,' I used the term so often," said Jane.

Stuart and her husband wanted their kids to derive a sense of strength and compassion toward each other from their unique family identity. Different traditions evolved as the children grew—special snacks for road trips, highs and lows before dinner, all kids sleeping in one room on Christmas Eve—and were modified as they grew out of them. Those traditions, Stuart says, created the family identity.

Maureen and her husband wanted their children to understand other cultures and points of view. A family passion for travel and a wide social circle of families with similar interests and kids the same ages enabled those cultural and social orientations. "I've seen how well the kids can participate in any social situation with ease," says Maureen.

"Over time, the need for autonomy grows and the gradual process of removing the scaffolding begins," says Quinn.

When their children made choices that created distance, the parents I talked to reacted with changes in their own actions. And when the scaffolding came down, their kids did well.

It's hard not to detect a correlation between family time and long-term closeness. But what is the formula for closeness if schedules don't permit nightly dinners, or resources don't allow for expensive vacations, or the energy to always "meet our kids where they are" has been exhausted by four in the afternoon? What if family time consists of an occasional dinner out, or an ice cream on a hot Sunday night?

In Quinn's observation about sibling closeness lies another formula.

"Family closeness is furthered by parents taking some responsibility for the relationship between their kids. Rules that clarify your expectation that siblings be respectful to one another create safety and reduce hurt. Consciously nurturing and shaping the relationship between siblings is a critical parental role. Parents can't force their children to be close, but they can reduce the barriers siblings might otherwise create through unkind words and actions."

This speaks to me in particular. When my husband and I started our family, I was sure about two things. I would teach our children to see their siblings as unconditional friends. There would be no personal attacks, no mocking, there would be no "shut up" or name-calling. They would not only be expected to apologize if they were out of line; they also would be required to discuss it.

And, because I know that a loved child will be who they are until they are discouraged, I would accept and know my children as well as anyone could. They would learn that I could be trusted with anything they told me and I would not destroy trust by comparing my children to each other, gossiping about them, or encouraging competition between them.

I would worry about plenty, but I wouldn't worry about closeness.

Our daughters, three years apart, clashed from the beginning. They were nothing alike and, as one of them put it, didn't want to be. There were fights and slamming doors, muttering and stomping. One cried when she got mad. The other one, "the attorney," never made statements but only asked questions until her exasperated sister indicted herself.

I worried about closeness for the first time.

One evening, the older one picked up the younger one at a play practice. Out came our younger daughter, sobbing, walking toward the car in a stupor. Her sister met her halfway, and learned that a bully in the chorus had been tormenting her for weeks.

"Which one?" said my older daughter, angry, eyes scanning the crowd.

"Let's just go," said the younger one. "Please."

Go they did, my younger daughter pouring out her heart, her older sister realizing in silence that if listening didn't soothe her own feelings of anger, it helped soothe her sister's agony.

Our sons, born eight years apart, were inseparable. When the older one went to college the younger one put a chart on his bedroom door to mark the days until his return. Keeping to himself in his room, he listened to his brother's music and followed his teams. Eventually, he made his own friends, found his own music, and stopped hitting fly balls alone on the lawn.

Again, I thought about closeness.

I overheard them talking quietly one night last year. They shared stories of their freshman years in college, far from home for the first time, the struggle to find footing, the loneliness, the disorientation among strangers from everywhere, finding and not finding acceptance. They had not described their experiences to me this way, but eleven years after they were separated by transition, they said it to each other.

There is an expression: best friends know all about you and love you anyway. The same can be said about parents, children, and siblings.

Asking families what makes them close is a bit like asking someone why they are in love. We talk about how we reinforce it more than what it is, and the deeper it is the harder it is to describe.

But in my family, and probably in all families that have not allowed growing up to mean growing away, it is fair to say: close families know all about each other and love each other anyway, no matter what, no matter when.

TRUST AND TRACKING

One way parents often feel they can keep their families closer together, or at least linked, is location-based tracking apps. Some families love these apps, as kids know where their parents are (how long until they are back from the grocery store) and parents can double-check that their newly licensed driver has arrived at school or softball practice. The apps can simplify communication channels by providing a technological connection and up-to-date location information at all times. Yet few topics spark more rancorous debate. Is this closeness or an unwelcome invasion of privacy? This tiny bit of code is the source of so much angst because it speaks to the very core of parenting: letting go, family connectivity, and how we show trust and love.

On the one side are the safety arguments. Using the signals emitted by their children's phones to keep tabs on their whereabouts enhances parents' abilities to keep their kids safe. If they go someplace they're not supposed to, have car trouble, or lose track of time, a map app can help us pinpoint their location and remedy the situation. Monitoring our kids allays not only their fears but also our own.

On the other side is the argument that rests on privacy, trust, and doubts as to whether we can actually keep them safe. They are not toddlers anymore, far from it, and their every move should not be watched over by adults at all times. As teens and college students, most of us were allowed bountiful freedoms that our kids have never known. Is it right, or fair, to take away what little freedom they do have with electronic tracking? By not tracking them, and giving them this freedom, we are asking them to take responsibility for their actions. We have found that many parents track their college students, legal adults, and it leads us to wonder at what point in life it stops. How will we know when they can take on more responsibility for themselves?

This can be a slippery slope, and we have to figure out where the tracking begins and ends. We can track their whereabouts on their phone, but we can also read their texts, emails, social media, and follow their trail across the internet. Should we track cars and measure their speed when driving? How are any of these activities measurably different from the others—and if some of them are desirable, where do you draw the line? There can be no doubt that our monitoring of our kids changes our relationship with them, but in what ways—and is it damaging?

Damour argues that like so many parenting questions, this is not one size fits all. Electronically trailing our kids, she explains, makes murky who is responsible for keeping a teen safe. Kids may have a fantasy that parents can magically protect them, that parents have the power to fix all their problems and that tracking helps a parent do this. By not tracking your teens, explains Damour—or by turning off the tracking and informing them of the change— you can send an empowering message to your kids: "I want you to understand that you alone are responsible for your safety."

Every teen handles their newfound autonomy in a different way, of course. Some are thrill seekers, prone to ignore parents' directives or veil their whereabouts. Only a parent, says Damour, can judge what will work for their family and their teens. Some may decide that reading their teens' texts or tracing their movements constitutes an invasion of privacy, whereas installing a speed-gauging device on their car is simply a matter of safety—and a recognition that teens are the least responsible drivers on the road.

While we offer up no definitive answer, there are important questions that hit at both the heart of family closeness and the tracking debate. How much privacy is your teen due? Have they given you sufficient reason to distrust them? Can you actually impact their safety, or is the ability to call you if they are in trouble enough? Are you going to discuss with them the ways that you track them? How will that impact your relationship?

There's no question that all these tiny lines of software code speak to the large heart of parenting: letting go, staying connected, and demonstrating trust and love on both sides of the generational divide. One approach might be to address the issue head-on: tell your teen you have faith in their ability to safeguard their own safety. Trust may be the ultimate tracking device.

If there is one message about family closeness that transcends every issue, it is communication. Parents often tell us that the single defining difference between their relationship with their kids and the one they had with their parents is talking. Our kids tell us stuff. We are far more transparent with them. Our communication is unimpeded by time or geography. We believe we remain close to our families because we never stop listening, commiserating, supporting, and sharing. And while all of this is unquestionably good, Jennifer Breheny Wallace, journalist and mother of three, explains what the research says and when and how it can go wrong.

COMMISERATING WITH YOUR TEEN

From Wallace:

Your daughter and her best friend can talk for hours about the mean girls at school or a crush's ambiguous behavior. Having a supportive friend to confide in about teenage troubles is important for building an adolescent's sense of self-worth and buffering against depression.

But mounting research suggests some forms of social support may actually do more harm than good. The very qualities that build closeness in relationships, like sharing personal thoughts and feelings, can be detrimental to a teen's mental health if predominantly negative and done excessively.

When adolescents routinely engage in co-rumination—rehashing and speculating about problems with a friend or parent—it can amplify stress and increase their risk of developing anxiety and depression.

Teen girls, in particular, are prone to co-ruminate: *Why didn't she invite me to her party? Is he about to break up with me?* Fixating on the negative, according to a 2016 study in the *Journal of Abnormal Child Psychology*, can cause a teen to perceive their problems as bigger and more serious than they are and lead them to behave in ways that can make a difficult situation even worse.

Researchers surveyed 628 seventh and tenth graders and asked them about depressive symptoms (such as sadness or feeling blue), experiences of stress (with peers or in romantic relationships, for example), and co-ruminating with a best friend (specifically, how frequently they rehashed problems, encouraged problem discussions, or dwelled on negative feelings).

"Nine months later, we assessed these adolescents again and found that those who co-ruminated with a best friend and felt even just a little sad reported having even more problems with peers months later," says coauthor Dr. Amanda Rose, a professor of psychological sciences at the University of Missouri who developed the co-rumination construct in 2002. Rather than letting a problem go, Rose theorizes, co-rumination may cause teens to act in counterproductive ways with peers, which then generates even more stress.

Adolescents can pick up this unhealthy style of communicating from well-meaning parents, namely mothers. In a 2013 study published in the *Journal of Adolescence*, Rose and colleagues surveyed four hundred fifth, eighth, and eleventh graders and found that adolescents who co-ruminated with their mothers were more likely to exhibit symptoms of anxiety and depression and more likely to co-ruminate with their own friends.

Talking about problems in moderation is healthy, says Rose, but if you and your child tend to continuously repeat details or feelings about a situation, dwell or speculate about a problem when no new information is being introduced, then you're likely stepping over the line to co-rumination.

"Parents who co-ruminate with their children are on the right path in building warmth and closeness in their relationships," she says. "They just need to learn to stop some conversations sooner."

Parents sometimes keep a negative situation alive by raising a painful topic long after their child has worked it through, says psychologist Dr. Michael Thompson, author of *Best Friends, Worst Enemies: Understanding the Social Lives of Children*. If your child has a fight with a peer, he says, resist the urge to ask lots of probing questions day after day, such as "Did he tease you again today?"

"Interviewing for pain does your child a disservice," says Thompson. "It focuses on the negative, paints them as a victim, and plants the seeds of unhealthy co-rumination. Instead, listen and respond with empathy like, 'I'm so sorry you have to deal with that mean behavior,'" says Thompson. "Then, after you've absorbed some of their pain and helplessness," he says, "refocus the conversation from being a victim to how they'll empower themselves, such as 'so, how do you think you're going to handle this?'"

One of the most effective ways to break the co-rumination habit is to be aware you're doing it, says Rose. When conversations turn circular, parents can suggest a walk or do something else to distract. She says it's helpful to share the research with your teen and important to be explicit about why you're changing the subject: "It's not that I don't care—it's that I want you to feel good, not stuck thinking about the negative." Encourage your child to do the same with friends.

"We live in a society that associates 'more' with 'better,'" says Rose. "But, when it comes to parenting, 'more' isn't always better—in fact, it can often backfire."

Ten Things to Do with Your Teen When They Are Barely Speaking to You

Emotions run hot with teens, except, of course, when they are freezing you out. So, if it ever seems like they barely want to share the same space, and that the feeling is growing mutual, here are ten ways to try to bring your teen around.

1. **Rediscover a taste of childhood.** Cook, order in, or go out for something they loved as a child and have maybe recently forgotten. This could be a favorite sandwich or pasta or a Halloween candy they no longer indulge in. Break the ice and start the memories flowing with a taste that will bring childhood back.

2. **Watch a game together.** Sports transcend anger, and discussing the game can be a nice rest from talking about grades, college admissions, and curfew.

3. **Put on some music.** Food can take you back, and so can music. Put on songs they used to dance around the living room to and share a memory and a laugh.

4. **Exercise.** Get on a bike, go for a run, kick a soccer ball. Sure, they are bigger, faster, and stronger than you, but it's a way to do something together that doesn't involve a lot of words.

5. **Watch a movie.** Lots of together time, not a lot of talking.

6. **Set aside for later.** No talking about SAT prep until tomorrow morning or a mutually agreed-upon time; no reminders about applications until this weekend. Think of it as a détente of sorts.

7. **Grab the siblings or friends.** Drop the intensity by diluting your presence. It is avoidance, but the problems will

still be there tomorrow and you might both be in a better mood.

8. **Take them shopping.** Sure, we shouldn't buy our kids' affections and compliance, but they can always use new socks and underwear. Run some sort of errand that gets you out of the house and focused on a safe topic like size or color.

9. **Face it head-on.** This one takes guts and often tears, but go for the jugular. Tell them you know things are tough right now. Tell them you love them. Tell them you remember being a real pain to their grandparents. Tell them that not talking is not acceptable. Share hard truths and try to get through to the other side.

10. **Walk away.** Sometimes we all just need to stew, and teens maybe even more so. Let them seethe, let them tell their friends that they have the worst parents, let them come to the end of their rope and just run out of anger. And then be there when they are ready to start over.

MOM IS MY BIGGEST ASSET

After a high schooler's sometimes miserable last year at home, and the guilt of feeling like it might be time for them to leave—interspersed with the fear that they are really leaving—we need to figure out how our relationship will evolve. They need us, but they don't *need* us. They share their problems but don't want us to help solve them (nor should we). They want to be close, but they need us to know that they are now totally independent, fully functioning adults—until, of course, they are not. We feel the push-pull, and so do they. One college sophomore, Sophie Burton, reflected for us on this dilemma and explained why a mom, or any parent figure, is the most valuable asset to getting through the college transition. This is an important lesson to keep in mind as our relationship with our kids moves into post–high school life.

After two days of trips to Target and Bed Bath & Beyond, my mom finally agreed that I had everything I needed and that it was time for her and my dad to head back to the hotel. We made it out to the dorm parking lot, and she pulled me in for one last squeeze. After what felt like hours, she released her grip, wiped her tears, and climbed into the passenger's seat of the rental car. I walked back to my dorm, struggling to contain my excitement. I felt freer than I had ever felt in my life.

My mom and I have what I like to call a "complex and ever-changing" relationship, which consists of some bickering, some sassing back and forth but, most prominently, a steady flow of unwavering support and love for each other.

We used to giggle like sisters when we watched Kristen Wiig on *Saturday Night Live*, and we shout at each other over the phone when we disagree—which is often. It is a roller coaster, as she often describes it.

Even though I love my mother, and knew I would miss her at times, watching her leave felt like a weight was being lifted off of my shoulders. I felt like Kevin in *Home Alone* when he realizes all the freedoms that come with a total lack of parental supervision.

Finally, there was no one to scold me for arriving home late (or in a questionable state), for eating nonorganic fruit, or for binge-watching Netflix when I had far more important things to do.

The first few weeks of school we barely spoke, and when I did call her, it was because I felt like she would be mad at me if I didn't. She kept her distance wonderfully, allowing me to bask in this newfound independence. Things were great.

But, then came the inevitable stress of freshman year. I started rush, my classes began to pick up in pace and workload, and I started to wonder about all the things that most freshmen question, at some point: How did I get into this school? Is it physically possible to retain this much material? Why am I even doing recruitment?

I was nervous about unloading all this onto my mom because, until then, I had been doing just fine on my own. *I am an adult*, I rationalized; *I should be able to handle these things without Mommy telling me how.*

The pressures continued to pile up. I finally caved. I called her in a panic, spilling out all my fears, stresses, and concerns. She listened intently. She told me that I was smart enough to be here, that I could manage all the material, and that the recruitment process would work out how it was supposed to. Even though I probably could have come to these conclusions on my own, it was the reassurance that only a mother can provide that enabled me to push through those freshman struggles.

As college students, we like to see ourselves as capable, self-sufficient human beings. And for the most part, we are. For those of us who are more stubborn, it can be difficult to admit that, sometimes, we just need our moms to point us in the right direction.

She might not know what a comm class actually entails, but she can tell you with absolute certainty that you are going to do okay on assignment one. She will overnight you socks when you discover that you brought none; she will send you delicious goodies on your birthday; and she will shower you with positivity—including every variation of heart-shaped emoji—when you realize you are dateless for formal.

I am not ashamed to admit that I am a sophomore in college and my texts to my mom, this past week, have included: "Should I go to bed now, and get up early to do homework, or should I do my homework now?" "I just partied with Madonna's daughter!" and "Does regular yogurt hurt your stomach?"

If I could go back to that sticky night last August in the parking lot, I would hug my mom a little longer, a little tighter, and maybe even shed a few tears to match her sobs. Because even though I didn't realize it then, nothing—not even soy mochas, office hours, or your very best friend—can get you through the college grind like your mother can.

TOO CLOSE?

Some of the clearest thinking about parenting comes from those who see its nuances from both a personal and professional perspective. High school teachers, college professors, psychologists, and physicians bring the heart of a parent and the head of a professional to many of the issues surrounding parenting teens. Here, Lori Smith, mom and higher education professional, shares six things you may want to sidestep when it comes to your involvement in your kids' lives. And while she is coming from the point of view of a professional in the college space, these points are equally true for those with teens still in high school.

As a parent, I know how hard it can be to let go and allow our children to manage the bumps and bruises of life. I wish

I could protect my daughter from every difficulty and shield her from every hurt. However, as a higher education professional, I know that I can't, and shouldn't, parent with that as my priority.

In my work, I see the effects of hyperinvolved parents who have been more concerned with preparing the path for their child than with preparing their child for the path. No doubt their overinvolvement stems from love, but in the end, it may not succeed in producing confident, capable adults. Here are five signs you may be overparenting your student—and a few suggestions for alternative courses of action.

1. **You contact your student's teachers or professors because you didn't like a grade / want to ask for clarification on an assignment / want to ask for an absence to be excused / want to ask for an extension on an assignment due date.**

   Unless your child is incapacitated (heaven forbid), this is not okay. It doesn't matter if you are paying your student's tuition; teachers and professors do not want to hear from parents. They want to hear from their students directly and engage them in these conversations. Maybe you're calling because your kid is so busy and you just want to help him out, right? We see through that excuse, so don't go there. Your student can handle those things for himself. (And if he can't, please teach him.)

   Pick up the phone, sure—but instead of dialing a professor, talk to your student about what is happening. Make sure they've thought through their concerns. And help them think through the resolution they are seeking. Encourage them to consult the syllabus; it may contain information that sheds light on the issue. Then help them formulate how to approach the professor, or high school teacher, and ask for what they want. This process of teaching teens how to deal with challenges in the classroom, on their own, needs to be learned in high school or earlier.

2. **You say "we" and "our" when talking about your student's school experiences. ("We got a bid from our first-choice sorority!" or "We really hope to get into the eleven a.m. section of Biology 101." Or the one we hear most often: "We applied to six schools but have heard back from only three.")**

   You are not joining the sorority, or taking Bio 101, or applying to college, so stop that! This subtle pronoun choice communicates a lot to your student. It can make them feel pressured to achieve the things that will make you happy. Conversely, it may hand your student a chance to elude responsibility for making things happen. After all, if "we" want something, "we" will handle it. Also, it sends a message that you are personally invested in these experiences to a level that goes beyond concern for your student. It sends the message that these things are about you, when they really aren't. (On a side note, these first-person-plural pronouns are red flags to higher education professionals that you are overly involved in your student's college life.)

3. **You read their emails and check their assignment grades on a regular basis.**

   Step away from the passwords, please; you don't need to know what they earned on every test, and you have no business finding out what their professors and friends are emailing them. If you are supporting your college student financially, it's reasonable to request final course grades at the end of each semester. Beyond that, stay out of the minutiae. Some parents argue that staying aware of course grades throughout the semester enables them to help a student get back on track before it's too late. I get that—but in my seventeen-year career I've never seen it happen.

If a student isn't responsible enough to make changes after earning a poor test or assignment grade, they won't develop that skill by your checking in on them and trying to make them manage it in the way you think best. They will learn through experiencing the consequences of their choices and by learning to ask for help. A little adversity goes a long way—and certainly a lot further than overparenting—in moving a student toward good habits. If final course grades are less than desirable, talk to your student about the changes he or she needs to make to avoid the same mistakes. Make sure they are aware of campus resources such as academic coaching, tutoring, and professor office hours. Reiterate your expectations for their performance next semester.

4. You call them to wake them up for class.

If they are bright enough to get into college, they are bright enough to figure out how to get themselves out of bed. This is a basic life skill. If they didn't learn it in middle or high school, it's high time now. From super-loud alerts to bed shakers to devices that fly around the room until you catch them, all sorts of wild reveilles are on the market. Send your student shopping for one if a regular old alarm clock or their phone isn't cutting it.

5. You beg them to come home frequently (with the bribe of doing their laundry).

Of all the items on this list, this one will probably be the hardest for me as a parent. My daughter is still a few years from being college age, but I already know the "mom" part of me will want her to come home to visit as often as possible. At the same time, the "college professional" part of me knows this is a terrible idea. Students who leave campus frequently don't connect as well with their institution and other students—a critical factor in college success and completion. Students who leave frequently also don't study enough. Especially during their first year, encourage your student to get involved on campus and to spend time on the weekends studying and working ahead on papers. (And tell your student to do their own laundry. You've done enough.)

When we smooth our students' way through every challenge they encounter, we deprive them of prime opportunities to learn how to address problems and handle adversity. We likewise short-circuit the confidence they will need to address entirely different sets of issues in the future. The bottom line is that children need to have their own experiences, separate and distinct from ours. We need to love them enough to get out of their way and know they can handle their lives. Trust them to do well, but know that mistakes will be made. Trust them to survive those mistakes, learn from them, and emerge as confident, capable adults.

We kept in touch with Janet, the mom who became the first to ask an anonymous question in our community, and she reported back to us that she had called her daughter Kate's college dean as well as her son Michael's high school to let them know what was happening in her children's lives. She was making every effort to keep their lives as normal as possible, but their father had stage 4 cancer, and she knew her kids might need help. Kate's dean was incredibly kind, offering to meet Janet and Kate on move-in day and arrange to have Kate driven home if an emergency arose. Janet now had someone she could speak with if she was worried about her daughter being away from home during this difficult and painful time. And Kate had someone who knew and cared about what was happening in her life before she ever set foot on campus, if she needed it. But we had never spoken to Kate, never learned about her experience of moving away from home. Here she tells her story:

It wasn't until the summer before my freshman year, that cancer would officially become a part of my life forever.

I remember sitting down at the dinner table with my family, and the mood changing. The air in the kitchen grew heavy. My mom and dad looked at each other and tried to explain that "Daddy is sick, but we are going to fight this together as a family."

Fight what together? How do I prepare for this battle? What is this? This only happens in the movies and TV shows I watch. The doctors are wrong. This isn't true. I don't want this. Take it back. Go back. *No.*

I was so confused. Where do I go from here? How do you react to when you find out your Dad has cancer? How do you fight that? I had all these questions and more swinging through my head, and yet no one had clear answers.

I ended up going to college to start my freshman year that September. As I was moving in and starting classes, I decided that I would keep what was going on with my Dad a secret. I hated to think about it and I didn't want anyone to know. Maybe if no one knew then somehow it wouldn't be real. I ended up confessing what had been going on at home to some friends in December. I finally felt comfortable and accepted it enough to tell them.

Coming home for winter break was not what I had expected. One January morning, I woke up early to go out and buy my brother a birthday cake. I can vividly remember getting a text while I was in the store aisle, saying that I needed to come home now. I don't know how but I knew. I raced home.

On that day my dad, Wayne, passed away. His fight with cancer was over.

Not only did I lose my father, but the world lost a husband, a friend, a mentor, a coworker, a churchgoer, a volunteer. That day the world lost the strongest man I had ever known. My dad was the sweetest, funniest, most caring person, and I couldn't understand why he had to go. I still had so much to learn from him. There were so many things he wasn't going to be a part of now.

These last three years have been the hardest years of my entire life. Little did I know at the time that my dad had laid a strong foundation for my family. He knew that we would be okay. And on days that we aren't okay, he sends little messages and signs from heaven.

I will forever aspire to try to be even a quarter of the person my father was. I will continue to grow and learn from my mom, the strongest woman I have ever met. And I will continue to laugh and learn from my brother, who is the most honest and funny guy.

I know that my dad is looking down and smiling at my family, and I know that he is so proud of us.

CHAPTER TWO

Happiness, Anxiety, and Mental Health

W e just want our kids to be happy. We say this habitually, tossing the phrase around so often that it's easy to forget how much we truly mean it. It is the one unshakable truth of parenting. But adolescence and young adulthood can be a tumultuous time. In the midst of much joy, teens can almost visibly simmer with anxiety and stress. One of Lisa's sons describes these years as ones of "high highs and low lows."

As we once taught our babies to soothe themselves to sleep and our children to weather the social ups and downs of the playground, one of the most important things they need to learn, as they transition through the teen and early adult years, is to be the guardians of their own happiness. For some kids, this seems to come naturally, as they have been optimistic and sunny from birth. But even those who have a natural source of joy have much to learn about dealing with stress, disappointment, rejections, and the roller coaster they are often surprised to find their emotions riding.

When we had our children, we didn't think much about teaching them about happiness. We hoped they would be happy. We were going to move heaven and earth to help make them happy, and if they still weren't happy, we would call in the professionals who knew about these things. What was there for a parent to teach?

As moms of now twentysomethings, this view seems hopelessly naive. Part of our job as parents is to show our kids how to manage stress, find joy, and understand how both of these things work best for them. Some of this is done explicitly, but much more of it is transmitted by modeling our own ability to experience joy even in the face of stress and frustration.

It is clear that anxiety and depression are becoming ever more present in the lives of young people. In the following chapter, we will talk about teaching them to cope with stress, to find help from teachers, professors, or mental health professionals when they need it, to set realistic expectations, and to understand the ways that parents can help.

TEACHING HAPPINESS

To start collecting some practical answers to the question of how to teach our kids about happiness, we consulted experts, among them a neurology professor, a high school teacher, and a pair of instructors who teach New York University's most popular elective course.

We began with speaker and performance coach Daniel Lerner and Dr. Alan Schlechter, a clinical associate professor at New York University and director of the Child and Adolescent Psychiatry Clinic at Bellevue Hospital, who share a classroom of 475 NYU undergraduates every semester. After team-teaching their standing-room-only Science of Happiness course for many years, they turned their course into a popular book called *U Thrive: How to Succeed in College (and Life)*, a campus-and-beyond guide.

We asked Lerner and Schlechter to share some of their research and findings about how parents can help teens and college kids cultivate happiness.

While we want our kids to be happy because we love them and care deeply that they find joy in the world, Lerner and Schlechter suggest that there is an additional reason we should care. "There is an increasing abundance of studies that talk about the direct effect of positive emotions on the way we perform," Lerner explains. "We looked at studies with college students who are primed with forty-five seconds of positive emotions. We prime them by asking them to think about the happiest moment they can before moving on to complete a designated task. And what we see when students are primed with positive emotions is that they retain more words when they are taught in a foreign language. They do better on creative tests as well as making improvements on standardized tests."

In these studies, students were asked to think about the happiest memory they had, and by doing this simple thing before undertaking a task, students objectively performed better on examinations. What does "priming with positive emotions" look like? "For some it can be a moment of joy, like remembering how amazing it was to get their acceptance letter to college," Lerner explains. "For others, it might be recalling a vacation with their family, perhaps sitting on the beach, something that is a much quieter moment. For each of them it is different, but it's important for students to understand that positive emotions work for each of us individually. As we are seeing from the research, there are real cognitive and physical benefits to experiencing these positive emotions."

Schlechter suggests that we can encourage our kids' happiness and consequently their success with even our most minor interactions with them. "Most parents call up their kids and say, 'How are you doing?' But they will quickly get to—'How's your work going? What are you doing in your classes?' When really their first question should be 'What was the most fun thing you did? When did you laugh the hardest today?' And if you start your conversation with your college students with a question such as that, you are actually priming them with positive emotions on the phone. After that, they are actually much more likely to want to talk about the more challenging things in their lives. When we prime each other with positive emotions, it increases the desire to negotiate, compromise, and trust each other."

As our kids go off to college, we may question whether they are academically prepared and whether they know enough about adulting to live responsibly on their own. And while both of those things are important, Schlechter explains that research points to something even more important: "The number one factor that predicts whether you are going to pass your first year in college is the feeling that you belong where you are," he explains. So after parents discuss the things that might have brought joy into their students' days, they should ask them about their connections on campus.

We hear from readers all the time that their kids have started college, are at the place they longed to be and were excited about all summer, and now they are sitting in their dorm room and won't come out. They are scared. They feel alone, and they are certain, beyond a shadow of a doubt, that they are having the single worst experience of any student on any campus. They have exiled themselves from their floor and every other social connection, and now they are leaning on us, their parents, through calls, texts, and every other modern form of communication to make it right—or at least listen to how wrong it is.

Schlechter suggests that the solution to this problem begins before kids even set a foot on campus. They need to get into the mind-set that they will in some way involve themselves in the life of the campus. There will certainly be trial and error as they find their way and discover where they belong, but Schlechter says that thriving in college "is not about looking through the course catalog, it's about looking through the intramural activities. It's about the clubs on campus. It could be about the Greek life. If you want to succeed in college, the number one question is, how are you going to connect with your campus? And how are you going to find the resources that are going to make you feel really comfortable on the campus?"

He explains further: "We know that those students who do the deep dive into work and only work are the ones who end up feeling isolated. They are the ones who have a bad first semester, but you don't really hear about that."

Parents need to watch themselves and the message they convey when talking to their teens. "The expectations of parents and what they say versus how they act don't always align," Lerner says. "They say, 'You should go off and join clubs and get involved on campus,' but then their first question is, 'How are your grades?' It's a default, because it's what got most kids to college in the first place."

Parents, he argues, should focus on more than their high school student's academic progress. If their kids are to be happy, well-adjusted college students, or successful in whatever they do after twelfth grade, parents need to remind their high school students how proud they are that they have a balanced life—that they've joined activities and spent time with their friends, as well as getting their work done. They can prime their teens with positive emotions through the kind of questions they ask as a way to establish real and meaningful communication. If we just praise our kids for their academic achievements, we send a message that these other things that bring us joy are not important, when, ironically, these other things will allow our kids (and ourselves) to perform better.

KIDS AND STRESS

After worrying about our kids' happiness, the second issue that parents tell us concerns them is their teen being under too much stress. Critics say we have babied our kids, disabled a generation from being able to withstand pressure and walk into adulthood with independence. But we see it differently. Parents have watched their kids endure more stress than they ever did at the same age, and for many this is a source of concern. Our kids took more tests, harder classes, needed higher scores, and weathered more competition—while we stumbled into colleges that most of us readily acknowledge would never accept us today. In *U Thrive*, the authors note that 85 percent of college students report feeling stressed *every* day. And at some point, 60 percent say they were so stressed they could not do their coursework.

So we have lived with our kids' stress during high school, watched it exhaust or even wear them down, and now as we send them off, we worry they are just jumping into the stress deep end. But Lerner and Schlechter suggest parents reframe the entire notion of stress.

Our goal in life, they explain, is not to take stress away from our kids, or, for that matter, ourselves. Our job is to help them understand the optimal level of stress for themselves and rethink what stress means. Until now, we may have been looking at stress all wrong.

Stress generally has negative connotations, when, in fact, stress can often be a positive force. "We need an optimal amount of stress to learn, perform at our best, or change," Schlechter explains. "Some people are living a life with so much fear of any stress that they actually never hit their peak. They may do very well, but they never really find out what their optimal performance is because they avoid stress. Some people get so overwhelmed by stress that they go over the peak and they end up feeling disorganized or overwhelmed." Each person needs to find the level of stress that enhances their performance without impeding it. The stress we can manage may improve our performance and enable us, yet as it rises beyond that point it can become unhealthy. But how can we help our kids discover the optimal amount of stress?

"I think when you hit the right level of stress, it should be challenging but not overwhelming, and afterwards there should be some level of fulfillment—like after a good run," Schlechter says. But, as with a good run, sometimes it all seems to fall into place, and you may be breathing heavily from exertion, but your energy level remains high. Other times, the run is simply grueling.

"The first thing is adjusting your mind-set," Schlechter explains. "We need to understand that stress is not the enemy. Jeremy P. Jamieson did a study that showed when people read a paragraph about the fact that stress actually allows them to perform better, they performed fifty points better on a practice GRE [graduate school entrance exam]. But the really cool part of the study is that two months later when they took the real GRE, they performed seventy points better than their peers who were not told, as they approached the exam, that stress could be helping them. Simply changing the mind-set around stress can impact performance."

The key seems to be in viewing stress in a different way. "Kids need to learn that even though they are feeling some nervousness in a given situation, they are also feeling some excitement," Schlechter reminds parents. "The work of Alison Wood Brooks out of Harvard showed that when people said, 'I'm excited' versus saying 'I'm stressed,' they actually performed much better—whether it was speaking in public or performing math problems."

Looking at stress as excitement and fear, joy and apprehension, and nervousness mixed with eager anticipation changes how we feel and thus react. As Lerner and Schlechter explain, just saying the words "I'm excited" helps us see the feeling as something far more positive than simply stress.

MANAGING HIGH SCHOOL STRESS

Even if you have a kid who seems to manage stress well and is able to maintain their equilibrium, there are times that high school will put them to the test. Lisa found a few reliable ways to help her kids whenever this happened.

The stress in my house ramped up in eleventh grade, a year that felt like the seventh circle of hell, a place so sinister and drained of joy that I despaired of my kids or I ever emerging from it. Although frankly, I may have felt their stress more acutely than they did.

I worried about my boys. When high school began they had their heads down doing what they needed to do: studying, playing sports, creating art, enjoying their friends, and sharing time as a family. Before long, however, as SAT prep kicked in and they began to meet with their guidance counselors, the stress level they felt at school and among their peers rose.

I had two choices here. Feed the anxiety beast, jump on board with them, and worry like there was no tomorrow (and I would be lying if I didn't admit to doing this sometimes)—or take a step back and try to remember that they were young, and while I had learned coping mechanisms for stress over my lifetime, they were still finding their way.

I came to see that my job as their parent was twofold. As one of the two people who loved them most in this world, I wanted to help ease them through this period by helping in small ways. I didn't subscribe to the school of thought that says if they can do it themselves they should. I was more than happy to do little things to lessen the pressure. But far more important, I needed to show them what I had learned about coping with stress in the years since I walked in their shoes. Research reveals that teens today feel stress even more acutely than their parents, so teaching them to cope is a crucial part of parenting adolescents. Here are the ways I tried to dial down the stress and teach them lessons they might be able to use for a lifetime.

FIND A STRESS-FREE ZONE. Everyone has a place where they can decompress, a place where the pressure seems to fade, if not disappear. Teens may not see their place so clearly. For one of my sons, it was working with his hands to create things; for another, it was listening to music; and for a third, I am sorry to say, it was computer games. Our job as parents is to recognize where that place is for them, if they cannot see it, and from time to time—as long as it isn't destructive— encourage them to make a visit when the going gets rough.

REMEMBER, IT IS ABOUT EFFORT, NOT RESULTS. Sports experts will tell you that we can master and control process but not outcome. The focus, any good coach will say, should be on practice and the mastery of skills, not the outcome of a game. With every set of midterms and finals, one of my boys and I would have the same conversation. He would ask if I thought he studied as hard as he could and should. I would acknowledge his effort, and then the two of us would agree that the rest was out of his hands and therefore not up for discussion. If he put in the effort and tried hard on his exams, I abided by my vow to shut up. This was much more difficult for me than I'm making it sound, but I've been well trained by a kid who understood that teens need praise not for what they've accomplished but for what they have at-tempted.

IT'S THE LITTLE THINGS. Helicopter parenting has crashed. All around us we hear the rallying cry for not doing things for our kids that they are perfectly capable of doing for themselves.

Most of the time, I am on board with this. But sometimes the best way to help someone with stress is to take a little something off his or her plate. I have done this by making my kids breakfast to take in the car in the morning, or filling a gas tank they've left near empty. I have packed gym bags when they have forgotten to do so the night before.

There are two ways I looked at this. I sometimes thought that I needed to stop babying boys who towered over me and were months away from leaving home. Yet, I also thought, this is how adults love and care for each other, by doing those little things that make someone else's day just a little bit easier. Isn't that the kind of behavior I wanted to model? Don't I want them to go out in the world and treat their partners, friends, and each other with small kindnesses to show love and exhibit care?

Yes, they are teens and could do this all themselves— and sure, some of these actions might be construed as enabling, and possibly even disabling, kids who are learning to bear responsibilities. But here's the thing: they soon will be gone. And our opportunities to make these little gestures that demonstrate our love and support will be gone too.

TEACH THEM TO TALK TO TEACHERS. So much school stress comes from worrying what a teacher thinks, wants, or expects. So much anxiety is produced through conjecture. Learning to speak up and ask questions of a teacher, whether it is clarification on an assignment, an explanation of a grade, or a request for more time, reduces stress. You can never remind your teen too many times that teachers actually like to talk to students. And while it is teachers now, later it will be professors and bosses. Learning to express their concerns to a figure of authority is a skill they will always need.

TREATS WORKED WHEN TEENS WERE LITTLE, AND THEY STILL WORK NOW. Rewards are not the same as bribes; they are simply your way of acknowledging the effort you see a teen making on behalf of whatever challenge happens to be in front of them at the moment. Whether it's a special coffee drink when you pick them up from work or school, or an offer to pay for something small you know they've been eyeing, the message is that you appreciate their endeavor, you applaud their efforts, and you love to see them smile.

DON'T TALK ABOUT THE PAST AND WHAT LIFE WAS LIKE FOR US AS TEENS. Parents like to reminisce about their teen years and recollect that the demands made on teens in another era were lighter or different. Sometimes we stray into inveighing against the demands that our kids now experience and opining that it should not be thus. But we no longer live in the 1980s or '90s, and our kids can't time travel. Telling teens they should not have to do what they clearly must is far from helpful. So rather than pining for a world our kids will never know, we should help them learn to navigate the one they actually live in.

PROVIDE A JUDGMENT-FREE ZONE. Peer pressure is perpetual and pervasive; teens feel it every day simply walking through the halls of their schools or thumbing through their phones. Let home be a true respite from the real or imagined judgments they perceive. Although I am the first to acknowledge that it is impossible and probably not helpful to keep all our opinions to ourselves, a parent's words should be weighed carefully given the onslaught of judgment that many teens experience elsewhere in their lives. Our home and our families need to be a refuge from the anxiety of the outside world.

EXERCISE WORKS AS A DE-STRESSOR FOR US, AND IT DOES FOR THEM TOO. Unless your teen is on a sports team, physical activity may be one of the first things to go as their time pressures rise. It needs to be one of the last, and ideally wouldn't be dropped at all. Exercise is a lifelong habit that cannot start too young, and research shows that its mental health benefits are substantial.

MAKE A SLEEP PLAN WITH THEM. I take that back. Sleep is the first thing to go, followed by exercise. Teens need a lot more sleep than they get, and part of the problem is their inability to plan their time and recognize that, at the end of the evening, they simply do not have enough hours left. "I'll do it later, I have plenty of time," is the familiar refrain that results in massive sleep deprivation. Ever try to discuss sleep at 11:00 p.m. with a teen who has not finished his homework? Not pretty. Teens need to be reminded that sleep is not what we do with whatever time we have leftover, but that, like every other activity, it has to be allotted sufficient time in their day. Their very safety depends on adequate sleep, as it impacts everything from driving to assessing risk. Dr. Jess Shatkin, professor of child and adolescent psychiatry and pediatrics at the NYU School of Medicine, says, "A good night's sleep reduces risky behavior among adolescents by allowing enhanced prefrontal control over emotional brain centers."

REMIND THEM THAT THERE ARE 168 HOURS IN A WEEK. IT IS ENOUGH TO GET EVERYTHING DONE, WITH PLANNING. With a teen who is feeling stress because of poor time management, it is tempting to act as their personal organizers. A better suggestion might be to model planning for them. Open up a calendar app and show them how twenty-four hours a day, or 168 hours a week, really is enough time to do what they need—or if not, help them decide what plans need to be abandoned. Talk about the time they are wasting and where that might be cut from their schedule. Discuss setting priorities and figuring out which activities are most important. Sometimes committing their time demands to a piece of paper or electronic calendar allows them to see, literally, how they will deal with their responsibilities and have time for the things they enjoy.

The anxiety never leaves; it is never totally gone. For so long, I thought I would eventually get to a place in my life where I would be free of worry. In high school, I thought that place would be college. Now that I am in college, I fall into a pattern of thinking that my graduation date will bring a sweet release from my anxieties. This is a dangerous way to think. I have realized in my short nineteen years that there is no place like this that exists. There will always be deadlines to meet, projects to complete, bills to pay. In fact, as you grow older, the list of things to cause anxiety just grows longer and longer.

The key to dealing with this is not working toward a place where anxiety is nonexistent—the goal is to be okay with what you have, where you are, and what you are doing. The worries will always be there, but you can develop ways to not let them control your life. And to all of the parents with kids suffering from anxiety, remind them to get out of that dorm room, and don't stop telling them how much you love them. We would never admit it, but we miss that every day.

—RACHEL, 19

PART OF THE BLAME IS ON US

So where does all this stress come from? Some of it comes from outside our homes. Our kids see markers of success and they set their own expectations based on the external messages they receive. Some of it comes from social media. When every person you know is having the most amazing, fun, over-the-top, perfect life, it is hard not to take your own expectations up a notch or two. But it is time to be honest about our role, as parents, in creating or exacerbating stress for our kids—because their expectations also come from us.

If we can't take a good long look in the mirror, we are ignoring our own responsibility for the acute pressure so many of our kids feel. And if we can't be honest with ourselves, we can't be the parents we hope to be. Lawyer-turned-writer and mother of three sons Helene Wingens analyzes this fraught dynamic.

I'd like to think it was carelessness rather than thoughtlessness that led me to create a culture of crushing parental expectations. But we need to choose our words carefully, especially those we offer our children. Over the years I developed a habit of saying things to my sons like, "You're going to do great things." Or "You're going places, kid." I expressed these sentiments in an effort to demonstrate that I had confidence in my children and their abilities. I also said these things with full knowledge of the detrimental pressure that society places on teenagers to be superlative in everything they do.

The pressure to excel is ubiquitous. Not just pressure to excel for the sake of mastery, but pressure to be "the best" for the sake of earning recognition. There is pressure on the sports field, in extracurricular activities, and certainly in academics. And often we are unaware of the yoke of expectations we foist upon our kids.

Making musical phenoms was never my aspiration. One of my sons took piano lessons for two years. He never practiced. I never cared. I wanted him to simply enjoy that one hour of instruction a week. It was my goal to expose him to piano, *not* to turn him into a pianist. As it was, after two years of my dragging him to lessons while he whined like I was boiling him in hot oil, I caved to his desire to quit. Did I worry about the serial quitting of activities? Sometimes, but not much.

I was equally uninspired about athletics. I suppose I was fortunate that my children declared early and often they would never excel on the sports field. Other parents told me in ominous undertones that if I didn't sign my child up for soccer by the age of three, his "foot skills" would be forever lacking and we could just forget about competing with the other boys. I didn't care; if they chose to play a sport, it was about learning to be on a team and getting some exercise—nothing more.

But academia was different.

School was our sweet spot, and I was swept up in the hysteria of best grades, best school, best job, and best life. With each good grade they received, I would reassert for my children my conviction that they were bound for glory.

And then came the day my son anxiously asked me, "But what if I don't do great things with my life? What if I just become a lawyer?" I realized then that I had no idea how insidious my words had been. They had been having an impact, but not in the way I intended. To my son, the

words I had so cavalierly uttered created a parental expectation, one he clearly felt he might not be able to meet.

That's why I no longer tell my sons that I expect greatness from them, and I no longer suggest to them that they
will set the world afire. I actually have no idea what their
future will bring.

Instead, I will tell them that I have the following parental
expectations:

I expect you to work diligently and to take advantage of
the opportunities life has given you. I expect you will fail,
but when you do you will pick yourself up and try again—
because success is a question of stringing together more
good days than bad, and the only way to do that is to plow
through and learn from the bad. I expect that you will prize
goodness above greatness, and that you will be kind and
thoughtful to all people. In that vein, I expect you to flex
your philanthropic muscle, even when you think you lack
the resources to do so.

I expect you to learn for the sake of knowledge, to play
for the sake of joy, to give of your time and money for the
sake of others, and to do it all to meet your own expectations and no one else's. In fact, to love and be loved is my
greatest expectation for you, and my highest hope.

SCHOOL-LIFE BALANCE

Lori Stratton lives the "academic-life balance" debate: she teaches
AP English literature and is the mother of a grown son and two
daughters, so she sees the pressure our teens face both at school
and at home. She wrote this piece when one of her daughters was
a high school senior at the same school where Stratton teaches.

As parents, we all want the best for our children. So when we nag them about getting higher grades, and when we lose sleep at night worrying about test scores, extracurricular activities, community service hours, and the whole college admission process, it stems from the best of parental intentions.

As a high school teacher, I see the burden of all this parental, societal, and high school stress on the faces of my high-achieving students every day. And as a mother, I fight the urge to gather my students in my arms, dole out warm cookies and cold milk, and put them down for much-needed naps.

High school students these days are often stressed, sometimes to the point of forgetting that being a teenager can be fun. Life for teenagers has become so complicated due to rising college tuition rates, unemployment scares, social media expectations, and no lack of urgent activities demanding their attention. How can we help them slow down and enjoy their last few years at home? How can we send them the message that life is meant to be savored and not conquered?

I did not fully understand the extent of the stressors in the lives of teenagers until my own children reached high school. Then, I finally got the opportunity to see the lives of teenagers three-dimensionally. Not only did my own children face high school stress over classes, grades, sports, and activities, they had the added stress of maintaining a successful social life, and making it look, at least on social media, that they had it all together.

They seldom made it home in time for dinner, because practices or work got in the way. They would stay up late in the night, studying for a test or writing a paper, fully cognizant of the fact that their parents could not pay for 100 percent of their college expenses and scholarships were necessary.

On the rare nights there was no homework, there'd be boyfriends and girlfriends to text, tweets to write, Instagram photos to edit. Rarely did they get even close to enough sleep.

This year, as my youngest child sits in my senior AP Literature classroom, I know how it will affect her and her friends when I assign an essay or schedule a test. I feel torn between knowing what I need to do as a teacher to prepare these students for college and the end-of-the-year AP exam, and not wanting to see my students' jaws tense and their eyes grow cloudy when I pile on obligations to their already overflowing plates.

I face the same issue when grading student work. If an essay deserves an 82 percent, I hesitate before marking the paper, fully understanding what that grade will do to the student who puts pressure on herself to never get less than a 92 percent. But analyzing literature is difficult, and an 82 percent is a good grade for students just learning the skill. So as a teacher, what do I do?

I try to convince my students that grades aren't nearly as important as their mental health or getting enough sleep at night. We discuss how grades will never, ever define them. I let them know that B's are perfectly acceptable, and achieving balance in life is what really leads to happiness. But I see the skepticism on their faces.

All around them are stories of how difficult it is to get into college, how hard it is to pay for college, and how tough it is to find meaningful, well-paying work after college graduation. And then there are their parents, losing sleep at night adding the cost of tuition and room and board in their heads, inadvertently adding to the pressure. All too often I hear my students say, "But my parents expect me to get A's."

Maybe as parents we can step back and model for our teenagers what a balanced life looks like. I have to check myself. If my daughter comes home for dinner, a rare occasion given her schedule, I have to set aside any work I had planned. Instead, I need to spend time listening to her, laughing with her, and demonstrating how successful adults spend their leisure time. This is difficult when I could so fully fill up my days and evenings with work.

But we owe it to our teenagers, don't we? After all, every parent I know wants his or her child to be happy. But so many of our teenagers aren't happy due to the amount of stress and fatigue they feel. Maybe instead of asking about his test grade, we can ask about his favorite band, or what movie he has been really wanting to see. It won't be easy. We are primed to be achievers and to raise achievers.

We only have these interesting and creative kids in our daily lives for a short while. Let's give each other permission to enjoy them and our time together. Let's realize that GPAs, a résumé full of extracurricular activities, and college admission letters are not the only marks of a successful and happy life.

IT'S ALL ABOUT THE BRAIN

So much of understanding our teens, and their anxiety and happiness, is understanding their brains. There are many things we assume, incorrectly, about how they think and function. We extrapolate from our own thinking or try, with mixed success, to remember being teens ourselves. Dr. Frances Jensen, chair of the neurology department at the University of Pennsylvania's medical school and the mother of two young-adult sons, says, "The teenage brain is not just an adult brain with fewer miles on it. It's a paradoxical time of development. These are people with very sharp brains, but they're not quite sure what to do with them. Adolescents are not, in fact, an alien species, just a misunderstood one."

In *The Teenage Brain: A Neuroscientist's Survival Guide to Raising Adolescents and Young Adults*, Jensen and coauthor Amy Ellis Nutt remind parents that the process of maturation is a long one: "Children's brains continue to be molded by their environment, physiologically, well past their midtwenties."

We asked Jensen about the challenges of parenting high school and college kids and how best to guide them through these years of turbulent but wonderful growth.

Q: Teens often become monosyllabic, refusing to elaborate or offer up much information. For parents, this can be scary. Is there something we can do to engage them in real, meaningful conversation? How can we discuss the hard stuff when they don't share much?

A: The more time you spend with your kids, the more desensitized they become to you and open up. Don't be that household where your kid comes home from school, gets a snack, and retreats into his bedroom with the door closed for the rest of the night. That is sadly a pretty typical modern family. Extract them for mealtime or some other family activities on a regular basis. That way, you are interacting. Let them see you being you. They are watching you, and let them see you make mistakes.

Being in the car together is wonderful because, blissfully for my sons, there is no eye contact. You are driving, they are in the passenger seat, and you can start to have the conversations that would be uncomfortable face-to-face. In fact, one of my favorite parts of the college-search process was going on trips with my kids. Over a several-hours-long car ride you would get to the bottom of a lot of "stuff."

Have a conversation with your kids about how they do not yet have very good split-second judgment. I doubt there is a single teenager who hasn't had one or two events where parents have said to them afterward, "Are you kidding? You are an A student, why did you do that?" It's not that teens can't reason through the question, but they don't have access to split-second reasoning in their frontal lobes like adults do. Their brain's activity isn't conducting fast enough for teens to say to themselves, "Oh, I better not do this." They go for the risk and afterward realize that they shouldn't have done that. Point out this weakness and ask them to try to think twice in the future.

They are going through a stage, and it is a natural stage. But point out the downside of taking risks that can cause excess stress and injury to the brain. Give them the data and facts rather than anger and orders. They love data! I talked to my sons about sad examples of DUI, deaths, and suicide, and I pointed out what went wrong. I would use these tragic examples in our community to tell them, "There but for the grace of God goes you."

Q: What are the specific subjects that we need to discuss with our teens before they go to college and are out on their own?

A:
- Illicit drugs: A drug like cannabis can lower a teen's IQ if they are smoking on a daily basis, so talk to your kids about frequency and the patterns of addiction. There can also be significant brain damage from drugs such as Molly/Ecstasy, which is especially true during the early twenties. Because the brain is changing and young adults have more receptors for these drugs, there is more potential for severe damage.
- Excessive alcohol: Your teen has only one brain and it is still growing. Binge drinking can cause cell death in a teen's brain at a level that would only cause intoxication in an adult.

- Stress: Stress can interfere with learning. With impulse control being weak in teens, they need to be careful about what they expose themselves to in terms of harmful situations that can cause stress.
- Mental illness: This is the time of life when depression, schizophrenia, and psychotic breaks can start to occur. Be aware of the signs, such as a deepening of a teen's mood swings, changes in eating or sleeping habits, loss of interest in seeing friends or participating in activities they once enjoyed, and the tendency to take more risks or act out more frequently. And stay connected with your kid. Discuss mental health with your teens so that they can better recognize problems in themselves or their friends and get the help they need.
- Learning machines: College is the best time in their life to learn, and these abilities will diminish over time. This is one of the last chances they have to memorize things so easily, so carpe diem! It is a golden age for them. They will obviously have fun, but tell your teen that college is a chance to set themselves up for the future and turn themselves around. If they are a C student in high school they can become an A student in college. It is a time when kids can work on strengths and weaknesses, and they should recognize they have a power they won't have later in life.

Q: While our kids are living under our roofs, we have a front-row seat to observe their every change, both physical and behavioral. But after we drop them at their freshman dorm, that view is limited. How connected should parents be during the college years?

A: Err on the side of being fairly connected, but not helicopter or bulldozer parents, which can create a child who has a sense of learned helplessness. Alienation is a problem if it grows from a bad relationship between parents and kids. Being angry or misjudging your teen by projecting adult capacity on him or her is a recipe for disaster in some cases. Don't be that parent who gets so angry that the relationship degrades. Recognize that your teen is going through a natural stage. They are not trying to be annoying all the time!

But try to stay connected. Be the parent who calls, shows up for the weekend, sends care packages. If I felt I was losing track of my child because he didn't check in, I would be over at his college campus for a visit. As embarrassing and goofy as you seem to them, you are making the effort, and that is really important.

Q: You discuss the dangers of binge drinking on young brains. But if we only have a chance to tell our kids a few points about why they should *not* overindulge in alcohol, what are those points?

A:

- College is a time for learning. Society is asking teens to use this time in their lives to learn. There is synaptic plasticity in the teenage brain that allows them to excel at learning, but alcohol can undo the learning directly.
- Alcohol disrupts sleep patterns, and sleep deprivation results in your inability to work at your potential. You are setting yourself up for the worst week ahead when you binge drink on the weekend.
- Alcohol diminishes impulse control, which can lead to extremely risky behavior.
- The same quantity of alcohol has a bigger effect on a kid than an adult. Teens are uniquely vulnerable to its effects. Alcohol toxicity in teens is more likely to cause brain injury because a teen has more synapses, which are more impacted by heavy drinking than adults' brains are.

Q: Any final takeaways about the teenage brain?

A: The teen brain offers major advantages on the one hand, but unperceived and often unacknowledged vulnerabilities on the other.

The brain is the last organ in the body to mature, which is done in the midtwenties. It is more vulnerable in this window of teenage years because of its underdeveloped state—including the frontal lobe (seat of judgment), which is not as accessible to teens as it is for adults.

Teens have a heightened ability to learn, and their brain synapses are functioning at higher levels, which is excellent and explains why they can learn so much in this period. However, addiction is another form of learning, and thus they are more susceptible to the negative effects of substances or stress.

How you treat your brain now will have lasting impact on the adult you are going to be. To the extent you can hold back on some of the risks inherent in this period, it is like paying it forward for your future self.

WHEN WE JUST DON'T KNOW

Even as we try to understand our teens by thinking about how their brains work, we know their impulse can be to mislead us, to hide from us what they don't want us to see. Depression and anxiety have soared among teens and young adults, and while few of us would want our kids to suffer alone, even parents who are professionally trained and close to their kids can miss the signs of their suffering. In the following story, one mom, a physician, offers us a look into the pain her son was silently suffering and the corresponding pain it brought her when she discovered it.

I am now confident that actual, physical heartache is real—it exists. I have to admit that I had my doubts until a year ago, when I jokingly asked my son what the Band-Aids on his arm were hiding, and he looked at me with tears in his eyes. In that instant, something within me broke, leaving a painful, gaping hole—anguish that I could not, as hard as I tried, mitigate.

To be left alone with my thoughts was to invite torrents of tears and such self-scrutiny that I invariably questioned my ability to parent and declared myself a failure. How could I have spent the greater part of my adult life trying to keep the world from injuring my children, to then have my son—my beautiful, funny, intelligent son—harm himself? How could he have been so thoroughly despondent that the sensation of slicing his own body was the only respite he could identify? I returned frequently to the same haunting question . . . "What did I miss?"

Our family had always seemed like a giant old tree to me, with a broad and stable foundation, secure and steadfast. The brightly colored leaves recalled our multiple good fortunes and successes, embellishing the solid base. I used to love observing each year as the leaves changed colors and gently floated to the ground when winter approached; I was secure in the knowledge that, much as our lives evolved, in the coming seasons the trees would renew with more, equally vibrant leaves, mirroring the flourishing of our family. But that year, as autumn enveloped us, I saw only the dearth of leaves, each one falling and removing with it a small but definite segment of the whole, leaving a shell of the radiance that was present what seemed like a fleeting moment before.

I spent the better (or actually, worse) part of the subsequent months with images flashing through my mind—my son as a small child at the beach posing for photographs while clutching his beloved plastic hammer; him sitting proudly in the middle of his intricate sand sculpture; him joyfully and spontaneously singing a fabricated love song to his younger sister; him crawling into bed with me to snuggle. There was so much delight; where had that boy gone?

I tried desperately to understand him. I ached to help him. Knowing the depth of my agony, I could only imagine how intense his suffering must have been—I was sad, woefully sad, but that is not the same demon as depression. I scoured Facebook, Snapchat, any available social media with the hope of catching a glimpse of him with a smile, or at least to have proof that he was intact for another day. I texted him trivial questions, and breathed a sigh of relief when he answered, and panicked when he delayed; could he be occupied with self-injury at that moment? What if this was a forever situation, and neither he nor I would ever again experience peace? And how would this experience impact his future—the promise of an accomplished, charming, confident, and capable young man? Was he permanently broken? Did he hold himself to an unattainable standard, and was therefore fated to fail?

Answers to my questions were few and far between. My son had thankfully sought guidance from an older sister, who wisely directed him to professional help prior to my husband's and my knowledge of the situation. With medication and therapy, at a painstakingly slow pace, he gradually grew stronger, and his self-harming behavior was eliminated and his depression lifted. He now has a new "normal" existence. I am perpetually concerned that his postdepression balance is precarious, and that a suboptimal academic grade, a personal insult, or an ended relationship will plummet him on a downward trajectory. I am fearful that neither he nor I will identify the signs of recurrence early enough to avoid a repeat performance; I have observed this tragedy once, was grateful for the curtain call, and have no wish to revisit.

I share my reality because depression in young adults is on the rise across every American demographic, and it is often difficult to recognize. The effects are devastating, not only to the individual, but also to family and friends. Depression somehow crept into our close-knit and communicative family, took its toll, and left its scars; I was blindsided, and it has become clear to me that none of us is immune. I have been fortunate in that both my son and I have gotten a reprieve from the pain with which we struggled to coexist. As the following spring arrived, my own tree again began to thrive. I am relieved, but know that it will be many years before I can again comfortably appreciate the beauty I once saw in autumn.

PERFECTION IS A PERFECT STORM

When we were growing up, we didn't need to be perfect. No one expected it of us and it never occurred to us. Perfect, by definition, was what one could never attain. But mountains of research show that not only are our teens and young adults haunted by the expectation of perfection, they also feel harshly judged by others if they fail to achieve it. They are expected to be academic stars, have résumés that resemble those who have lived a decade longer, and all the while keep up a thriving social life, which is displayed on social media for all to see. And they are expected to make it all look easy. Effortless perfection.

Social media makes their life an open book whose pages need to be curated to show flawless selfies and reveal an unending string of activities that will stoke the envy of their followers and friends. At the same time, it is an incessant reminder of the parties to which they were not invited, clothing they cannot afford, or places they may never visit.

Teenagers come to believe perfection is possible; after all, they see it online every day, and no one makes the dissenting case. And there is no respite in the push for perfection, no moment when it turns off, shuts down, and just doesn't matter. The pressure of perfection is certainly the cause of some of our kids' emotional struggles, and psychologists and researchers tell us that our daughters battle with this even more than our sons. Rachel Simmons, educator, mom, and author of *Enough As She Is: How to Help Girls Move Beyond Impossible Standards of Success to Live Healthy, Happy, and Fulfilling Lives*, looks specifically at the pressure on girls to achieve. In her work she has found that "girls have to be superhuman: ambitious, smart and driven, physically fit, pretty and sexy, socially active, athletic, and kind and liked by everyone." She explains that young women take the message that they can do anything to mean they have to do everything.

In the following section, Simmons offers further insight into why girls are so vulnerable to the pressures of the college admissions process, and what parents can do to help.

Girls today live a painful paradox: they get better grades and go to college in greater numbers than boys, but they outstrip boys on measures of depression, anxiety, loneliness, and stress. At a moment when they have never enjoyed more opportunity, girls' mental health has bottomed out.

What gives? Part of the answer lies in a deeper look at the college admissions arena where, at first glance, girls appear to be champions. But in my work with girls, parents, and teachers over the last decade, I've seen something very different. In the college application industrial complex, the cruel system that tells teens their worth and potential are contingent on the "right" college acceptance, girls encounter a process that exploits vulnerabilities they already bring to the table: fear of failure, low confidence, and the desire to please.

"If life were one long grade school," Stanford professor Carol Dweck has said, "girls would rule the world." She means that success in school comes to those who can follow the rules, passively wait to speak, and do whatever someone else wants them to do. This, of course, is precisely how most girls are socialized to behave.

Although these habits give girls a leg up in the classroom and on their report cards, they often undermine girls' growth as individuals. As they absorb what it means to be a culturally acceptable "good girl," girls learn to please others at their own expense. They worry more about what other people think of them than what they think of themselves. They become dependent on the opinions of others, basing their self-esteem on their likability.

The need to get everything "just right" in their relationships often extends to their academic work and can lead to crippling perfectionism, fear of failure, and a lack of resilience in the face of challenge. Meanwhile, a pervasive sense that they are not enough as they are—that they must be smarter, prettier, more liked and so on—stokes resentment and jealousy among their peers, cleaving them from the crucial support systems they need to thrive.

To parent well during this time, it's critical to understand the precise ways college admissions mania intersects with girls' psychology and development. This section will explain how, and offer strategies to bolster your daughter against the most toxic elements undermining her potential.

Curiosity, the willingness to ask a question and go wherever the answers take you, is a crucial element of learning. But in the college application industrial complex, excellence is paramount. Every stumble "counts," as many students will tell you, on their college application. No surprise, then, that healthy risk-taking in learning—a willingness to enter a situation where you don't know the outcome—is an immediate casualty. In high school, risk avoidance can look like choosing not to raise your hand if you're not sure you have the right answer, avoiding a class where you may get less than an A, or declining to apply to a school where there's a chance you might get rejected. And while boys and girls alike are damaged by the pressure to excel at all costs, research shows that girls don't need any more help avoiding healthy risks.

Gender differences in this domain are prominent. A meta-analysis of 150 studies by James P. Byrnes and colleagues found that men were more comfortable taking risks in almost every category. The widest gender gap, notably, was in intellectual risk-taking.

Girls need extra support in taking risks as they face the message to play it safe in order to get into college. Try asking your daughter if she feels pressure to choose success over challenge. If she cops to it, sympathize and don't judge. She's likely only doing what she thinks is required to survive. Keep asking questions: Is she taking that class or pursuing this activity because she really wants to, or because she feels like she has to?

If there were no pressure to get into college, what would she be doing with her time? What would she do if she wasn't afraid? What matters to her more than success? Start a conversation about what she values in her life beyond college acceptance.

To encourage healthy risk-taking in your daughter, reward her when she's brave. Make a big deal out of it at a meal, or take her somewhere special to celebrate. Better yet, take a risk together and teach by example. Throw yourselves into a situation with an unknown outcome. Cook or bake something new, host a dinner party, go to an escape room. Learn a new skill. Do something you've never done. Go through an adventure together and celebrate the singular exhilaration that comes with proving to yourself you are smarter, braver, or tougher than you realized.

When she does fall short, teach her to celebrate the fruits of the process. I call this the "minimum benefit" question: What is the least good thing that came out of this? If we want girls to resist perfectionism, we have to pry them away from an obsessive focus on the outcome and teach them to appreciate the journey—even when it doesn't end up exactly where we wanted it to.

In his book *Drive: The Surprising Truth About What Motivates Us*, Daniel H. Pink writes that we're most likely to want to do something when "the joy of the task [is] its own reward." This is called intrinsic motivation, and it's a learner's most precious resource. A raft of studies find that intrinsically motivated students are more resilient, less anxious and depressed, and have lower levels of burnout. They get better grades and have higher levels of psychological well-being, to name just a few benefits.

But when we suspect someone is trying to control our performance through extrinsic motivators—say, by offering rewards, threatening punishment, or tendering certain kinds of praise—our intrinsic drive declines. We're not doing it anymore for ourselves; we're doing it for something, or someone, else. Success in the college application industrial complex is largely dependent on obtaining external rewards like good grades and high test scores. For too many students, the drive to learn is constantly disrupted by the fear of failure.

Girls are more vulnerable to losing their intrinsic drive when they are offered a reward or punishment, say Professors Edward L. Deci and Richard M. Ryan. Because girls are socialized by adults to please others, they tend to care more about feedback from teachers and parents.

Females, Deci and Ryan have found, "pay particular attention to evidence of having pleased the evaluator when praised." Multiple studies find that girls show more negative outcomes when they are praised in ways that encourage them to keep performing at a high level. In one study, praising elementary school students for fixed traits and abilities, like being "smart" or "nice," undermined intrinsic motivation for girls but not boys. Other studies have found that emphasizing "extrinsic values" like good grades, college acceptance, and financial success is particularly damaging for girls' wellness.

To help girls reconnect with their intrinsic motivation, consider helping them find purpose in their lives. Stanford University's William Damon defines purpose as the "intention to accomplish something that is at once meaningful to the self and of consequence to the world beyond the self." Purposeful pursuits can include volunteering, caring for animals, inventing an app, or starting a business. When you have a sense of purpose, you know why whatever you are doing matters to you personally, and why it matters to the world. Purpose is the deeper reason we pursue our everyday goals. Research has shown that teens with purpose are more confident and comfortable with themselves and have higher self-esteem.

When you ask your daughter about her day, listen for signs of excitement about anything inside or outside of the classroom. What lit her up? Why did she like it? What would she like to do about it next? Then, offer to help her deepen her interest.

Gender differences in self-criticism intensify in adolescence. Girls tend to be more self-conscious, harder on themselves, and more prone to negative self-talk than boys. They overthink their setbacks and spend too much time wondering what they could have done differently. Many interpret "no pain, no gain" as something to actively inflict on themselves, feeling certain that beating themselves up will motivate them to change, and that without self-criticism, they will be immobilized and unable to perform.

By their logic, you can't move yourself forward, racking up achievements and building out your résumé, without beating yourself up.

The problem, researchers say, is that while self-criticism may give us a swift kick in the pants, it elevates symptoms of anxiety and depression in the long run. Enter self-compassion, a trait identified by psychologist Kristin Neff of the University of Texas at Austin: the practice of treating yourself with the same gentleness when you are in distress as you would treat others. Self-compassion has three components:

1. Self-kindness: Approaching yourself in a soothing, comforting way. Talking to yourself the way a close friend might talk to you in this difficult situation.

2. A sense of common humanity: Recognizing that all humans are imperfect and make mistakes. Rather than deciding you are the only person who is struggling (a common reaction that leads to isolation and shame), you connect your own experience with countless others who have struggled before you or who struggle now.

3. Mindfulness: Naming how you think and feel right now, in the present moment. You don't deny what's happening, but you don't blow it out of proportion, or ruminate (overthink) about it endlessly.

Self-compassion can be uniquely helpful for girls for several reasons:

- Girls tend to ruminate about their problems. Rumination is defined as repetitively thinking about the causes and consequences of a problem, instead of a solution. Ruminating is associated with anxiety and depression, and a decrease in problem-solving abilities. Practicing mindfulness stops the cycle of ruminating and pulls girls into the present moment.

- Girls tend to feel more shame than boys. Shame is the feeling that you're a bad person (as opposed to guilt, the feeling that you've done a bad thing). When girls feel like a bad person, two things happen: they tend to isolate themselves from others, and they believe they are uniquely messed up or bad. The second step of self-compassion—connecting with common humanity—can dislodge girls from shame by helping them resist the urge to isolate. And mindfulness discourages catastrophizing thoughts, like "I'm the worst person," by pushing girls to stick with what's true in the present moment.

- Girls often interpret and respond to failure in self-destructive ways. Studies have found significant gender differences in this area: girls, for example, tend to be more "debilitated" by failure. They are more likely to get upset when confused by a challenging task and question their ability. They are also more likely to interpret a failure as a sign of lack of ability. The issue here is not ability itself; it's how girls think and respond in the face of failure. Self-compassion gives girls a cognitive tool—perhaps even a weapon—to combat the self-destructive thinking that can accompany challenge and failure.

Self-compassion can make you braver. Facing down a difficult challenge isn't just about what you do in the big, scary moment. What you do after that moment—how you deal, no matter what the outcome—matters just as much. If you don't know how to talk to yourself in the face of a setback, and you let mistakes fill you with shame, overthinking, and a desire to isolate . . . well, who would want to bother ever trying to be brave?

As with most behaviors and character traits, it always helps to model what you want to teach your children. Just as our kids mimic our words and phrases, they also pick up on how we interpret and respond to stress.

The next time you share a setback or self-critical thought with your daughter, try integrating the three components of self-compassion (or even one or two of them) into conversation. For example, I might say to my daughter: "I'm really mad at myself for not getting what I wanted. But I tried as hard as I could, and there were some other stressful, time-consuming things I was dealing with at the time."

By demonstrating a healthy way to respond to difficulty, you offer a vital script to your teen that she'll use in countless ways throughout her life. And what if you've been saying all the wrong things? Parenting is nothing if not humbling, and you are entitled to change course. Admitting where you've been wrong won't compromise your authority with your child; it will only amplify their trust in and respect for you. Mistakes make you real, and teens gravitate toward people who can be authentic and vulnerable.

WHEN IT DOESN'T LOOK LIKE DEPRESSION

We think we know when our kids are happy. We have watched over them from the time they first gurgled with joy. Can we actually stare right at their depression or anxiety, even as they live in our homes, and miss it? The answer is, of course, yes. Our teens may be hiding these painful feelings from us. Their symptoms may not manifest in what we classically think of as signs of depression. They may just seem like "a teen": moody, volatile, or shut down. Symptoms of depression in teens can include poor performance in school, rage or anger, lack of concentration, or changes in eating or sleeping patterns—and can easily be missed by parents because they look like other issues.

Like so many of us, when Tracy Hargen, writer and mom, looked at her son, she saw a well-adjusted high schooler who was managing his life just fine. But his four simple words came out of left field and shocked her profoundly.

My son said, "Mom, can we talk?"

Every mom who has heard these four words knows what follows may be a serious and possibly difficult message from your child.

These words are meant to be a warning, a chance for you to brace yourself because something big is about to be said. So when my son walked into my bedroom, on a break from studying for finals his junior year, I knew he needed my full attention.

"Mom, there's something I need to tell you. For the past year or so I've been depressed, seriously depressed. Recently, I've been talking to Ms. ___ at school [a teacher he and I both adored], and she's encouraged me to talk to you and Dad. In fact, today she insisted. She said you would both listen, and you were the only ones who could get me the help I need—and I need help."

I'll be honest—this was not what I was expecting. "I'm struggling with studying for this final"; "I'm worried about what I'll do all summer so I'm not bored"; "I'm exhausted from everything I've got going on"; "I'm stressed about senior year and getting into college"—any of these I might have seen coming. But not depression.

I know what adult depression looks like—can't get out of bed, no longer enjoying favorite activities or friends, sad, angry, and lethargic. None of this behavior described my son in the least.

I work from a home office that is directly across the hall from his room, where he studies and hangs out every afternoon. I could literally hear him laughing out loud at a funny video he was watching—daily. I saw him interacting with friends, playing sports, involved in theater, getting up each morning bright and early, ready to go.

I wanted to blurt out, "You're not depressed; I hear you laughing. You're not withdrawn—we talk and laugh all the time. You get up every day and seem great." What I didn't know in that moment was teenage depression shows itself differently—it can manifest as numbness, apathy, no feeling at all for anything, a darkness they don't understand—even if outwardly they seem okay.

What I did know in that moment was that he was serious and this conversation was very difficult for him. My husband was coaching a lacrosse game and was not home, so it was up to me to handle this, and I knew the stakes were high.

In the back of my mind I was also thinking about the friend whose child committed suicide. An "all-American boy" in his first year at college. A boy who loved school and his friends and was very close to his parents. In fact, his parents were in town—where he was in college—for a wedding. A wedding he was planning to attend. A wedding where he promised his mom the first dance. They'd spoken to him hours before he killed himself. He was upbeat and happy and was asking his mom if she brought the cuff links he needed for his tux shirt—she had. They talked about meeting the next day so the whole family could go to the wedding together.

They were absolutely shocked to learn just a few hours later he took his own life.

Knowing this boy and his family, and having two boys

of my own, this haunted me. His father speaks at colleges now—he bravely shares their story to help others understand what his family has learned about depression, anxiety, and suicide in young adults. They have set up suicide hotlines and they are saving lives, and I took notice of everything they shared. We'd talked with both of our sons about what happened to this family and asked if they ever felt depressed. At that time, they both said no.

I realized sitting there that night, after my son asked, "Mom, can we talk?" that it was quite possible that my happy-go-lucky son was feeling much different inside.

I chose my words very carefully. "I'm so sorry you're going through this, but I am so very glad that you told me. Thank you so much for trusting me. I promise that Dad and I will help you—you are not alone. Please, tell me what's going on. What are you feeling; why are you depressed?" Was it exactly right? I don't know, but it was the best I could come up with at the time, and it seemed to be what he needed to hear.

What followed was the two of us sitting there while he shared everything. I'm telling you—I thought I knew him inside and out. He was so open with us, and we spent a lot of time together—I really thought I would know if something this serious was wrong with him, but I didn't. He'd hidden it from us very well, whether intentionally or not, so I was blindsided.

That night, he was so clear and articulate about how he felt, what he was going through, and he asked for help. We talked about options. I knew a wonderful therapist who would see him, and he could decide if she was a good fit for him or not (thankfully she was). We agreed I'd make an appointment for him to see his primary care doctor to determine if medication was needed, and I asked him if I could reach out to his teacher to thank her for supporting him and guiding him to talk to us. I assured him we would be here for him.

We would do whatever it took to get him the help he needed. I told him it could take a few tries to find the right resources, but we'd all do it together—this was no longer a secret he had to keep inside. He was so visibly relieved it was like a huge weight had been lifted off his shoulders.

When his dad got home our son filled him in, and we all talked about our plans. Over the next few months we met with experts, I did endless research to learn everything I could, and we talked. It was hard not to check in every few hours, asking, "Are you okay? How do you feel?" I needed to know, but I didn't want him to withdraw. He wasn't suicidal, but my friend's son was in my mind, and I didn't want to miss any signs. We talked honestly about how he was doing and we talked about his treatment. We made changes until he was on the right course of action.

It took time, but slowly things got better.

There were many times I cried—I cried thinking about how long he'd suffered alone. I cried wondering how I couldn't have known. I cried imagining what could have happened if he hadn't told us and hadn't asked for help. I cried grateful tears for his teacher—who was supportive and insisted that he tell us. I cried as she said to me, "I told him I could listen and I could understand, but I couldn't get him help. I told him I knew you would listen to him and you would do anything to help." She will always hold a special place in our hearts.

He's in college now. At orientation all the freshmen did an exercise called Dear World—every person tells their story in a few short words written in black marker on their bodies. They are paired up, and they help each other do the writing while sharing the story behind the words. Then they have a professional photo taken to capture the moment. Our son sent us his photo without telling us what he wrote—and in the photo he has his left arm out to the side and in bold letters is written "I CAN FEEL THE DAYLIGHT" and on his open hand the word "AGAIN."

When I saw it, I cried—I cried because of how far he's come and because he's openly and willingly telling his story to others. He said he hoped that by talking about what he went through someone else would be helped. He was thrilled when I asked him if I could share his story. I told him I thought it could help other parents who might not know that their kids are suffering. He immediately said, "I would love it if you wrote about it. I absolutely agree it could be great."

Here's what we've learned: talk openly about depression and anxiety; share your experiences and encourage your kids to share theirs; listen for verbal clues and watch for signs of struggle; ask them what they do to relieve stress, and tell them repeatedly that you are there to help if they need you.

And please, tell them my son's story and ask your teens if they've ever felt this way—numb, like nothing matters, like there is just a darkness around them. The research we've read shows that talking about depression and anxiety won't make it manifest in your child. Talking about it brings it out into the open and puts words to their feelings—the first step to getting help.

"Mom, can we talk?"

"Always, any time, day or night . . ."

FINDING HELP

As we've seen in this chapter, the high school and college years are a challenging time for coping with depression and anxiety. As Dr. Jess Shatkin, a child and adolescent psychiatrist, explains in his book *Born to Be Wild: Why Teens Take Risks, and How We Can Help Keep Them Safe*, "The prevalence of mental health illness skyrockets during the teen and early adult years. Major depressive disorder affects one in six adolescents by the time they reach eighteen, and anxiety disorders affect up to one-third of adolescents aged thirteen to eighteen."

These conditions mean that our kids sometimes need professional help and they need our help finding it. While most experts recommend the on-campus mental health services as the place to start, every student has individual needs. We asked clinical psychologist and *Under Pressure* author Dr. Lisa Damour to answer some practical questions about how to find the right resources.

Q: How do I find a provider?

A: College counseling centers are staffed by well-trained, seasoned clinicians who are excellent at supporting undergrads. If your student is facing a crisis, this should be the first stop. Counseling centers offer walk-in appointments, are free of charge, have clinicians who are plugged into relevant resources at the college, and know how to collaborate with faculty and administrators, if needed, to help students who have hit a rough patch.

In general, college counseling centers are terrific at providing short-term support—usually fewer than ten counseling sessions—and are not designed to offer ongoing psychotherapy. If forming an ongoing therapeutic relationship makes the most sense, you may want to consider clinicians in the community surrounding your son's or daughter's college.

Q: How do I locate a nearby clinician?

A: Phone the college counseling center! All college counseling centers are familiar with the local resources and are happy to connect you to them. Call the main number, tell them what you are looking for, and you should get a quick call back, often from the counseling center director, with suggestions of clinicians who are known by the college to be excellent at addressing the needs of college students. If you'd like, you can call anonymously; you need not disclose your name or your student's when connecting with the counseling center. Alternately, use your own resources to track down a reputable therapist near your son or daughter. Phone your child's pediatrician, trusted clinicians near you, or psychotherapists you know elsewhere. Many clinicians have broad national networks and can spare you the trouble of picking a name blindly from a web directory.

When seeking a psychotherapist, there are several variables for your college student to consider in order to secure a good fit. Does your student or young adult have a preference for working with a man or a woman? Does the clinician's age matter? What about the clinician's theoretical orientation? There are many traditions within the world of psychotherapy and different approaches suit different clients. Here's a quick primer:

- Psychodynamic psychotherapy: This brand of psychotherapy takes an open-ended, supportive, and exploratory approach. The emphasis centers on unconscious processes, interpersonal relationships, and understanding the origins of repeated, unhelpful patterns.

- Cognitive behavioral therapy: This brand of psychotherapy is problem-focused and solution-oriented. It illuminates how patterns of thought and action contribute to psychological distress, and how they can be changed to bring about relief.
- Dialectical behavioral therapy: This relatively new form of therapy aims to help clients develop healthy skills for managing difficult feelings. It's especially appropriate for clients who turn to self-destructive behaviors—such as drinking excessively or harming themselves—when distressed.

Don't worry about the letters behind a psychotherapist's name. The nature of a therapist's graduate training often says little about his or her quality as a clinician. Just make sure that the clinician is licensed by the state and comes recommended by a trusted source.

Q: What about specialists?

A: Any seasoned clinician should be able to help clients with depression, anxiety, or relationship challenges. If you're unsure about whether a clinician will be a good fit, you or your teen, college student, or young adult should feel free to ask prospective therapists if they address the concerns at hand. Some challenges call for a specialist in a particular treatment area. If your college student is struggling with substance abuse, an eating disorder, or trauma, let your referral sources know.

Q: How does confidentiality work?

A: In general, psychotherapy is like Las Vegas: what happens there, stays there. Your teen or college student has the option of signing a consent form that will allow you to speak freely with his or her clinician if you, your student, and the clinician deem that appropriate. If your son or daughter chooses not to sign such a form but you feel that there is pressing information the clinician should know, you have an option: you can call the therapist and leave information in a voice message. Ethically, the clinician cannot return your call, or even acknowledge that your child is a client. Most therapists, myself included, would alert the client to the call and address the information, and how it arrived, as a part of the psychotherapy. Accordingly, you'll want to weigh carefully the costs and benefits of making such a call before doing so.

Q: Can I use my insurance?

A: Here's the short answer: it depends. To save yourself, and your student or young adult, some trouble, you might start by calling your insurance carrier to see what coverage they provide for in-network and out-of-network clinicians near your student. In general, insurance coverage of psychotherapy is stacked against the consumer: insurers usually offer limited coverage for a limited number of clinicians. And therapists who can maintain vibrant practices without taking insurance (usually the more skilled and seasoned clinicians) have no financial incentive to belong to insurance panels. If your resources are tight, you can ask clinicians who are not covered by your insurance if they offer a sliding-scale fee.

Good psychotherapy helps young people build their independence, learn to take excellent care of themselves, and consider healthy choices and possibilities that previously seemed out of reach. By the time your son or daughter seeks psychotherapy, things are already moving in the right direction.

A View of the Pressure on Teens from the Front of the Classroom

Jess Burnquist teaches creative writing and English near Phoenix, and she reflects here on the pressure teens face and the power of letting kids be kids.

My AP Lit seniors entered my classroom exhausted, sick, or both. We stared at each other for a few minutes.

As the mother of two teens and a high school teacher, I witness firsthand the effects on students of our testing culture, our early start times, our competitive roads to higher education.

Mariah entered class with slumped shoulders and bags under her eyes. She was exhausted from having worked until eleven the night before.

Erick, our student-body president, was still recovering from a state convention where he contracted the flu.

Kaila arrived to class and placed her books in the corner of her desk, folded her arms, and put her head down on them—she had also worked the night before and had another shift that afternoon.

When the bell rang and I took attendance, several students began to prepare to take our weekly AP Literature practice essay test.

"Stop," I instructed.

Jaylee's eyes widened. Mia raised an eyebrow.

"Why?" Kris asked.

I looked at each of my students and decided to follow my instincts.

"It's third quarter," I said. "This is the hardest time of year no matter what grade level, and for teachers too—but especially for seniors. I just want to know how you are doing."

I will never forget what happened next.

The students seated in the back moved up to seats near my desk. Mariah and Dani sat on the floor near me.

Erick sat on his desk and announced that he had just been accepted to NYU. He stated this news as if he was ordering off a menu. When I asked him how he felt about such a prestigious acceptance, he responded that he didn't really know. He is the first in his family to attend college.

"New York is very far away from Arizona. I haven't really had time to process it yet," he said.

I noticed how his classmates responded to his news with positive affirmations but also very gently. They were being sensitive.

"Are you sick of being asked about what you're doing after high school?" I guessed.

They responded in a resounding chorus: "Yes!"

For the next fifty-five minutes, I listened. I permitted them to share their stress about not letting parents down, about not being able to afford college, about wanting to get out of Arizona and see the world, about classes they were struggling in.

I listened to them sweetly tease one another and even permitted them to take out their cell phones so they could share their favorite videos.

I laughed with them. I broke the rules and let them eat

their snacks. I responded to their questions, which covered everything from what I was like in high school to how I parent my two teens.

And it was magic.

I think provisions in curriculum and college acceptance must take into account the whole student. Not just math and English aptitude. Not just extracurricular involvement.

I wish teachers could be consulted beyond a simple one-page letter of recommendation about their students. I wish colleges and universities had time to interview every applicant.

I was an average student in high school, but I've gone on to accomplish some extraordinary things as a teacher and writer. Even at the age of eighteen, I had a sense of my own possibility. I am also an idealist. I see potential in students who have been written off because they don't meet the current definition of educational success stories.

My AP class is mostly comprised of students who have never taken an honors course. Their improvement has been remarkable. Perhaps they won't pass the AP test this spring. The numbers will indicate gaps and areas where understanding failed. I will know just how ready these young adults are to contribute to their communities, to take risks with grace and humor, and how excited they are to change the world. I will know because I took one day to simply listen.

When the bell rang at the end of our fifty-five-minute class period, I watched with pride as they made lunch plans and smiled when they vowed to catch up on their reading.

Mostly, I noticed something that I find myself seeking out in my own son and daughter, the older they become—the elements of childlike wonder and joy in my students' demeanors, as they laid down their armor for one class period and got to be kids again.

There is no aspect of raising kids and teens that leaves parents feeling more helpless than watching our kids struggle with their mental health. We are often at a loss to know how serious the problem is, what kind of help might be needed, and where to get that help. Compounding the problem is the fact that parents can feel utterly alone at this moment, as if everyone else's kid is thriving while yours is in pain. This is the stage in life when some forms of mental illness are most likely to appear, and as we have said, it is also when we have less contact with our experts (teachers, doctors) and parent community. We do not want to be glib about how serious or intractable mental health problems can be, or how urgent it can be to get professional help for a teen or young adult who may not be asking for it. We hope we have covered some of the ways that parents can understand when their kids are in need of help and how to get that help. But what parents have told us countless times is that they need help too, and the kind of help they often need is what other parents—who have been in similar situations and who have come through the other side—can provide.

CHAPTER THREE

Health

Of all the transitions we go through with our children, handing off to them the care of their own health may be the most abrupt. Up until age eighteen, we have been the guardians of their well-being. We have taken them to the doctor, filled their prescriptions, and doled out over-the-counter remedies. There is no shirking this role: the one time Lisa sent her seventeen-year-old to the pediatrician's office alone, his doctor called actually laughing with the news that Lisa would have to come into the office—her son could not authorize his own tetanus booster.

But then comes the morning they turn eighteen, and in a single day, the legal responsibility switches entirely from us to them.

While the law may not allow them to authorize their own care before eighteen, that doesn't mean we can't be preparing them for the day it will. The best time for much of this teaching and preparation is during the high school years, although some of it will inevitably spill over into those first years away from home.

Here are the four main topic areas our teens need to understand when it comes to their health.

Where do you go if you are sick? When our kids were small, the emergency room of the local hospital was probably the only after-hours health service we could access. Over the last decade, however, urgent-care centers have sprung up as natural outgrowths of doctors' offices, hospitals, and pharmacies. Which is the best resource to use in a noncritical situation? For a sore throat, should you see the nurse who works in the pharmacy or the doctor who works in urgent care? If you are bleeding and need stitches, does that have to be done in an emergency room? To help your kids answer these questions, share your reasoning with them while they are still in high school; explain the circumstances in which it's best to visit a physician's office, an urgent-care facility, or the emergency room. For college students, the answer might be the student health center, but even then, they should have a predetermined backup plan for hours when it is closed.

How do you know you are sick? We need to talk with our kids about the serious signs of illness that they cannot ignore. One of the surest markers of illness is, of course, internal body temperature. And while the process may seem reflexive to parents, not every teen knows how or when to take their own temperature. As parents, we know that running a fever cannot be detected merely by feeling warm or experiencing clammy skin; instead, our kids need to know that a thermometer is the only way to officially determine elevated temperature. (And they shouldn't leave for college without one and the knowledge of how to use it.)

The larger question to address is when to seek medical care and when to take a wait-and-see approach. Deciding when to go to the doctor is always a judgment call, and our teens should feel free to call us and consult after they've moved away. But in the meantime, it's also a simple matter to talk through why we are taking them to the pediatrician: "It's been two days and your sore throat is no better," or "I'm concerned about your fever because it is so high, and I want a doctor to see you."

What do you take when you are sick? Walk into any pharmacy with a headache or a cough and the number of remedies can easily overwhelm you. While our kids are still at home, our default behavior is to hand them the medication we (or their doctor) decide they need to take. Each time we do this, however, we pass up an important teaching opportunity. Lisa explains from her own experience:

> When my son got sick freshman year of college with a nasty cold, he headed to the closest drugstore and bought something for his runny nose and something else for his aches and pains. Each medicine was a multi-ingredient remedy, prompting his phone call home a couple of hours later reporting that he felt light-headed and queasy. When I asked what he had taken, I realized he had consumed the same thing twice, doubling the proper dosage.
>
> I had missed many teaching moments, and this was the unfortunate result. Buying and taking over-the-counter remedies can be dangerous. I should have taken my kids with me when I bought medications. I should have discussed their usage and dosage while they were in high school instead of just giving them what they needed to take, and I should have warned them away from using anything but the simplest medications because of the complications that can result from mixing and matching meds.

What do you need in order to access health care? The area of health care our kids often know the least about is insurance, medical records, and even their own medical history. Until now, all three of these things were likely largely invisible to them. We as parents managed the insurance, and their doctors held their records. But over their high school years, it is important for them to familiarize themselves with their own medical history (they may need to recall it in an emergency setting) and understand how their insurance coverage works. They need to be knowledgeable about any major medical or mental health episodes, chronic conditions, medications that they use regularly, or medications that they may be allergic to.

This is a lot to cram into a single summer before college, and we've found that the health care learning process is best spread over the high school years, as a multiyear handoff. At the beginning of this transition, we have complete control over their health; by the end we should have none. Along the way, however, it's our job to give our kids more and more responsibility.

How to Pack a First Aid Kit

A first aid kit is a staple on every list of dorm essentials. You can buy one preassembled, but gathering and packing the necessary items yourself gives you a chance to talk about their proper use with your college-bound teen. The following list of recommended first aid items is incredibly comprehensive—and rightfully so, as it was compiled by Gretchen Sionkiewicz, at the time the mother of a freshman, who works as a certified immunizer, diabetes educator, and registered pharmacist. "The pharmacist in me made up a first aid kit and supply list for my son, which I put in a plastic box for him," Sionkiewicz says. "It seems like a ton of stuff, but our son is eleven hours from home. I also included a sheet of instructions of what to take/use for what ailment and how to do so safely." When our young adults get sick far away from home, instructions from Mom or Dad may be easier for them to follow than the tiny print on the package.

Here's Sionkiewicz's exhaustive list, which can be used for inspiration in compiling supplies for your future freshman—and for teaching your teen how to use the proper medications and treatments *before* he or she leaves home:

GENERAL FIRST AID SUPPLIES
Acetaminophen (for fever/pain)
Ibuprofen (for fever/pain/inflammation)
Instant ice packs/reusable ice packs
Thermometer (look for the digital version with a flexible tip; it is both accurate and durable)
Band-Aids in various sizes
Antibiotic ointment
Hydrocortisone cream
Antifungal cream and powder
Rolled gauze
Sterile gauze pads (2×2 and 4×4)
Ace bandages in various sizes
Scissors
Tweezers
Nail clippers
Nail file
70% rubbing alcohol
Hydrogen peroxide
Lip balm
Petroleum jelly
Pain relief patches
"Artificial tears" drops
Styptic pencil (for nicks from shaving)
Sunscreen
Bug repellent

Aloe vera gel (for burns and skin conditions)
Cream for insect stings
Oral anesthetic gel
First aid disinfecting spray for minor cuts or burns
Wound-wash saline
Surgical tape

COUGH AND COLD SUPPLIES

I'm no fan of multi-ingredient products; they often get combined with other products containing the same ingredients, causing problems. (In the case of acetaminophen, problems can include liver toxicity and overdose.) I listed decongestant, expectorant, antihistamine, and pain relievers separately, because any medicine a student takes should address only the specific symptom(s) they have.

Saline nasal spray
Decongestant
Cough suppressant
Expectorant
Mentholated topical ointment
Antihistamine
Cough drops

STOMACH AILMENT SUPPLIES

Antacid
Loperamide (diarrhea medication)
Simethicone (anti-gas medication)
Meclizine (for motion sickness or nausea/vomiting)

REPRODUCTIVE HEALTH SUPPLIES
Condoms (to avoid the need for the next item)
Morning-after contraceptive (I sell a lot of it on Sunday mornings.)

OTHER ADDITIONS

Copy of health-insurance card in a ziplock bag. (The original stays in his wallet; I keep a second copy at home.)

Copy of immunization records and important health information in a ziploc bag. (The school has one, sure—but it's never a bad idea for the student to keep a copy as well.)

Vitamin supplements. (An individual choice—as is melatonin or any kind of sleep aid. Athletes, please note that any product you plan to ingest as a supplement or medication should be cleared first by trainer and coach. The NCAA guidelines are strict on this score.)

For areas of the country susceptible to tornadoes, earthquakes, or floods, an emergency survival kit with essential items may be in order.

STAYING HEALTHY ON CAMPUS

We hand our kids control of their health care at a challenging moment in their lives. Housed in cramped dorms, they share germs with the other students and are often sick. They don't always eat well or sleep enough. They may be exposed to illegal drugs and alcohol for the first time, or in far more readily available quantities. Stress is rampant, and most students feel its effects to some degree. For all these reasons, and more, parents have ample cause to be concerned about their student's health—but what, if anything can they do?

We spoke with Dr. Marcy Ferdschneider, executive director at the Columbia University Irving Medical Center Student Health Service, and she shared her insights about how college students, with perhaps some guidance from their parents, can stay healthy during their time on campus.

A healthy college experience begins even before freshman year begins. To start, students and parents should make themselves aware of the breadth of on-campus services while they are looking at colleges, or revisiting them once the teen has been accepted.

If a student has a preexisting medical, chronic, or mental health condition, Ferdschneider urges "parents and students to connect with on-campus resources, call the director of medical services, or find the person who should be made aware before the school year even begins." At many colleges, if the school is aware of a condition the student has, student health services will reach out the summer before matriculation to help ease the transition and put the student in touch with the appropriate campus services. She makes clear that, even if the management of a medical condition will not be taken on by a physician at school, parents or the student need to share medical records with the university so that if there is a time-sensitive or emergency situation, the school can help provide what Ferdschneider calls "continuous collaborative care."

Although in most cases colleges want students, rather than their parents, to manage their own health care, transitioning their health care issues to campus might be an exception. Ferdschneider says that "some kids arrive on campus at seventeen or barely eighteen and might need their parents to help explain some of their health history. Students are at different developmental stages, and the parents know their child the best. I don't have a problem with the parents helping them get settled. It's a transition. It doesn't mean the student can't handle something on their own."

Parents can play an important role in the early days of college by just keeping in touch with their teen. If your kid doesn't sound like themselves, encourage them to seek out the on-campus student counseling center. Often it is a more minor issue like homesickness or stress of the new environment, but it can be more serious. This is one of the reasons to check out resources before they are needed. And the help is there and available. There is no other time in your life that someone is going to offer you free counseling, so if your college student needs it, Ferdschneider urges parents to suggest their teen take advantage of it.

As they watch their new enrollee making this transition, many parents are tempted to ask roommates and friends to watch out for their teen or for each other. Friends and roommates do need to watch out for one another, but they cannot be asked to assume responsibility for another student's physical or mental health. Ferdschneider tells students, "If someone tells you they want to harm themselves, don't take responsibility for that, seek out help. As a college student, you cannot take on the burden of responsibility for another person. Seek out residential advisers or the student health center. Despite how much you may care, you are not their parent or health care provider, you are just a friend."

Also on our checklist for campus health is a discussion with your teen around privacy and confidentiality. Talk about these issues with your incoming freshman before they arrive on campus. Suddenly lacking access to medical information about their teen, some parents ask their kids to sign consent forms for record release, while others choose not to. This is a personal decision, of course, but it should be discussed before the issue arises in an acute medical situation. Compelling your teen to sign such a release has implications and potential unintended consequences that parents should consider. There is the very real risk, for example, that a student might hesitate to access much-needed medical or psychiatric services knowing their parents may learn about their condition. They may forgo treatment out of fear that the insurance bills will be sent home. For these reasons, some colleges simply don't charge for services like STD screening and mental health services.

One major health topic that often gets overlooked is sleep. While our kids live with us, the house winds down in the evening, younger siblings go to bed, and lights are turned off. In a college dorm, sleep may not be regulated on such a predictable rhythm. "Sleep is one of the more underestimated factors in a successful academic career," Ferdschneider explains. "College kids are almost competitive about sleep, bragging that they studied so hard that they only slept three hours the night before. They seem to forget that the kid who will do the best is the one who has slept a full night. They need to remember that they are overloaded with activities and academics and can only get this done if they learn healthy sleep habits."

Finally, parents need to teach their teens to advocate for their own health. When they know something is wrong, they need to seek out care and make their needs known. If a health professional does not understand the seriousness of their complaint, they need to assert themselves. When there are facts from their medical history that are relevant to the current situation, they need to speak up. While we teach our kids respect for expertise and authority, it is also important for them to understand that no one knows their body and mind better than they do.

A Visit to the Gynecologist

Mary Dell recalls: It was not clear to me if I was more nervous than my sixteen-year-old daughter as we sat in the waiting room for her first visit to the gynecologist. She was there at the recommendation of her dermatologist, who had suggested birth control pills for severe acne. Although I was working hard to look nonchalant, with decades of annual pelvic exams and two pregnancies behind me, I was uncomfortable thinking about the potential for my daughter to undergo such an intimate exam. Fortunately, the doctor invited us both back to her office, explained that this initial meeting would give my daughter a chance to discuss her health care needs (without my presence) and would not involve a pelvic exam. If there was a silver lining to the misery of teenage acne, it was a chance to know a gynecologist and establish trust before a more intrusive physical exam.

Here are some guidelines:

When to go: Many high school parents face the question of when to take their daughter for her first visit to the gynecologist. We asked Dr. Adina Keller, an obstetrician/gynecologist at CareMount Medical for some guidance. The American College of Obstetrics and Gynecology indicates that the right age for a first visit is between the ages of thirteen to fifteen. However, Keller reminds parents that they know their daughter best and should look for indicators that she is ready for a visit. How mature is your daughter? Is she fourteen going on eighteen? Or is she fourteen but sometimes seems like ten? Is she having any problems with her period? Many girls will report this to their pediatrician, who then refers them to an ob-gyn. Has she asked about seeing a gynecologist? Keller suggests that once a teenager asks, she should soon be given an appointment. She should also be brought in for a visit if the parents have any reason to believe that their daughter is sexually active. And if none of these circumstances has arisen and college looms in the fall, parents should use this as an opportunity to arrange a first appointment with a gynecologist.

What to expect: For girls who are not yet sexually active, this first visit is fully clothed and usually does not include an examination. It is a chance to develop a relationship with their new doctor, seek answers to any questions they may have, and gather some advice on preventing sexually transmitted diseases and pregnancy, as well as discuss any issues around menstruation.

Keller suggests that parents think about a number of things before taking their daughters for a first visit. Is this a doctor with whom she will be comfortable? Is it someone who works well with teens? Taking her to your own doctor, someone you may have selected decades ago, may not be the best choice for her. Does she understand the issues surrounding her privacy and the importance of total honesty with her health practitioner? Visiting an ob-gyn for the first time can be frightening, and parents can reassure their daughters by telling them what to expect from the visit, and that the doctor will not do anything without a full explanation and the patient's consent. While doctors will test teens for STDs if the patient is sexually active, the guidelines suggest that pap smears do not begin until after age twenty-one.

The importance of communication: Parents should emphasize that their teen should be totally honest with their ob-gyn, telling the physician everything relevant about their health, knowing their privacy will be protected, in most states, even if they are under eighteen (the exceptions to this include major medical procedures or cases of abuse). They should emphasize that even if their teen is not comfortable discussing their reproductive health with them, their physician is the person with whom they should have this discussion and to reveal any concerns or ask any questions. Because it is so important that a physician know a patient's family-health background, such as a history of cancer or early strokes, parents might be asked to remain in the room for this part of the visit and asked to step out later.

As parents send their daughters off to college, they might be tempted to include over-the-counter treatments for urological or gynecological infections. Keller suggests that parents not encourage their daughters to self-medicate but rather urge them to see a practitioner in the student health center and have the appropriate lab tests. Sexually transmitted diseases are increasingly prevalent and can only be properly treated if they are accurately diagnosed.

HELPING THEM STAY SAFE WHEN WE CAN'T KEEP THEM SAFE

Maureen Stiles, writer and the mother of three boys, went through some harrowing moments when her freshman son had to visit an emergency room without her. Her experience yielded important lessons for those anticipating or entering this next stage of parenting. Foremost among them: work with your kids in advance on a plan B.

Stiles explains:

The tone of my son's voice was different than it had been earlier in the day. His breathing was labored, and he was so congested that I could barely understand what he was saying. Yet I managed to make out some key phrases, such as "tingling in my legs" and "really stiff and sore."

I was processing this as quickly as I could while trying not to panic. He had gotten a Z-pack from the campus health center just a few days before, but now—6:30 p.m. on a Thursday—there was no alternative: my freshman son had to go to the local emergency room. Without me.

Fortunately, his roommate was there to help him get to the ER quickly, which made me feel somewhat better. It was the most comfort I would experience for the next twenty-four hours.

So what does a parent learn from their child's ER visit—and subsequent hospitalization—when they are seven hours from home? I hope you never need to find out—but just in case you do:

1. **In a situation like this, a student's friends are the linchpin of their safety.** Not only did my son's roommate drive him to the ER, he bowed out of a fraternity commitment to stay at the hospital (where he was joined by another friend and my son's girlfriend). The three remained at the hospital until my son was admitted and settled in his room—which was not until 1:00 a.m.

    They communicated with me constantly, patiently fielding all my questions. As soon as my son was diag-

nosed with an infectious disease—viral meningitis—
another friend went to his dorm room and washed his
bed linens. Small mercies: having chosen his friends
wisely, my son now has a family away from home.

2. **Someone should know your kid's phone password
   and how to contact parents in an emergency.** My
   son's friends knew the passcode for his phone, making
   it much easier for them to call me, answer my texts,
   and get info for forms. This small bit of knowledge
   can make a huge difference in an emergency. Many
   phones now also have a medical ID capability that
   can be accessed without having to unlock the phone.
   Make sure your student has the necessary information
   and contacts listed there if so.

3. **Pick a hospital in advance.** My son was in a major city
   and had options, but that's not always the case. If there
   are multiple facilities, look at online reviews of their
   ERs. My son faced a fortunate choice—hospitals that
   had earned ratings of 2.6 and 2.4 out of 3—so he went
   with the one he knew how to reach. I wish I had inves-
   tigated the area before we needed an ER, so a plan could
   have been in place.

4. **When a student is over eighteen, parents are not
   contacted before treatment, even if said parents are
   responsible for payment.** My son had an EKG, a chest
   X-ray, a CAT scan, and a spinal tap while I sat home,
   unaware of these tests, in Maryland, five hundred
   miles away. Eventually I spoke with a nurse, but only
   because my son had handed her the phone and said,
   "Please talk to my mom." According to the university,
   my son must request and complete a form authoriz-
   ing me to see his records and get information about

his case every time he is seen by a health care professional; no blanket authorization is available.

5. **Get informed about other urgent-care facilities, as the campus health center is limited in capability and appointment times.** My son attends a large state university and routinely has to wait a day or two for appointments. There is no urgent option no matter the situation. My son could not get a same-day appointment at the health center when he had complications upon release from the hospital. Instead, he had to go back to the emergency room again and be evaluated there. Research ahead of time nearby facilities like a MinuteClinic (at CVS) or other walk-in clinics. In nonemergencies, it is helpful to get checked out somewhere other than an expensive and time-consuming ER.

6. **Empower your child to raise objections if anything contradicts a previous medical order, or simply seems "off" in a medical situation.** My son was not confident enough to argue with a medical professional. Those diagnosed with viral meningitis are instructed to lie flat for an hour after the spinal tap, but my son neglected to mention that he had received this directive when an orderly came in to fetch him for a chest X-ray well before the sixty minutes had elapsed. (This movement, I believe, brought on the complications he suffered days later.)

7. **It may be difficult to get answers.** Even if you give your student a list of questions to ask doctors, there is no guarantee those questions will get asked—or that your child will retain the answers. I texted my son some questions to ask the nurse when she came to

check on him; exhausted and distracted by dehydration and fever, he was able to recall only very sketchy details afterward. His friends filled in what they could, and the rest I gleaned by calling our family doctor (and, in a moment of weakness, consulting WebMD).

8. **Take advantage of hospital resources.** Scan the hospital website to learn what resources are available to you from afar—then push to gain access to them. After this whole episode had (more or less happily) concluded, I noticed that the hospital system offers an online patient portal; knowing about it would have helped reduce my anxiety.

9. **Most hospitals require a credit card (to cover the copay for urgent care) as well as an insurance card.** Thankfully, my son had both. Ideally, the card in your child's possession will have a reasonably low credit limit. (Ours did not. We will be changing that ASAP.)

10. **It's important to keep track of all the papers they hand you in the hospital.** Each of my son's professors seemed to ask for different documentation. The hospital gave my son a medical excuse with no mention of meningitis; to inform his professors of the full scope of his illness and recovery time, he therefore combined that note with his discharge instructions. And lacking a scanner, he simply took pictures of all those hospital documents and attached them to an email. (The pics came in handy later on as well, when the papers get lost in the organizational nightmare known as a dorm room.)

11. **If your gut says go, then go help your student recover.** I ended up on an airplane the next day because there was a lot to unravel and my son was seriously ill. Even

amid the best medical care in the world, there's no re-
placing Mom. I began asking questions, signing forms,
and taking charge as soon as I stepped off the elevator,
allowing my son to focus on healing. (And the joy and
relief on my son's face when I got there? Priceless.)

Left to his own devices, my son coped just fine—
which means we both must be doing something right.
I'm grateful to the ER nurse who got him through a bad
spinal tap and some other tough procedures without
me, and I know my son is too: before being discharged,
he filled out a form nominating her for a performance
award.

While none of us wants to think about the emergencies that can
befall our kids once they leave home, it is imperative that we plan
ahead. Discussing available medical resources, how much medical information your teens are willing to share, and how you will communicate if they are unable to do so themselves are good places to start.

COLLEGE STUDENTS AND ALCOHOL

Illness is only one of the health risks that new college students face
in the early weeks of a school year. According to the National Institute of Alcohol Abuse and Alcoholism (NIAAA), "the first six
weeks of freshman year is an especially vulnerable time for heavy
drinking and alcohol-related consequences because of student expectations and social pressures at the start of the academic year."

The facts about college and drinking are staggering. According
to the NIAAA, almost 60 percent of college students drank alcohol
in the past month, and almost two out of three of them were binge
drinking during that period. They estimated that drinking among

college students will result in 696,000 assaults, 97,000 sexual assaults, and 1,825 deaths in any given year. Fully a quarter of college students say that drinking alcohol adversely affects their academic performance, including "missing class, falling behind in class, doing poorly on exams or papers, and receiving lower grades overall."

"Although the majority of students come to college already having some experience with alcohol," the NIAAA survey concludes, "certain aspects of college life—such as unstructured time, the widespread availability of alcohol, inconsistent enforcement of underage drinking laws, and limited interactions with parents and other adults—can intensify the problem." Indeed, the survey points out, college students have higher rates of binge drinking and drunk driving than do their noncollege peers.

And while this paints a very bleak picture of drinking on campus, parents are far from powerless to influence their student's behavior. Medical experts insist that parents can continue to play a positive and influential role as their student learns to adapt to the more freewheeling existence of campus life. Even from afar, parents' high expectations about their college student's conduct can have a constructive impact. Experts urge parents to discuss alcohol use with their college-aged children, emphasizing not only its well-documented risks but also any factors that make its use safer (moderate drinking being the most reliable). "Students who choose not to drink," say NIAAA researchers, "often do so because their parents discussed alcohol use and its adverse consequences with them."

"Even if you're the parent of the kid who hasn't ever—wouldn't ever—overindulge, talk to your kid openly and honestly before they arrive on campus," says Ferdschneider. "Maybe your kid is not going to be drinking—but they will be among others who are, so they need to know the costs, among them sexual misconduct, blackouts, and violence. Let them go into [the college experience] with their eyes wide open."

In particular, she urges parents to talk realistically about alcohol. "Yes, the legal drinking age is twenty-one," says Ferdschneider, "but the reality is that college kids have access to alcohol—and they are likely to drink. Speak to them about not leaving their drink unattended, about drinking water, drinking slowly, and making sure they eat something before going out. Tell them not to 'pregame' to save money."

Alcohol abuse and binge drinking (the latter defined as consuming four to five drinks in about two hours) peaks during the college years, explains Dr. Frances E. Jensen, chair of the neurology department at the University of Pennsylvania's Perelman School of Medicine and coauthor of *The Teenage Brain: A Neuroscientist's Survival Guide to Raising Adolescents and Young Adults*. We asked Jensen for guidance on how to discuss alcohol abuse, and in particular binge drinking, in a way that will really deliver the message to our college-bound teens. Here are some highlights of that conversation.

Q: In *The Teenage Brain*, you write about the harmful effects of alcohol and binge drinking on developing brains. How can we explain it to our teens and have them better appreciate these physiological risks?

A: Alcohol affects how our synapses function. The synapses are where your brain cells connect to each other and send signals to get thoughts to happen and where memorization occurs.

With more synapses than the adult brain, the teen brain has more "real estate" where ingested substances can interact. The effect is stronger and the duration longer than on the adult brain. Given how "impressionable" teen brain cells are, it's no surprise that everything—good and bad—gets amplified in the teen brain.

Here are four things to keep in mind about the teen brain, alcohol abuse, and binge drinking:

1. Alcohol's disproportionate effect on the teenage brain means that the same amount of alcohol that merely puts an adult into a dormant state might inflict brain injury on a teen. Binge drinking, in particular, has been shown to cause brain injury in a teen where it would not in an adult.

2. A teen's big advantage over adults—faster synaptic speed—can be inhibited by alcohol, depriving students of this fleeting chance to learn more at a time when they have the best ability to do so.

3. Addiction is also a form of learning—it is repeated use of the same circuit, which builds a bigger synapse (same as when you're trying to learn a golf swing or memorize Spanish vocabulary). Addiction to a harmful substance comes from repeated exposure to a drug that causes a strengthened response and can become hard-wired in a brain. Unfortunately, addiction can happen faster in a teen, just like learning happens faster.

4. Alcohol can loosen inhibition and result in "opening up" behavior. Drinking can impede the functioning of the frontal lobe, which is an area that can prevent risky behavior. Teens' frontal lobes are not fully connected, and they won't be until their late twenties, especially in males. Even fully connected adults can be disinhibited by alcohol, which can cause them to do risky things. If you are starting off disinhibited because your frontal lobes are not connected, alcohol will get you to the place of disinhibition even faster.

Q: We teach our kids to drive safely. Why can't we teach them to drink responsibly?

A: It's an interesting point. We know that risk-taking behavior is a part of adolescence, so something considered taboo often has the allure of big risk. It's unfortunate that binge drinking comes from a lack of experience with alcohol; given sudden access to it, some teens drink impulsively and excessively. That's why binge drinking is such a problem in college—and such a critical discussion point for parents. Other societies have different approaches to alcohol, with many other countries allowing earlier drinking ages. Whether this earlier experience and more relaxed approach leads to better outcomes requires more studies, which are ongoing.

It's important to give teens information and facts about alcohol and examples of what can happen. That is what I did with my kids. We may not be able to control whether our kids abstain from alcohol before the age of twenty-one, but we do need to arm them with facts first.

Parents can also give their kids a "frontal-lobe assist" to understand why excessive inebriation is not a good thing, especially with driving, and try to get them to be aware that they are very prone to impulsivity and risk-taking. Teach your teen that their limbic system (emotions, rage, succumbing to peer pressure, wanting to be liked) gets connected years ahead of the full connectivity of the frontal lobe. Talk about how peer pressure can push kids to take further risks in groups—teens will be tempted; they will want to be like everyone else, but there are dangers on the other side of risky behavior, and they should know that their brains are more vulnerable.

Q: You write that 50 percent of the risk of alcoholism is genetic; what actions should parents take if there is a family history of this disease?

A: It is crucial for parents to have conversations with their kids if there is history of alcoholism with direct relatives within a family.

They need to know that they potentially have a higher risk of alcoholism, and they should know what the warning signs are. Likewise, mental illness traits (depression, bipolar disorder, schizophrenia) are highly hereditary, so if there is a family history, parents should be more vigilant for the warning signs and aware of changes in your teen because they may have a higher risk.

Q: What advice did you give your sons, as a mom and neurologist, when they were going off to college?

A: I told them that they are in an amazing window for learning that they won't have again. This generation of high school and college kids is the first to know that they can get more accomplished now than later. I reinforced that they would be able to learn faster, longer, and stronger in this period than at any other point in life. I told them they would be more susceptible to peer pressure, like they were in high school, but now they are on their own.

The first day you drop your kids off at the college dorm shouldn't be their first taste of freedom. Phase in independence and let them have opportunities to make choices and have some freedom before they go off to college. Camps or semesters abroad are really good ways to let teens experience being on their own. They have to go through trial and error, and failure, and parents need to wean themselves from swooping in to solve their problems for them.

I also told my kids about how mental illness can occur when kids get to college, and to be alert to their friends who might need help. Recognize that they might have a friend who will have a psychotic break or severe anxiety issues. Be empathetic, be a friend, and help them seek help if they need it.

A BAD NIGHT WITH ALCOHOL
CAN HAPPEN TO ANY KID

We've had all the right conversations, reviewing the dangers of drugs and the teenage brain, peer pressure, and covering important warnings about alcohol use. Our kids have shown us that they are smart and sensible. They worked hard to get into college, and for the next four years we expect and hope that they will use sound judgment. And when they manage to keep up with athletics, academics, and activities, it's easy to fool ourselves into thinking there won't be a problem.

But that would be folly, as the story recounted here makes clear. It was shared with us by a parent who prefers to remain anonymous.

As parents, we were not naive to the issue of alcohol among college students or to the fact that our son drank before he even set foot on campus. I had a vague awareness of a possible fake ID, but I never saw it or confirmed it.

We had all the important discussions.

We stressed safety and responsible drinking.

We thought we had covered our bases.

Yet none of those fireside chats prepared me for getting the phone call that my child was being transported to the hospital after becoming severely intoxicated. At eighteen he was technically no longer a child, of course, but he was still my baby—and he had gotten himself into a very dangerous situation.

In hindsight, I'm not quite sure what made us answer the phone that Monday evening. When the landline rings in the evenings we rarely look at caller ID, certain that it's just another telemarketing call. Was it intuition? Fate? Something made my husband glance over.

His face fell as he mouthed to me that the caller was the venue hosting the concert my son was attending. My heart pounded as he listened, rubbed his temples, and nodded his head. *He should be asking questions*, I thought as I paced. I had so many questions.

My son had been "found" alone and drunk. He was vomiting and needed assistance walking. That is all we knew. We didn't know how he had lost his friends, who discovered him, where he was discovered, or what shape he was in.

We were simply told that they were transporting him to the hospital nearest the arena and that we should meet him there. My husband is not calm in these situations, so he stayed home with our younger children. I gathered keys, the insurance card, and enough sense of stability to drive. Before pulling out of the garage, I texted the roommate I knew was at the concert to tell him my son was on the way to the hospital.

Concerts are loud, and the roommate didn't hear his phone right away. When he called me back about thirty minutes later, he was genuinely confused. He had left my son with other friends and said he seemed fine—not sober, mind you, but fine. Their seats were separate, so not seeing my son after that raised no alarm bells in his head. He felt genuinely awful.

Walking through the ER entrance, I steeled myself for whatever my son's condition might be. I had read all the articles; I had seen pictures of kids on ventilators from alcohol poisoning. All I could do was pray that we were not going to be the next cautionary tale.

What I hadn't expected was that my son was not there. At all. This threw me into a panic: Was he so bad off that they had taken him to a more acute facility? The hospital had no clue, so I took a chance and called my son's phone.

I will never forget the blackness that enveloped me when a strange voice answered the phone and said, "Is this Mom?" Was this the police officer or doctor who was set to deliver the worst news of my life? Was this how it felt to have your world ripped to shreds? Suspended in the purgatory of not knowing, I stopped breathing.

An orderly explained that my son had been diverted to another hospital only a few minutes away for no other reason than "sometimes ambulances do that." I cried so fiercely and gutturally that the orderly asked that I not drive until I had regained my composure. My son was stable but needed me to be coherent when I got there.

I sat in my car for a few minutes, texted an update to my husband, then set off for the second facility. There he was, finally, in the emergency room cubicle, looking like a stinkier, disheveled version of himself. On the chair beside him was his wallet, his phone, and all of his belongings, perfectly intact.

According to the doctor, he had been able to converse with them well enough, handing over his insurance card and telling them his name and some other basic info. Then he passed out.

They monitored him but mostly let him sleep it off. His blood-alcohol level was 0.27 (more than three times the legal limit), but he had stopped vomiting and had urinated when he arrived at the hospital—both good signs. They decided not to give him fluids, which was fine by me. I wanted his hangover to be real and lasting. As long as he was hydrated and not in danger, I had no desire to make him comfortable.

We got that first call at 8:00 p.m. I left the hospital with him at 5:00 a.m., having sat in a chair and watched him sleep for seven hours. I alternated between anger and primal love over the course of his stay. But I couldn't stop wondering: How had my responsible, never-been-in-trouble-before child ended up here?

It turned out he had no idea either. He retraced the evening as far as he could through pictures on his phone and remembered conversations, but there was no memory of being drunk and alone, covered in vomit and in true peril. My stomach still flips every time I think of how truly alone he was despite knowing at least fifty people at the event.

My husband and I had to think long and hard about how to approach this. We started by grounding him. He needed to have a short leash for a while, if only to make up for the upheaval to our family. He would be responsible for the hospital bills. And we made him read a *Sports Illustrated* article about a football fan beaten to death in a stadium parking lot because he was incapacitated by alcohol, alone, and rooting for the rival team.

I could not let it die, which of course is the greatest punishment of all. I could not shake the panic and pain of that night. I made him answer tough questions about his drinking habits and the way he was managing—or not managing—his life.

THE RECKONING

As parents, we had some reflecting to do as well. There were red flags that we had ignored because he'd always been such a good kid, handling everything with aplomb.

The sheer amount of credit card charges at bars should have tipped us off early in that first freshman semester. He was clearly going out nearly every night, but since he was making it to class—even the eight-thirty one—we did not act. Surely, he could not keep that up if he was getting trashed every night.

Wrong. He could.

We thought back to Parents' Weekend, when my son had invited us to a mosh pit of a tailgate party—rife with vodka shots and sloppy drunks—rather than one of the many events hosted by school organizations and designed for families. We left the muddy chaos to head into the game but told him to stay. He texted when he got to his seat to ask where our seats were, yet we didn't see him the rest of the day. (He did keep texting us though, so in our minds he was trying to catch up with us.)

At breakfast Sunday morning he looked horrible and apologized profusely. We let it slide because he had stayed in constant touch with us and had been sober Friday night. We chalked it up to the excitement of a big event in a new environment.

Instinctively we probably knew his life was out of balance, yet we incorrectly assumed he had it under control. But realistically, how could he? The partying and the long nights eventually take a toll, and you run out of luck. Or land in the ER.

THE AFTERMATH

To our son's credit, he thought long and hard about his drinking patterns and began to recognize the factors that led to trouble or pushed him over the edge.

Armed with this enlightenment, he returned to school in January much more self-aware. He had seen his limits firsthand, and being that drunk scared him almost as much as it scared me. He went out much less, studied more, and made the dean's list.

The saddest part? The hospital staff was nonplussed by the whole episode; they admit hundreds of drunk teens every year, coming from concerts and games. Good kids, just like mine, who made bad choices one day.

I had expected to be met at the hospital by a police officer brandishing citations and court dates, but the concert venue simply used its own security personnel to whisk my son from the premises. All signs indicate that he never even made it inside.

What I do know is that I'll be much more proactive in the future when I see what could be a pattern of irresponsibility and recklessness. My children—no matter how many talks we have, no matter how wonderful they are—are still just that: children. They are prone to lapses in judgment that can have dire consequences.

We dodged a bullet for sure. I share my story so other parents, tempted to shrug off that nagging feeling, will act on it instead. Even if your kid has always been the levelheaded type, don't let chatter about "helicopter parenting" stop you from following your gut.

There is no more high-stakes aspect of parenting teens than the hand-off of responsibility for their health. It's easy to postpone this until packing a first aid kit for freshman year. Even simple things—like understanding which cold medicine helps with a stuffy nose, learning how to take a temperature, or knowing where to go in a physical emergency—are teachable, and we need to convey all we know about how to stay well and what to do when we're sick while our teens are under our roof. You may still get the call at 2:00 a.m. from your college student when they feel rotten, but they should know where to find their insurance card and be able to tell you if they are running a fever. And at least they—and you—will have some sense of the resources available to them in case of an emergency.

CHAPTER FOUR

Love and Sex

We have always taught our kids about love: family love, filial love, sibling love, the love we feel for friends. As they entered the tween and teen years, we began to teach them more about sex and romantic love. So much of this was discussed in hypothetical terms, events and feelings that we hoped would happen to them in their lives. Then suddenly it seemed we were talking in the present tense. When we talked about love, or even sex, there may have been a real girlfriend or boyfriend in the picture. While these conversations can get awkward (okay, *do* get awkward), we are firm believers that this comes with the parenting territory.

It's easy to be misled by the popular press into thinking our teens are not really interested in what we once called romance. It's easy to think they live submerged in the hookup culture with little regard for getting to know each other or building sustained loving relationships. But the reality is not the stuff of headlines. While hookups are not uncommon, and friends with benefits is a real thing, the typical college student is looking for something far more meaningful.

"Hooking up" is a term that means everything and nothing. For teens and young adults, it is a way of saying that something happened while leaving the specifics undefined. For parents, it is a term that denotes a baffling world of übercasual sex overfueled by alcohol and potentially a cause for real concern. While our kids are still in high school, we worry about their behavior but hope that by staying close we can keep a conversation going and remain a positive influence. Our concern compounds as they head off to college, where both parents and teens have heard that hooking up has replaced dating as the dominant route to "romance."

Recent research from the Harvard Graduate School of Education suggests that parents' worries are sorely misplaced. Based on a multiyear study of more than three thousand young adults and high school students, the Harvard project, known as Making Caring Common and led by Dr. Richard Weissbourd, discovered that kids are hooking up far less than we (and they) think. Sure, some teens and college students thrive on impersonal or casual sexual encounters, but this new report finds that this is "far from the norm."

After being asked about their ideal Friday night, respondents in the survey were given the following choices:

- sex in a serious relationship
- sex with a friend
- sex with a stranger
- hooking up (but not sex)
- going on a date or spending time with a romantic partner
- hanging out with friends
- spending time alone
- something else

About 16 percent of the respondents chose an option related to casual sex. The remaining teens and young adults (84 percent) reported either wanting to have sex in a serious relationship or chose an option that did not involve sex.

According to the Centers for Disease Control, a little more than a quarter of eighteen- to nineteen-year-olds nationally had more than one sexual partner in the previous year, whereas only 8 percent had four or more partners. So despite the belief that many college-aged students hold that their peers are all hooking up with each other, the facts do not square with their perceptions.

Yet this myth of the pervasive "hookup culture" has taken hold, with damaging consequences. The media highlights it, and students hear the stories on college campuses. Young people who are not opting for casual sex can feel as though they are out of step with their peers when the truth is that their behavior is far more typical. And parents, concerned about the uncertain implications of hooking up, may be failing to focus on what is important to our teens, forgetting to teach them about what will really matter in their lives: how to develop caring, healthy romantic relationships. Finding and nurturing such relationships will be one of the keys to their lifelong happiness, yet as parents we spend frighteningly little time talking to them about how this might be done.

Here is the good news: the vast majority of teens and college kids *want* some guidance and insight from their parents or teachers on the emotional aspects of their romantic relationships. They want to talk about falling in and out of love. They want to discuss how to get along in a serious relationship and how to communicate within it. They want us to share what we have learned and to listen to their questions and worries. The Making Caring Common report points to a few things parents can constructively do to help guide and advise their kids on this very important part of their lives:

1. Spend time talking to your teen about the importance of mature, reciprocal relationships based on respect and trust. Explain how these differ from more immediate forms of intense

attraction. Over 70 percent of the respondents in the Making Caring Common survey wanted more information from their parents on some emotional aspect of a romantic relationship.

2. Talk about what constitutes a "healthy" relationship. Ask your teen to think about whether the relationship makes both partners better and more compassionate people. Does each partner listen to and support the other? Describe explicitly what some of the red flags in an "unhealthy" relationship look like.

3. Discuss the very real danger of sexual assault, including what steps your teen can take to prevent or stop it in any given situation. While most parents are fully aware of the many risks that exist on college campuses, Making Caring Common suggests that many of us do not delve into this topic with our sons and daughters.

4. Speak up when you observe your teen in a destructive or degrading relationship. Our silence may be misconstrued as tacit permission or approval. While teens are very much entitled to privacy, they are also still learning to be adults—and in this role, we have much to offer.

THE LESSONS OF LOVE TEENS LEARN FROM US

So much of what we teach our children and then later our teens about love is taught through our daily lives. If we are in a marriage or relationship, we have modeled what that looks like, for better and, on some days, for far worse. So often we wish we could have done better, wish we had showed more kindness and compassion. Christine Burke, writer and mother of two teens, knows that we lead by example on this—and that when our relationship causes our kids pain, honesty is truly the best teacher.

As I sat on the soft leather couch and looked at the Zen garden planters, I wondered how my husband and I had wound up in a therapist's office that smelled faintly of patchouli oil and lavender. I glanced at the framed diplomas and certificates and wondered if the man we were about to unload our marital stress on was really as qualified as he seemed. I looked over at my husband of twenty years and was shocked by how much of a stranger he seemed to me. Somewhere between midnight feedings and paying for braces, we'd lost our way.

After a particularly contentious argument on a hot summer afternoon only weeks earlier, I had finally waved the white flag, announcing that I was done fighting. As our teens lounged on the patio, their faces lit by the screens of their devices, I quietly asked my husband for a divorce.

Our marriage was broken, and no one was more surprised than me.

Thankfully, the therapist with the Zen plants and lavender incense was indeed qualified to help us in the way we needed to find our way back to each other. Two years into couples therapy, my husband and I have learned not only how to communicate again but we've also rekindled the kindness in our marriage. The bricks of anger and hurt are gone, replaced with a new foundation of mutual respect and compromise.

While it's better now, our journey to the "new us" has been hell. And it's still not easy some days.

Our struggle in the last two years and over the course of our marriage makes me wonder how I can prepare my teens for the inevitable stresses that a long-term relationship brings.

When I see my son texting with a girl who makes his face light up, I realize he's at the very beginning of a lifelong ebb and flow of relationships. He's on the precipice of falling in love for the first time and likewise on the verge of having his heart broken. And that's just the first time around. He's about to throw himself headfirst into the dating scene, and he has no idea what's coming.

I met my husband when I was twenty, only a few years older than my son and daughter are now, and that blows my mind. I couldn't balance a checkbook or drink legally when my now husband entered my life. We were babies with raging hormones, much like my son.

When mutual friends set us up on a blind date, my idea of a "perfect" relationship was vastly different from my definition today. But that's the natural order of things, as there's no way for a young person to truly know what to expect when they start dating someone they can build a life with. And though I wouldn't trade the experiences that led me to where I am in my relationship today, I do wish that the Cinderella fairy tale included *And she slammed her door because Prince Charming had forgotten to pick the kids up from day care for the second time this week.*

I wish I'd known more about the dark side of relationships. As my husband and I settled into dating and the honeymoon phase, I wish I was more prepared for the reality of spending my life with a man who doesn't share my obsession with Broadway musicals and celebrity gossip.

As I stood at the back of the cathedral, my father at my side and my vision gently blurred by the Irish lace veil that covered my face, I had no idea that marriage was going to slap me into reality. I was marrying Prince Charming in a fairy-tale wedding. My personal "happily ever after" was starting, and I simply expected that our lives would continue on the perfection continuum.

That's when reality delivered a crushing blow to my world. The honeymoon was soon over and there were days that I wandered around asking why no one tells you that "don't go to bed angry" advice that your grandmother gave you is actually a crock. Prince Charming doesn't put the toilet seat down, and Cinderella loses her patience when life gets tough. And those glass slippers don't fit any longer after kids completely ruin your body.

In short, marriage is hard. And it's not always roses and romance and dinners by candlelight. Cinderella lied to all of us.

Marriage is new dishwashers on a tight budget and googling concussion symptoms at 2:00 a.m. while your kid pukes in your partner's lap. It's balding heads and hairy chins. And yes, it's furtive sex when the kids are finally asleep and quiet moments in front of the television where you hold hands. Marriage is sitting at the kitchen table as your kids yammer on about their hatred of broccoli and sharing a conspiratorial smile that says, "Yep, this is our life now."

Marriage with the right person, on the whole, is pretty great during the good times.

But it's also the hardest thing I've ever done.

And when I found myself wanting to leave my marriage, my first thoughts were of my kids and their feelings.

What would they think if we told them Mom and Dad might separate? How would they feel if we proceeded with the divorce? Would they hate us for the rest of their lives for breaking up their home? Probably. And most nights that thought brought me to my knees.

I wanted to shelter them from the worst of our arguing, from the worst of both of us as we unleashed salvos of anger and resentment at each other. I wanted to hide the fact that their father and I couldn't behave like civil adults, often choosing sullen silence in the evenings long after the kids went to bed. And, for a long time, I wrote "Accountant" in a biweekly 5:00 p.m. slot on our family calendar in order not to tip the kids off that their father and I were in therapy.

But as my husband and I unpacked our emotional baggage in therapy, I realized the best gift we could give our kids was honesty about how much our relationship sucked right now or might suck in the future. By hiding our struggles, by tucking our arguments and irritations under the carpet, we were raising kids who had a false sense of what a genuine relationship looks like.

Not to put too fine a point on it, but we were setting them up for their own future relationship slaps.

And that's when I decided to be honest with our kids when it comes to relationships.

There wasn't a moment of reckoning where we sat down on the couch in starched khakis and perfect hair and said, "Hey, kids, your father and I have something to tell you." We didn't suddenly announce that we'd been on the edge of divorce, nor did we discuss the intimate details of our lives with them. Because we are still their parents. We still want them to feel safe and secure, even when their parents are acting like selfish idiots.

Instead, I started to look for opportunities to talk about the struggles their father and I have had over the years, sometimes with humor. Because the story of their father and I arguing over the crown molding we accidentally installed upside down in our first house really is hilarious, even if it involved me chucking a hammer across the room in annoyance.

When my son asked about his birth story on the morning he turned fifteen, I told him the less-edited version. I told him about his traumatic birth and my difficult recovery. His eyes bugged out of his head when I told him it was his father who had to help me shower for the first time after his delivery. And I told him about my battle with postpartum depression, about how his father helped me seek the help I needed to ease my way into motherhood.

I've taken the time to relay stories from when we struggled financially and times when I wanted to tear my hair out because of my husband's stubbornness. And when I compliment my husband around my teens, I am honest. I say, "I'm grateful that your father realizes that I will never, ever dispose of a bug in this house," or "Your father is a saint to put up with your mother's inability to keep up with the laundry," instead of "Your dad is the best!"

Because, let's face it: neither of us are the best at anything, and the sooner our teens realize that relationships are made of humans who are disorganized, messy, and chaotic, the better.

I know I can't save my kids from relationship heartache. But I also know I can help them see that relationships take work and effort to last long-term.

I can help them deconstruct the notion that we are owed the fairy tale when we walk down the aisle or enter into a partnership with someone we love deeply.

I can be honest with them in the moments when I'm annoyed at their father, and I can openly show them that

I still love him with wild abandon, even if he rolls his eyes when I flip on *The Bachelor*.

I can teach them balance and compromise with my actions by showing them the good, the bad, and the ugly in my relationship with their father.

And if my kids ever find themselves on a therapist's couch with their partner, I want them to know that therapy is an opportunity to rewrite their happy endings, page by page, word by word, with the person they've chosen.

WHEN THEIR HEARTS ARE BROKEN

Love can be the single greatest source of happiness in our lives, but we have all lived long enough to know that when it goes wrong, it can lay us low. It's hard to know where to start when our kids come home or call us from school to say they are devastated by the end of a romance. Sometimes they may need to talk to someone less emotionally invested in their lives, be it a best friend, their resident adviser, or someone professionally trained, and we can guide them toward these support systems. But sometimes they just need their parents. The pain of heartbreak does not get any easier no matter when it happens, but our ability to put it into some sort of perspective does. Elizabeth Spencer looks at what we have to offer as parents, along with our love and support.

I'll never forget the night in my freshman year in college when the guy I thought I was going to marry told me he'd met someone else. It was only a little over a month into the school year, and I was sitting on the floor of the bathroom I shared with my suitemates, the cord from the wall phone in my dorm room stretched as far as it would reach. Hunched on the cold tile, through my rather hysterical sobbing, I heard him tell me we were over.

At the time, I thought I couldn't possibly know any sorrow worse than that . . . until it happened to my daughter. And until it happened in our house, where I could watch her pain unfold right in front of me.

Of course, there are all different kinds of heartbreak. Our kids' significant others break up with them. Friendships end. Dreams don't come true. Plans are derailed. We lose loved ones. Whatever it is that breaks our kids' hearts, as parents there's often not much we can *do*—which is where the power of our words has to carry the day.

I offer you ten things that might help to say when your son's or daughter's heart is hurting.

1. **I'm so sorry.**

   Whether we as parents have played any part in what's broken our kids' hearts, we want them to know that when they're hurting, we're hurting right along with them. Usually when I say "I'm sorry" to my girls, they respond, "It's not your fault." And I tell them, "I'm not sorry because this is my fault. I'm sorry because what matters to you matters to me. And I want you to know I'm in this with you."

2. **Do you want me to . . . ?**

   Mail you a care package? Hold you while you cry? Listen while you vent? A couple of days after my breakup, my dad called me at school. This was a big deal, because even though I had a great relationship with him and he was always a loving, affectionate parent, it was usually my mom who I talked to first. But on the phone that day, my dad asked, "Do you want me to come get you and bring you home this weekend? I could take Friday off and drive down."

Even all these years later, I still get choked up thinking about it. That my dad would have this thought. That he would make the call. That he would be willing to take the day off and drive all the way down to school and then bring me all the way back after only one full day at home. I didn't really need him to come get me, but until he asked, I had no idea how much I needed him to offer to come get me. His willingness to show his love in this sacrificial way launched my heart toward healing. Your broken-hearted child might not need you to do anything, but they might need you to offer to do something.

3. You won't feel like this forever.

But go ahead and feel like it for a while. There's a time for feeling, and there's a time for fixing. Our hurting kids need encouragement to spend some time in sadness or anger or bitterness, along with assurance that someday, they will feel better.

4. Do you want to try again?

Maybe this is only a bump in the road of this relationship, not the end of it.

5. If you want to give this another go, what can you do now to get ready for what comes next?

Whether "this" is a personal relationship or a college application or making the cut for a team or achieving some artistic goal, if our disappointed kids want to take another shot, what action can they take to improve their aim? Rehearse what they'll say to that other person? Rewrite their admissions essay? Work out harder? Take more lessons?

6. Do you just want to be done?

We live in a "never give up" culture. But maybe your heartbroken child needs you to tell them there's no shame in moving on when that's the wisest decision. You're not necessarily denying them their future happiness; you might just be preserving their present happiness.

7. Do you want to try something else?

Another sport or another college or another friend? If letting go is the best first course of action, taking hold of something new can be a healing follow-up.

8. Something good will come of this. (But it's okay if that seems impossible right now.)

After our hurting kids have had time to grieve what they've lost, there's hope to be found in thinking about what they can gain. It didn't take me very long after that night on my bathroom floor to realize that as spouses, my former boyfriend and I would have been a disaster, because we both had uptight, over-reactive personalities. If we'd gotten married, we would have lived in constant crisis mode. Instead, I married a man who counteracts my reactionary, freak-out nature with his own calm assurance that everything will be fine. As partners in life, we generally meet in the middle and balance each other out. I lost something I cared about that night in college, but I gained something greater because of it.

9. This is not all of who you are, and it is not only who you are.

Your hurting child may be the ex–love interest or the wait-listed student or the understudy or the benchwarmer. But what describes them in part does not define them as a whole.

10. I love you.

It's what we say as parents when we don't know what else to say and even when we do know what else to say, because it's the beginning and the end and the foundation for everything worth saying in between.

HAVE THE HARD CONVERSATIONS

Our conversations about love and sex are not all designed to mend hearts, strike fear, or discourage destructive behaviors. As our kids head off to college, it's time to talk, at a far more granular level, about the joys adults find in romance and a happy sex life. For some of us this conversation is as easy as discussing what we are having for dinner. For others, the words don't come as effortlessly. If you want some "crib notes," or just a little refresher (and after all, who couldn't use a few suggestions), here are one mom's thoughts. This is a letter that Kari O'Driscoll, writer and mom, wrote to her two daughters, but the message is largely genderless.

Dear Daughters,

I know the last thing you want me to talk to you about is sex, and while that is the primary reason for this letter, let me assure you that this is about so much more than that. I also know that I could abandon this talk and just hope that the education you get about sex from school or books or your friends is enough, but I've decided to come at this head-on instead. It's the least I can do for the two most important people in my life.

I am under no illusion that you want details of my past sexual experiences and, frankly, I don't want to know about yours, either. But I do want to encourage you to think a lot about what sex means to you, and I want you to understand ten important things.

1. *"Sex" encompasses a broad category of behaviors.*

Our culture sends out some pretty heavy messages about sex. When I was your age, I defined sex as something that could potentially result in a baby: basic missionary-style stuff. This led to a couple of errors: first, that any kind of sex act that couldn't produce offspring wasn't "really" sex, and second, that the worst thing that could happen was getting pregnant before marriage. In that light, any kind of fooling around outside of intercourse didn't carry the same weight as the "real" sex act, and so long as I avoided pregnancy, things would be okay.

Nobody told me that other sexual acts could be just as weighty as "the Real Thing," and that any type of intimate contact was likely to produce just as many conflicted and pleasurable feelings.

2. *Sex is a normal, healthy part of life when you choose it freely.*

The tricky part is the second half of that phrase. Choosing sex freely doesn't mean agreeing to do something because you think you are the only one of your close friends who hasn't done it yet. Choosing sex freely doesn't mean pleasuring someone else because you "owe them" or you don't want to disappoint them or "leave them hanging."

Choosing sex freely doesn't mean lying there quietly while someone else takes advantage of you because you are too drunk or too high or too timid to say no. Unfortunately, it also doesn't mean blindly riding the wave of physical pleasure that starts with kissing or hand-holding, without at some point (or several points) asking yourself, "Am I ready to go further than this?"

Choosing sex—and by sex, I mean any intimate contact—means that you know the risks and you are forging ahead without reservation. You're going ahead because you feel a connection with this other person and you trust that the only agenda for both of you is expressing your feelings for each other in a mutually respectful way. You are going ahead with the certain knowledge that if at any point, any point, you feel uncomfortable or change your mind—even if your underwear is halfway across the room and you've said yes sixteen times tonight—you can put your clothes back on and walk away. Choosing sex freely means that you have asked yourself the question, "Why am I doing this?" and answered honestly. If the answer involves improving or enhancing your social status, doing someone a favor, or punishing yourself or someone else, that is not choosing freely.

3. Making clear decisions about things like sex when you are a teenager is a challenge.

Your brain has been hijacked by emotional Stormtroopers that are holding your powers of logic hostage. Do yourself a favor and think about sex when you're alone in your room in the light of day. Ask yourself what you think you might say or do if you find yourself in a questionable situation. Ask yourself what a questionable situation might feel like, what it might look like. Figure out what you might say or how far you'd be willing to go to walk away from a questionable situation and who your trusted allies are—the people on speed dial who won't hesitate to come to your aid if you get into trouble. Do this at least once a month, once a week if you are in a committed relationship. Talk to your partner about it. Talk to your best friend. Or talk to your mother. Remember that the most important person here is you and the most important voice is your own. And if you get into a situation where your mental preparation eludes you, listen to your gut. If it's twisting in fear and the hair is rising on the back of your neck—or if you simply feel unsure—take a breath and stop. Your gut is always right, and there will be time to try again when you're ready.

4. *You will make mistakes. We all do.*

We all make choices that seem utterly ridiculous twelve hours later. At least once in your life, you are likely to choose intimacy with someone for the wrong reasons and regret it later. Breathe. Learn from it. Move on. Arm yourself with information and a plan to prevent STDs and unintended pregnancy. Learn to identify and avoid people who might take advantage of you and resolve to do better next time.

5. *Sex is not something to be afraid of, nor is it to be taken lightly.*

Like any other important life decision, it simply requires clear thought and some effort to define your values. Relationships are both difficult and rewarding, and, when you are ready and choosing sex freely, it can deepen and enhance your connection to someone else. Your sex life is yours to own; it doesn't belong to your peer group or your partner or your parents. You have every right to make the decisions that serve you, to ask for what you need, and to change your mind at any point. If you are honest with yourself about why you want to have sex and you feel good about the answer, you are probably on the right track. My fears for you are less about you getting pregnant than they are about your choices and values being co-opted or manipulated by someone else.

6. *Remember the other person in this equation—your partner.*

You can't be responsible for his or her choices, but you can be patient and kind and recognize that sexual intimacy is a big step for everyone. Just because you might be ready doesn't mean someone else is. Always err on the side of the most cautious person's wishes, even if it means you have to take a cold shower or go for a brisk run to calm down. The fact is, there is plenty of time and sex should be rewarding for both of you. It should make you feel good about yourself and the person you're with.

7. You can't trust someone's word about whether or not they have an STD, even if you love them.

They may not know they have one, they may be afraid you'll change your mind about being with them if they admit to having one, they may not care if they pass one along to you. Again, ask lots of questions and, when in doubt, pack condoms. Protect yourself.

8. Birth control is not shameful or secretive. It is a necessity.

There are many different options when it comes to birth control, so ask lots of questions to figure out which method is right for you—and use it. If the person you are with doesn't want to use it, you need to have an honest conversation about why it's important to you. As a young woman, the consequences of unintended pregnancy are monumental to you. You deserve to be with someone who understands that and isn't willing to take a chance on your life or your health.

9. Sex is confusing for everyone.

It conjures up strong emotional reactions and deserves thoughtful deliberation. Everyone has a unique reaction to and threshold for sexual intimacy. What feels good to you today with one person might not hold true in your next relationship. Tread carefully and respectfully with yourself and your partner.

10. Shame has no place in any sexual relationship.

If you are with someone who makes you feel ashamed, they aren't doing it right. If you use jokes or share confiden-

tial details or photos to shame someone else, you aren't doing it right. Intimate relationships are about trust and mutual respect, and they should feel good. You deserve to feel good about yourself and your choices. If you don't, change something. If you don't know what to change, stop everything until you figure it out.

Just one more thing. I remember what it was like to wrestle with tough decisions at your age and how much easier it seemed to leave things to chance or let someone else choose for me. If you can't love yourself enough in the moment to slow down and think, ask yourself this question, "What would Mom want for me?" The answer is always, always to be true to you. No matter what.

WHEN THEY ARE READY TO TALK

Even when we know what to say to our kids, it can be a dance to figure out when they are ready to talk and listen. The conventional wisdom suggests talking to teens in the car. The closed space creates the intimacy appropriate for any sensitive subject, and the lack of eye contact is just what many may need. We have tried this often-suggested tactic and are here to say: it works. But sometimes the issue isn't one of location or even having the right words; sometimes it is a question of figuring out when your kid is ready, and when just the slightest nudge will get the conversation started. Marianne Lonsdale, mother and writer, found that moment.

My son, Nick, recently had an appointment to take his senior high school photos. Since he's been driving for nearly a year and seldom wants my company or advice, I figured he'd get himself to the portrait studio. Until he texted me at my office the day before the appointment, in the late afternoon.

"You're coming with me tomorrow, right?"

"No," I responded, slightly annoyed at the interruption. "I have to work."

"I think parents are supposed to come," he texted back. A bell went off.

"Are you nervous?"

Senior pictures are no longer a couple of poses in a cap and gown—they've morphed into modeling sessions with different outfits and fake backgrounds.

"A little," Nick answered.

I looked at my calendar—two back-to-back meetings at the scheduled time. Of course. I swung into Mom mode, canceling one and rescheduling the other. Not such a big deal after all. Dang, my son wanted me to go with him. I couldn't remember my last invitation from him.

The photo shoot was fun, but Nick, it turns out, was very nervous. I hovered behind the photographer making goofy faces, trying to humor him into candid smiles. Then I embarrassed him by purchasing a key chain with a large photo of him, which was printed right on the spot. Nick thought it was tacky. I told him he should count his blessings that there was no charm bracelet option.

On the way home, I asked Nick how he was feeling about going away to college the following year. He played it safe for a few minutes, talking about how he hoped to end up somewhere with warm weather and fun dormmates. Then, texting away but not looking at me, he launched into how glad he'd be to live his life the way he wanted, without me pushing him to always be doing more, doing better.

I couldn't argue much; he had valid criticisms. The conversation was difficult and important. It probably wouldn't have happened if I hadn't made the time to be with him that morning, or if I hadn't gently probed him on how he was feeling.

Nick seldom volunteers information, but he'll open up to questions. This really hit home about a year earlier, March of his junior year.

It was a Friday night, and Nick and I were walking our fluff ball of a dog. He'd just arrived home after going to a sweet-sixteen party for his friend Sophie at a Chinese restaurant.

"Who was at the party?" I began.

Nick rattled off the names of about nine girls.

"Were you the only boy?" I asked. Nick nodded.

"Were you comfortable?" I knew he'd say yes, but I wasn't ready to cut to the chase.

"Yeah," he responded.

"Have you had crushes on any of those girls?"

He shook his head, looking at me and looking away, holding the leash and walking ahead of me.

I wasn't consciously thinking about where I was going with this line of questioning. I was more listening to my intuition that this was the right time. And my gut told me Nick needed a push.

"Do you even know yet if you get crushes on girls or boys?" I continued. "That can be confusing."

"Uh. Hmm." He cleared his throat. "Boys." Very clearly stated. There was no trace of doubt in my son's voice.

We kept talking that night and throughout the weekend. There was so much we wanted to say, to share, to question that we'd both been keeping a lid on. Nick said he'd wanted to tell me for over two years but just couldn't figure out how to bring it up, couldn't decide what the perfect moment would be. And I'd been feeling like I shouldn't ask, that I should wait until he was ready. He ended up feeling that my asking the question created that perfect moment.

I stare at the plastic framed picture of my beautiful boy dangling on my keychain. It's not as easy as it used to be. There are no clear signals—no tears, no scraped knees, and no easy answers. Most of the time he doesn't want or need my opinion, but he still wants my support, my acceptance, and my love. I'm going to keep asking questions, making sure that invisible tether between our hearts keeps pulling us together and apart.

> I had moved to Chicago for college from the Bay Area. In middle school and high school I wasn't yet out, but I wanted to fit in. Even when I first got to college and was out I didn't know how to fit in. I had to step away from the societal norms at college (frat parties, lots of drinking) and not worry what everyone thought of me to find what made me happy on my own. I had adopted the heteronormative idea that I had to find a partner in college. Now I realize I have more time to find companionship and I can ask myself at every turn in my life if each thing is important to me. It would be icing on the cake if I find someone, but it's not essential.
>
> —NICK, 21

NOT KNOWING HOW MUCH TO CARE

While our parenting goals might be to stay neutral, letting our
teens figure out how they really feel, and keeping our opinions
to ourselves, that is far harder to achieve than we ever imagined.
When your kid falls in love, it can be hard not to fall a little in love
yourself. Here is a person who is bringing such great joy to your
teen's or young adult's life, and sometimes it is almost impossible
not to love them for that. But Marlene Fischer, writer and mother
of three sons, asks, where do you draw the line?

The other day I ran into the mother of my middle son's
former girlfriend. Our kids, who had started dating in high
school, broke up at the beginning of their sophomore year
in college, after dating for nearly two years. Our encounter
was not awkward, and I was glad to see her and hear how
her daughter was doing; when she was my son's girlfriend, I
had enjoyed her company.

I have a friend who told me that until a ring is offered
and accepted, I shouldn't get too attached to the young
women my boys are dating. I had heard this advice from
other people as well. While that may be good advice, it's
hard to follow—at least it is for me.

Perhaps it's because I don't have any daughters that I
love when my boys bring home their girlfriends. The entire
atmosphere in the house changes when there are girls here.
I get to learn about the new fads and fashions in which my
boys have no interest or clue. I hear what the girls have
been up to, as well as news about my boys and their friends
that I might otherwise never know. My oldest son's girlfriend recently told me that one of his good friends had

gotten engaged a few months earlier, a bit of information my son didn't think worthy of mention.

My son and his girlfriend visited us shortly after they had attended a wedding. I asked my son how the wedding was, and he said, "Fine." I asked his girlfriend the same question, and she gave me a litany of specifics, like how many people attended and how the food was. I don't think my boys are withholding details on purpose; they just don't see the relevance in relaying such details. After living in a household with minimally communicative males, these morsels of information are like a few sips of water to a person who's been wandering in the desert.

After my oldest son first started dating his girlfriend, he told me, "You're going to like her too much, and it's going to be a problem." I am not entirely sure what he meant, but I am guessing he knew I would get attached.

When my sons' girlfriends are around, I get to see a side of my boys I don't normally see. The "young and in love" thing is really sweet—it is good to know my boys can be considerate and silly and tender, different from the rougher versions I typically observe. I have been fortunate because I like the girls my boys have chosen to date thus far. They have been smart, kind, caring, family-oriented, and unspoiled. They are young women with excellent characters, and I am happy to know my boys have such good taste.

My sons' girlfriends have been present at holiday meals, celebratory dinners, and have spent more than one New Year's Eve with us. They remember to text me on my birthday and offered me comfort when my father died, attending his funeral and shiva. They have encouraged me with my writing career; my oldest son's girlfriend even made me business cards. How nice is that?

So how in the world am I *not* supposed to get attached? How do other parents not get attached? How do they distance themselves from these terrific young people who become (perhaps, temporarily) part of the family? Is there some sort of guidebook or manual for this that I don't know about? Do I really have to wait until they are engaged or married before I get attached? What if they do get married and later get divorced? Isn't it all just a moment in time?

After my middle son and his girlfriend broke up, even though I knew that the reasons for their breakup were sound ones and they parted as friends, I found myself missing her. I know that I had only myself to blame because I had broken the cardinal rule by getting attached.

For a little while after my son and his girlfriend parted ways, I decided that my friends who told me to hold off until things were "official" before getting attached had the right idea. I thought I had learned my lesson. I was determined that the next time I was going to play it cool. But then . . .

My son met a girl during his junior year at college and we had a chance to meet her when we visited him at school. A few months ago, he brought her home for a weekend, so we could get to know each other better. As I spent more time with her, I could see what he loved about her and how much they cared about each other. Despite my best intentions, when I saw how happy he was, I started warming to her. I just couldn't help it.

I admit that I'm just not good at keeping people I like at arm's length. I really don't know how other people do it. I find it hard to imagine that my feelings toward these young women would change the moment after a marriage proposal. My emotions are not like a light switch that I can easily flip on and off.

Another friend of mine is fond of saying, "You are who you are"—as you can see, my friends offer a lot of advice—and maybe she is right. I guess what matters most is that my sons want me to know their girlfriends and they feel comfortable bringing them home. And if getting at least somewhat attached is the price I pay, then I'm okay with that.

SEXUAL HEALTH AND STDS

Our discussions of sex and love need to touch on the subject of our teen's health. Sure, they have probably had health classes in school that covered the various risks when it comes to sexual health, but that doesn't get us off the hook for this discussion. Marybeth Bock, MPH, writer and mom, walks us through how to approach these conversations.

Right out of the gate, here's a content warning. Reading this may make you feel a little squeamish, awkward, and uncomfortable. That's kind of the point. Too many of us are being cowardly and need to be called out. Pause for a second, take a few slow, deep breaths, but stay with me, as this is important. We need to talk about sexually transmitted diseases—STDs.

Let's start at the root of the issue and briefly go back in time to think about our own childhood experiences.

Picture yourself as a twelve-year-old and imagine the word "sex" being spoken aloud in your house. Would the feeling in the room have been one of casual conversation and open discussion? Or would all eye contact suddenly cease and the topic abruptly change, while any adult in the room pretended not to have heard the word?

For many, my childhood experience was the norm—a couple tidbits about anatomy mentioned here and there, albeit never using the correct anatomical terms, and a small pink booklet about "Becoming a Woman" passed to me with a box of feminine products. End of story, with message received: we really don't want to talk about sex or anything related to it.

Today, we live in the age of erectile dysfunction commercials, dating apps, and unfettered access to information on the internet. Yet many of us are still too uncomfortable to talk to our kids about sexual health, or we wait way too long to begin the conversations. We either leave it to teachers and coaches in schools, or we live in a state of semidenial and hope the kids will eventually figure it out via Google. Some proactive parents hope that leaving a box of condoms in their son's room or bringing their daughter to the doctor for birth control pills will be the beginning and end of their involvement.

When it comes to simply preventing pregnancy, these tactics seem to be working. According to Power to Decide: The National Campaign to Prevent Teen and Unplanned Pregnancy, "between 1991 and 2017, the teen birth rate declined by an impressive 70 percent nationwide. It has declined in all fifty states and among all racial/ethnic groups."

Despite access to more information in today's world, the rates of sexually transmitted diseases (STDs) are at an all-time high, with young people and gay and bisexual men at greatest risk for becoming infected. In 2017, for the fourth year in a row, increases were seen in all three nationally reported STDs—chlamydia, gonorrhea, and syphilis. The

Centers for Disease Control and Prevention estimates that "nearly twenty million new sexually transmitted infections occur every year in this country, half among young people aged fifteen to twenty-four, and account for almost $16 billion in health care costs."

The complexities of discussing sexual health with our kids is that we must also address issues like oral and anal sex. Periodic, confidential sampling conducted by the National Survey of Family Growth shows sustained increases in oral and anal sex rates starting in 2002, when both men and women ages fifteen to forty-four began survey participation.

The reality is that infections can be transmitted from any kind of sexual conduct involving genitals, and there are some risks even if condoms are being used. Kids need evidence-based facts, and we can't just hope and pray they learn the facts from other sources.

So, if up until today, you've been one of the many parents too embarrassed to discuss sexual health with your kids in any great detail, what steps can you take now?

- Whether your child is twelve or twenty, arrange a first discussion—preferably where eye contact is minimal. Start off with acknowledgment that it's going to be awkward, hopefully a bit humorous, but free of judgment and solely focused on their health. Key attitude: sex is normal! Let them know they can ask you anything now and going forward, and you will help them find answers if you don't know them.
- If you have any reason to even suspect your child is sexually active, make sure they see a doctor, have access to birth control, and have them get tested for

STDs. If you can't stomach the details yourself, tell the doctor beforehand that you'd like a longer appointment so there's time for them to talk in greater detail with your child.

- Emphasize the extreme importance of always being completely honest with health care providers. I often remind my kids that medical professionals have seen and heard it *all!* Even if it is not offered to your child, suggest the option of talking to the doctor without you in the room, especially if you suspect they aren't being honest with you.

- Talk often about how alcohol and drugs alter decision-making when it comes to sex of any kind. Sexual health and history need to be discussed honestly with a potential partner when both are sober. Mutual consent is a must. Yep—if you're not mature enough to talk about it, you really shouldn't be doing it.

- Finally, highlight the fact that decisions made about sex today can significantly affect someone's health far into the future. As with learning to drive a car, emphasizing safety can be achieved without undue fear.

SEXUAL ASSAULT

When it comes to sexual assault, we turn to the experts for advice on how to keep our kids safe. Here are some of the guidelines developed by RAINN (Rape, Abuse & Incest National Network) that we can share with our teens.

- Trust your fear. If something frightens you, listen to your instincts and seek a safer situation. You do not need a reason.

This could mean leaving a party, a dorm room, anywhere. If you are uncomfortable with a situation you see someone else in, speak up as well. RAINN reminds college students that "it's better to lie and make up an excuse to leave than to stay and be uncomfortable, scared, or worse. Your safety comes before someone else's feelings or what they may think of you."

- Be very careful about using geo-tagging or other online methods of letting people know your physical whereabouts. RAINN stresses that "if you would not share the information with a stranger, then you shouldn't share it online."

- Don't assume that someone is a good, honorable, or honest person just because you were admitted to the same university. The people you are meeting are strangers until you know them well enough to offer them your trust. Proceed with abundant caution.

- Prevention is the most important advice, but we must also sadly prepare our kids for steps to take if they or a friend is assaulted.

Sexual assault on college campuses is a very real problem—and until recently, a somewhat hidden one. It is often hidden from parents, the police, and school authorities because so many victims are reluctant to report the crime. Friends or roommates may be the first and only people who know that a crime has occurred. A report by the Department of Justice indicates that "about two-thirds of the victims tell someone, often a friend (but usually not a family member or college official)."

So if your student calls from school to say they need advice for a friend who has been the victim of sexual assault or rape in college, or that they themselves have been a victim, what should a parent suggest? Call 911, the victim's gynecologist, resident adviser, or the campus health center? Tell the town police or the campus police? Take the victim to the local ER immediately or wait until morning or the next day when she or he might be feeling stronger? Find the university's policy on sexual assault and follow that? And where would that policy be? Does it change anything if the victim is still seventeen? What steps can a friend or parent suggest that, taken early, will lead to the best emotional, physical, and legal outcomes? And what, if any, decisions need to be made immediately?

After long conversations with a gynecologist, a detective in a special victims unit, and the head of a large rape counseling service, we have gathered their knowledge and experience. We are not experts in any of these fields—we are just moms who asked questions and are sharing the results of what we found. This should not be construed as medical, legal, or psychological advice but rather food for thought and possible first steps if you should find your college student seeking your advice or your care. Each expert reminded us that at times of crisis, as in the aftermath of a sexual assault or rape on a college campus, parents can play an important role as a calming and reassuring voice, and should have knowledge and suggestions of next steps to take.

Each victim is different. Every situation varies, and there's no cookie-cutter answer. What follows is some advice from three experts familiar with victims' bodies, minds, hearts, and legal rights. It would be impossible to suggest the best action for every person who has been the victim of sexual assault or rape in college, but here are a few things parents might want to think of when their teens (or teens' friends) are in moments of need.

PROVIDE UNQUALIFIED SUPPORT. All the experts we consulted emphasized the same starting point. Whether a parent is speaking to their kid as a victim, or advising their own child as a friend of the victim, our experts said it is paramount to let victims know that you believe them, will support them, and that all the decisions are theirs. Tell them you will respect their privacy and discuss this with no other person without their explicit permission. Reassure them that you will stick by them and help them in whatever way they judge is best. Only they can decide what steps to take, but point out that there are experts (medical, legal, psychological) with whom they can consult to make these decisions, and that they are not alone or without resources. Try to understand that they may be in a very complicated situation and that they more than likely know their assailant. According to the US Department of Justice, "90 percent of college women who are victims of rape or attempted rape know their assailant."

BECOME FAMILIAR WITH THE COLLEGE POLICY AND RESOURCES. Most colleges post their sexual assault protocol and list of services, including counseling, health, and legal services. Universities are required to have a Title IX coordinator, and if you search the college's name and the term "Title IX" (or sometimes the words "sexual assault") it will often lead you to the right site. College Title IX sites often have numbers to contact for medical and legal help, as well as confidential counseling services that are usually available to students around the clock. Many have extensive FAQs that can offer first steps and important contacts for dealing with a sexual assault. Students may well have been made aware of these online resources and parents can find them through a quick search. It is ideal if both parents and students are familiar with this site before it is needed (something parents might suggest to their college students).

FIND A COUNSELOR. One place to start is the National Sexual Assault Hotline that's run by RAINN, available twenty-four hours a day, seven days a week: 1.800.656.HOPE (4673). Calls to this number are automatically rerouted to a local affiliated rape counseling center, but the phone number of the caller is not stored. This allows victims, friends, or family to ask questions anonymously about resources, laws, and procedures in their immediate area and at their local hospital. The one caveat is for callers who are under eighteen and share personal identifying information; in this situation, there is a requirement to report the call to authorities. The counseling center we spoke to is happy to consult by phone anonymously to answer any questions and offer guidance and will meet with victims at the emergency room, their offices, or other locale.

HELP SEEK MEDICAL ATTENTION. In cases of sexual assault or rape, there are a number of issues to consider surrounding medical attention. A parent might ask: Has the assault been violent, and does the victim need emergency medical attention for any physical injuries that might require X-rays, stitches, or wound care? Is there a fear of pregnancy or sexually transmitted diseases? Our physician experts suggested that victims visit the emergency room for treatment because hospitals offer twenty-four-hour care, including morning-after pills, antibiotic injections, STD testing, and medical care for any injuries. While a call to a personal physician might provide direction, our experts agreed that most physicians are not as well equipped as the emergency room.

Not all emergency rooms are the same, but many are equipped to provide (1) an expert nurse specifically trained at medical treatment and evidence collection in cases of sexual assault, (2) specialized evidence collection materials, otherwise known as a "rape kit," (3) rape or assault counseling services from a local counseling center with specially trained counselors who will remain with the victim throughout their medical care, and (4) psychological services.

The physicians and detective we spoke to emphasized that immediate medical care is desirable, but the victim should understand (and this is a point that parents can make) that they can stop the process, even in the midst of the physical exam, at any point they wish. Those caring for the victim should stress that no one will do anything that they don't want done, and that they can change their mind at any point and call a halt to the medical, legal, or counseling process.

The earlier that medical attention is sought the better, as the quality of evidence collected is better and the effectiveness of the morning-after pill is improved. Some hospitals will forward the collected evidence kit to their local police department with only the name "Jane Doe," date, and hospital identification number. These kits are stored for many years for use if or when the victim wants to pursue legal action.

All the experts we spoke to felt it was important that someone accompany the victim to the hospital and stay with them for the duration of the visit. Rape counselors will also often accompany a victim, and the hospital usually calls them to be of assistance. They are trained in hospital procedure and can be helpful in explaining to the victim what the examination will entail, the reason for each procedure, and, importantly, that at any point the victim can terminate the process.

UNDERSTAND WHY VICTIMS FEAR SPEAKING UP. One of the main reasons victims of sexual assault do not want to involve law enforcement is that they feel that they will not be believed. A second reason victims do not want to come forward is the fear of social ostracizing. Because "acquaintance rape" is more common than a sexual assault by a stranger, victims may fear social reprisal from their peers. Rape in college is made even more painful as victims may cross paths with their attackers in their daily lives. Victims need to understand that they have a very long time, even years, in which to make any decision on legal action.

SEEK SUPPORT SERVICES. Friends and family can play a crucial role in giving support, but students who are victims of a sexual assault should seek out professional psychological help. The emotional scars of rape and other sexual assault can be long-lasting, and there are people trained to help victims. Parents can play an important role in urging a student to seek this care.

If your child is the carer, rather than the victim, do not underestimate how much this experience might shake them. Continue to keep in touch by phone, or visit, or help in whatever way your child wants help, and make sure they have someone to talk to about their own concern for their friend or fears for themselves.

Watching our college kids and now young adults enter into the first serious relationships of their lives has very much changed our thinking about love and sex. As adults, we have watched marriages we *knew* would last crumble. We have watched couples spend decades happy together who seemingly have little in common. If we know anything now, it is that the landscape has shifted and is continuing to shift. And what we hope for our kids is simply that they find partners who care for them deeply and treat them with kindness, who feel lucky to be loved by our children and will put in the rewarding effort it takes to remain a couple. We hope our children find love that is deep and healthy and rewarding—and forever.

CHAPTER FIVE

Academics

The academic struggle is real. While some of us might remember wandering through high school a bit aimless and perhaps underprepared, many of our kids live in an academic pressure cooker where talk of college admissions and test prep starts as early as middle school. As parents, we are caught between wanting to lower that pressure (and perhaps return our kids to an earlier era) and feeling like the forces creating it are so big that there is little we can do to mitigate them. When our kids are working tirelessly and are stressed out as a result, we worry. And when our kids are trying to skate by and are working well below their potential, we worry then too.

This chapter is not about the ways we can change the world our kids inhabit—frankly, we have no idea how to achieve that. Instead, we will try to look at ways that we can support and guide our kids during their academic lives toward whatever goal they have chosen for themselves.

As parents, we know it is crucial to celebrate our kids for who they are, while at the same time urging them to become their best selves. Even as we write these words, we realize that they smack of clichés. How does one know how to be his or her best self? What does that look like—and isn't that their job to figure out?

Here is our truth: we're really not sure. But the best answer we can come up with as two moms who are avid listeners in a massive community of parents and who are constantly consulting the experts is that it's our job to show our kids what trying your best feels like. It is our job to establish the values that are most important to our families. In some families, education is right near the top of that list, while in others it will be philanthropy, athletics, or religion. But regardless of how those values line up, it is our job to call our kids out when, because of laziness or apathy, they underperform.

It is not our job to define their interests for them or to pursue those interests alongside them (though we are always happy to expose them to a wide range of endeavors). It is not our job to blindly prop up their self-esteem—our kids are too smart not to see through that artifice. It is not our job to thoughtlessly cheer everything they do, though we are here to applaud their very real efforts when we see them putting that forth. Our role is to guide, to help them set their own aspirational goals, something we recognize is much easier said than done—especially when it comes to schoolwork.

Here are four key lessons we tried to impart to our kids to help with their academics, both in high school and later in college.

LEARN HOW YOU WORK BEST. It is important over the high school years that our kids come to understand themselves and the working conditions under which they are most effective. Do they need the silence of their own bedroom? Do they study best from note cards? Are study groups useful for them? How many times do they need to review the material to feel exam-ready? The answers to all of these are personal, and students who succeed know themselves well enough to know what works for them.

DEFINE YOUR OWN EXPECTATIONS. Our teens know our expectations for them, and there is nothing wrong with them becoming accustomed to high yet realistic goals in any sphere of their lives. At some point, however, it's essential that they learn to set their own expectations for themselves. The source of these may be external, like a minimum GPA for keeping a scholarship or a spot on a sports team, while at other times they will arise from an intrinsic motivation to master a new skill or pursue an interest. Either way, setting goals and standards, whether for short-term tasks (finishing an assignment) or long-term aspirations (getting into graduate school), is a critical skill to develop.

TALK TO TEACHERS. In high school, your teens should learn to communicate with their teachers or tutors; in college, it will be their professors, TAs (teaching assistants), or academic advisers. Many a seemingly insurmountable problem in the classroom can be solved simply by talking to those who stand at the front of it. Most teachers love to teach, and they are happy to clarify an assignment and quick to suggest ways to get more help (or offer it themselves). Learning to talk to those in a position of authority is a crucial life lesson that can never be taught too early.

MANAGE YOUR TIME. For many kids, the biggest challenge with their academics isn't the substance of the material they are being taught but rather being able to organize and manage their time. In high school, they may be tempted to leave projects and studying until the last minute. And perhaps this works for high school. But if college is next, with fewer yet more time-consuming assignments, it is all too easy to slip behind over the course of a semester.

Lisa struggled with one of her sons when trying to teach the skill of time management. The "teaching" often degenerated into nagging and arguing, and homework assignments were still slipping through the cracks unfinished or late. She recalls:

One of my kids struggled to plan his time well, so I hung a huge whiteboard on his bedroom wall. Originally, he marked his assignments down in a planner or a calendar app on his phone or (worst of all) on small pieces of paper shoved into every pocket. These methods proved far too easy to ignore. So instead, I insisted he write down assignments, tests, quizzes, and due dates each day, as soon as he arrived home from middle school and later high school.

By hanging the whiteboard over his desk, right above his beloved computer, it kept him from ignoring assignments and kept me from having to say, "What work do you have?" Planning is a skill that for some teens comes naturally and for others needs to be modeled. By requiring him to document his to-dos and plan every day, I was very slowly teaching him to practice his skills in much the same way he practiced soccer.

This story should have a happy ending where I tell you he went off to college knowing how to successfully juggle the requirements of freshman year. But no, that is not what happened. He struggled some more during freshman year and even into sophomore year, but he was equipped with the tools to solve his time-management issues and, over the course of his college career, he was able to begin to master this skill.

As parents, one goal is for our kids to understand how to maximize their academic opportunities, but we often find ourselves needing more explicit ways to help our kids do this. So, we sought out the wisdom of two experienced educators: a high school teacher of AP English and a college professor of political science. We asked each instructor to give us concrete, actionable pieces of advice that parents can offer and kids can follow. For example, what can a freshman actually do, whether in high school or college, to ease their transition and begin to thrive academically? Their answers were full of common sense—and uncommon insight.

A GOOD START IN HIGH SCHOOL

The following insights come from Emily Genser, a mom who has taught high school for more than fifteen years (and who has seen it all).

There are two things teens need to remember when it comes to getting a good start to high school: (1) build relationships from the very beginning, and (2) be honest. These two rules are the most important building blocks, but here are some others that help.

KNOW WHAT IS EXPECTED OF YOU OVER THE SUMMER. Many of your classes (not just English) now require summer reading, or some sort of summer work in preparation for the fall. Coming into class unprepared on day one makes a poor first impression on the teacher.

However, if you haven't done the work, cop to it right away. I would always rather a student come up to me on day one, and say, "I didn't do the summer reading, what can I do so that I am prepared?" This shows maturity and ambition—both of which are necessary to do well in any class.

WORK HARD ON THE FIRST ASSIGNMENT. This is your chance to show your teacher what you can do and what they can expect going forward. You should read thoroughly, write as well as you can, and participate fully in the activities of that first week.

It is hard to change someone's impression of you, and you want the person grading your work to feel that you are trying from the very beginning. They will be more accepting of slip-ups later in the year, if you have shown a willingness to work hard from the start.

PARTICIPATE. This is how we get to know our students. Your teacher doesn't care particularly that your answers are 100 percent correct, but we do want to see that you are putting effort forth and paying attention to what has already been said. Don't speak just to speak, speak to add to the discussion.

ASK QUESTIONS WHEN YOU DON'T UNDERSTAND SOME-THING. If you have a question, odds are someone else has the same one. It's likely that many people have the same question, but they are too shy to ask. If the question doesn't get asked, it probably won't get answered. Don't be left wondering.

BE HONEST IN ALL AREAS OF YOUR WORK. I have forgiven many transgressions on the basis of honesty. No matter how close you think you are to your classmates, nine times out of ten they will throw you under the bus to save themselves. The truth will come out. I understand that mistakes get made. We all make bad choices when under stress or overwhelmed. It is the way you deal with the consequence of your choices that tells me who you are.

If you cheat in my class, I will be upset. But if you are honest about it when caught, or (better yet) before being caught, I will more than likely either give you another assignment to make up for part of the grade, or help you to find a way to strengthen your grade after the fact. I want you to understand that what you did was wrong, but I don't want you to fail because of a momentary lapse. No teacher wants that. Your honesty will help me help you.

IF THE CLASS IS A REACH FOR YOU (AN HONORS CLASS OR AP CLASS YOU WANTED TO TRY), BE PREPARED TO ASK FOR HELP. You cannot grow on your own. Advocate for yourself. Help can come from any number of places, but it should always start with the teacher. She may already know that you are struggling, and she definitely wants to know that you care about your own success.

If you find that you don't get the help you're looking for from your teacher, find another resource. But always let your teacher know you are working hard. Mention that you purchased (or borrowed from the library) an AP practice book. Tell her that you've been getting tutored by an older student or an adult.

If your teacher knows you are trying to grow, they will be more likely to help you achieve your goal.

IF YOU DON'T DO AN ASSIGNMENT, OR HAD TROUBLE WITH AN ASSIGNMENT, DO NOT WAIT UNTIL CLASS TIME TO TELL YOUR TEACHER. Seek them out before first period, and, once again, be honest.

Your teacher knows how stressful your academic workload can be and may be more understanding than you think about the pressures of extracurriculars and/or family stress.

DEVELOP A RELATIONSHIP WITH AT LEAST THREE TEACHERS BY THE MIDDLE OF JUNIOR YEAR. You will need at least two teachers to write a college recommendation (or serve as a reference for an internship or job), and you don't want to put yourself in a precarious position when the time comes to ask.

Know who will be your best advocate and talk to that

teacher face-to-face. The worst thing that can happen is that a teacher says no. That's why you want to have that third teacher in your back pocket.

GET TO KNOW YOUR GUIDANCE COUNSELOR. It's easy to forget that each guidance counselor has hundreds of students for whom they are responsible. Don't wait until a crisis to seek out her help. The better she knows you at your best, the better she can help you at your worst. Make appointments to check in, see that you're on the right track, and ask questions about what might be missing in your high school schedule.

Guidance counselors are experts in their areas, but it's hard for them to guide you if they don't know you.

A GOOD START IN COLLEGE

This next section of advice, on how to start college on the right foot, has been honed by many experienced parties over the years. Michelle Miller-Adams, mother of a teen and a professor of political science at Grand Valley State University, explains:

This list began as an eighteenth birthday gift for my nephew who was headed to college. Five years and one degree later, it has benefited from feedback from more than twenty colleagues, friends, and former students who pointed out some important lessons I had missed and added their own reflections.

SHOW UP. Attend every class session unless you have a contagious illness. Chronic absenteeism is the number one reason a student will do poorly in my classes. Know yourself and be strategic—if you have a hard time waking up early, don't sign up for early classes. Choosing your own schedule is one of the best things about college! And don't sit in the back; I can practically predict a student's grade based on where he or she sits. Slacking in the back row will equal lower grades with very few exceptions.

Showing up will also help you develop a relationship with your professors. It's hard to be noticed when you're not there. And showing up can improve your grade. I am not the only professor to give credit just for being there (and being awake). And if a student is in a gray area when it comes to final grades, I will look to their attendance record, with perfect or near-perfect attendance tipping me toward the higher grade.

But showing up is not just for making a good impression or for a better grade. My colleagues and I believe that what happens in the classroom has value (that's why we're there, and that's why we prepare). Bonus advice: When writing to tell your professor why you weren't in class, don't ever ask, "Did I miss anything important?" We think you did!

INTRODUCE YOURSELF. Find an excuse to go to your professor's office hours, not just once but two or three times a term. Take a draft of your essay in for review; once graded work has been returned, go back and ask for advice on how to improve it. Your professors will be your referees, advocates, and possibly even friends later in life; you want them to remember your name once the semester is over.

Some professors may seem intimidating or reclusive, but most of us got into this business because we care about students and enjoy interacting with them. We can't do that if we don't know you. Visit your assigned academic adviser too, and if you don't feel good about that person, find another faculty member who will play that role. Part of our job is to help you make good choices about classes and careers, and steer you toward resources that can help you succeed.

Finally, if your professor is giving a talk or performance, show up—and make sure he or she knows you did. If your professor cancels a class to attend a conference, ask her how it went. We're human, we like the attention. Helpful hint: Always remind said professor or adviser of your name when you encounter them. Over the years we have taught a lot of students—plus, our memory is not what it used to be—and we will be grateful for the help.

ENGAGE. Come to class sufficiently prepared to ask a perceptive question or make a useful comment. Don't be a wallflower, but don't dominate either—your fellow students will not love you if your hand is always the first one up. And don't be afraid to disagree with the professor or with your fellow students. Most of us welcome debate and new perspectives, provided you can back up your arguments with evidence.

Turn off your cell phone and do not text during class. We can tell. When you email your professor, do it for a good reason and with respect. (A colleague says, "There are no stupid questions unless the answer is on the syllabus.") Don't address us as "dude" or use our first names unless we've asked you to. We went to school for *many years*, long enough to earn "Professor" as our salutation.

EXPLORE. Don't stress if you don't know what you want to do after college. This is your chance to find out. The odds are good that you will hold many jobs and even several careers after you graduate, so the key is to get the skills you will need to navigate through all of them. Employers and graduate programs alike will want to see evidence of the sort of critical thinking, communication, and analytical skills that are taught within many majors.

Your college advising office may encourage you to pick a major (and maybe some minors) as soon as possible, but this can be a mistake. Unless you are absolutely certain of your future plans, work first on your college's general education requirements or take a class or two in your possible field of interest to see if you really like the major before committing to it. I have never seen multiple majors or minors pay off, so don't spend extra time acquiring labels that no employer or grad school admission committee will care about.

Once you settle on a major, try to avoid changing it—changing your major can keep you in school longer than necessary, and the costs can add up. Use the time saved to gain experiences and skills—study abroad, gain foreign language competency, improve your quantitative skills, carry out a complex research project.

AFFILIATE. Take advantage of what your campus has to offer—you will find clubs, events, service trips, religious groups, and more for every interest and aspect of your identity. Join a group as early in the semester as possible, the first week if you can—student activities start up right away, and there is no better way to meet non-freshmen. Try out any and all groups that seem interesting until you find your niche. Affiliation enriches the experience and gives you skills and resources that will serve you well in the real world.

LEARN A LANGUAGE AND LIVE ABROAD. Language skills are among the most in-demand credentials for students entering the workforce; cross-cultural experience, the kind you get from spending time in another country, is up there too. In the real world, learning a new language is expensive and hard to do. Take advantage of the daily classes and language labs that are included in the price of your tuition.

Try to study abroad. Even if you can't get away for a whole semester, find a short-term spring or summer program; study abroad can be as brief as a few weeks. And don't decide you can't afford this experience until you do some research. Many colleges and universities have grants or scholarships available specifically for study abroad—and if you are willing to try someplace unusual, your experience may be fully paid for. (I have students who spent a year in Slovenia, Ghana, or Poland for less than the cost of staying home.)

STAY HEALTHY. Don't neglect your health. Eat well and be sure to get enough sleep. Getting sick means missed classes, missed deadlines, and missed fun. The recreation center, gym, yoga classes, or intramural sports are great ways to meet people and will help keep your mind clear. Do not abuse substances or binge drink. And don't get in a car with anyone who has had too much to drink or who texts while driving (and don't text while driving). Auto accidents remain the number one killer of college-aged students.

Practice safe sex! Nothing can interrupt your college experience, and that of your partner, like an unplanned pregnancy or an STD.

And every college has a counseling center—be preemptive about talking to a therapist if you have any concerns about your mental health.

TAP INTO RESOURCES. Career and professional advice; funding for internships, overseas study, or travel; opportunities to work with professors on research; mental health counseling and disability support services—are all offered by most schools, but it is up to you to recognize your needs and make use of such resources.

At the university where I teach, there are people standing by to help you formulate a research question, analyze your data, improve your writing, identify a suitable career path, prepare for a job interview, find an internship, manage a bad breakup or roommate trouble, track down a hard-to-get library resource, and help you apply for postgraduate fellowships—among other things! Avail yourself of the many research resources provided by your college or university. You are paying for them, after all!

BE SOCIAL. If you are living in a dorm, leave the door of your room open much of the day and cultivate a broad group of friends. Look up from your phone and make eye contact while walking around campus and before class. Set up a study group of a few people to share ideas, questions, and notes if you have to miss a class.

Many of us regret that our social circles in college were not wider. It's tempting to hang with your assigned roommate or suitemates, or if you are not living on campus to come and go without putting yourself out there, but this is a mistake. Your college is filled with interesting people like yourself, and some of them may become lifelong friends or important networking resources. Open yourself up to meeting a wide range of people; engaging in campus life can help with this.

SAVOR YOUR INDEPENDENCE. College is a time to grow up. Make the place where you live a home away from home with a measure of personal comfort. Create a positive atmosphere that will nurture you. Keep your support system—friends, family—in place, and call them when you need them, but don't be afraid of loosening the ties. Make the most of each day. This I promise you: the years will fly by.

THE JOY OF AN "AVERAGE" KID

Part of the blame for the academic pressure is on us, not on our kids or external factors. We watch the parade of students lauded by our teens' high schools and wonder why this isn't happening to our child. When they are born we feel that our kids are destined for great things. And they are—but those great things must be on their own terms and in their own time and may not include being an academic standout. Coming to terms with the fact that our kids are doing just fine, even if they are not given the accolades of a standout, can sometimes be a greater challenge for a parent than for their teen.

Sharon Greenthal, writer and mother of two young adults, gives an honest look back at raising an "average student."

One of the most challenging aspects of raising my son was accepting the fact that he was an unmotivated student. Though his father and I tried not to let his grades define how we saw him, especially during high school, his academic performance did impact how we viewed ourselves as parents. We had moments of self-doubt and, at times, questioned the way we had raised him. What had we done wrong? What did we fail to do to motivate him to succeed?

Nothing really, it turns out. It was never up to us to

motivate him, as hard as we tried. He had to find the motivation within himself.

In the hypercompetitive world of high school, with AP classes, honor roll, valedictorians, students of the month, perfect SAT scores, 4.0-and-above GPAs, scholar athletes, and myriad other ways for students to stand out, having a child with average grades is considered a serious problem by many parents and can even be looked upon by some misguided moms and dads as embarrassing or shameful. A C student's application, they fear, will get tossed aside without a glance by admissions offices at most competitive colleges.

It's not surprising that parents of average students—parents like I was—grow frantic with worry that their child won't succeed. But here is what I learned. Just because a student earns average grades in high school doesn't mean they won't succeed in college—and, more important, in life.

My son was an average high school student, graduating with a GPA just shy of 3.0. There were a few reasons for his mediocre performance in high school, among them his ADHD and a stubborn lack of motivation. His father and I did everything we could think of to ignite an interest in academics in his intelligent but disinterested mind. One of the people we enlisted to help was the English teacher at his high school who had been so inspirational to our older daughter. As I eavesdropped on their tutoring session each week, I was struck by how utterly bored my son was, despite the fascinating (if somewhat exasperated) way the teacher explained the novel my son was reading for class. For me, a voracious reader with an English degree, my son's disdain for literature was both sad and also a little terrifying. How would he ever make it through college without the skills to interpret complex writing?

Parents of average students might want to consider doing things differently than we did and fight the urge to push their student to perform better in high school. Many teenagers don't reach a level of maturity to find the impetus to work hard until after high school. The fighting and arguing about getting him to work harder, study more, and do better was futile and frustrating and caused unnecessary stress for my son and for my husband and me.

Sports and competition did motivate my son. His father and I felt the life lessons he learned playing football in high school—commitment, discipline, respect, and teamwork—would be of great value later in his life, so we supported our offensive lineman and his team. Even when it might have made sense to pull him from football to spend more time on his schoolwork, we let him continue playing because we knew how important it was for him to be part of something bigger than he was. Belonging to his high school football team gave him a focus and a sense of purpose that academics did not, and instinctively we understood that this was not something to take away from him. We were right about that.

When it came to sports, my son was also a passionate and curious fan who wanted to understand more than just the rules of the game. His command of baseball and football statistics was encyclopedic. He could dissect and evaluate every play in a football game the way mathematicians solve complex equations. What good would all this information be for him? his father and I wondered. We hoped that his zeal for learning about sports would someday translate into academic pursuits as well.

The belief that attending an elite college with a single-digit acceptance rate is the sole path to success is not just untrue but also impossible for the 95 percent of high school students who lack the grades or the financial ability to attend one of these institutions. And there are thousands of excellent schools that will admit average students and offer them the growth experiences and education that are the best reasons to attend college in the first place.

My son had the good fortune to be accepted by one of those schools. He majored in American history and wound up graduating in four years. He succeeded by finding the right support and counseling throughout his college experience, along with simply growing up. His senior thesis was about the Mexican baseball league and its impact on the sport in the United States. He received a B plus on his paper. He left college with two jobs waiting for him, one as a team manager and offensive line coach for a junior college football team and the other in public affairs for a large energy company. After a few years of working, he decided to return to school—this time to get his high school teaching credential.

My son, the average student, will make a wonderful teacher—and he plans to coach high school football too. One of his dreams is to create a high school class that interweaves the history of sports in the United States with the history of our country's politics.

It's unlikely that his high school GPA will come up during a job interview—and it shouldn't. There is so much more to him than his average grades in high school.

BATTLING THROUGH THE TOUGHEST YEAR

The road to college runs right through the most difficult year of all, eleventh grade. It was a year when we saw our otherwise even-tempered teens melt down. It was a year when we melted down. Much of this was because we didn't know what to anticipate or how to plan our way through the gauntlet of tests and activities.

We took many trips through eleventh grade, and we learned a lot along the way. First there were our own journeys decades ago. More recently we endured this tortuous year, the seventh academic circle of hell, with each of our kids. It is an exhausting process for both parent and teen. It is a nine-month tangle with our kid's academic, athletic, and social schedules while trying to fit in college visits, navigate a minefield of standardized tests, and teach them to drive.

It was also the moment we could see the end. A blurry vision that loomed in front of us became much clearer, and we could almost feel how close we were to the day our kids would leave. This is a warning signal from the parenting gods reminding us to savor every day, to get to know our changing child even better, and to prepare ourselves to send them on their way. This intellectual realization turned up the emotional temperature on all that would follow from here.

On each trip through eleventh grade, we picked up one or two pearls of parenting insight. Here they are, in no particular order:

STUDY FOR THE SAT AND ACT IN SUMMER. If your teen has completed the requisite math courses or if their English studies are far enough along, the time to start studying for the SAT is the summer between tenth and eleventh grades. Your child may not have reached their ideal intellectual maturity by this stage, of course, but they will not have this sort of concentrated time to focus on test prep once school starts up again in the fall. Whatever your preferred method of study, let them begin with some of the easier practice materials. If they haven't yet taken the PSAT, encourage them to take a diagnostic test before the chaos of junior year descends.

For many students, eleventh grade is the most challenging year academically, and it helps if some of the college entrance exam studying has begun when school begins.

WRITE THE COLLEGE ESSAY WITH AN ENGLISH TEACHER. For our families, the best person to work with our kids on their college essays was an experienced high school English teacher. A teacher will ask all the right questions and help move the process along ("Is that what you mean to say here? This is not clear to the reader. Do you have more details you can add to bring your story to life?"), but they will not write one word for your child. Urge your teen to find this English teacher (or a college counselor/other trusted adult) during eleventh grade and ask them if they can provide some essay help and guidance over the summer before twelfth grade. Many parents, even those who write for a living, find that acting as a reader for their teen's college essay can be a fraught experience and that having a different adult involved can do much to diffuse the process.

DON'T VISIT COLLEGES IN EARNEST UNTIL JUNIOR YEAR. One of the easiest ways to lighten the pressure on teens is to ban serious conversation about college and college tours until sometime during eleventh grade. Many of these early conversations and trips are wasted earlier on because teens change so much over their four years. If kids concentrate on their studies, activities, and standardized tests, they will have done themselves a favor once the college research process begins in earnest. High school needs to be about high school, not four years of college prep. As adults, we remember that it's an incredibly special time in life, and we don't want to ruin that time with a constant focus on college. Behind the scenes, parents can do some research about which colleges will best suit their family's budget and their child's interests, but until junior year, students should just focus on the job at hand. That is hard enough.

DO SOME SOUL-SEARCHING. The one way high school juniors can prepare for their eventual college search is to think about themselves as a college student and ideally in what kind of environment they thrive. While your junior will eventually learn a great deal about specific colleges from counselors, other students, and visits, it can be helpful to gain some self-knowledge before the process begins.

Some of the questions that juniors can ask themselves include:

- How do I like to learn?
- Do I need much interaction with faculty and teachers?
- Do I feel comfortable socially in a large environment, or am I happier when I know a sizable proportion of the people around me?
- Do I like the rambunctious atmosphere of a big sports school or is that social scene uninviting?
- How much can my family afford to pay, and what other means might I have for gaining scholarships and loans?
- How far from home do I want to go? Do I want to be able to

easily drive to my college from home, or would it be okay to take a plane or train each time?

- Do I like big-city life, suburban idyll, or a rural setting?
- What academic and extracurricular interests do I have now, or might I have over the next four years, and which schools will best suit these?

A student who can answer some of these questions (recognizing that the answers may change over time) will find that time spent with guidance counselors is far more productive.

Once your junior has met with their counselor, it is time for the road show. This can be a wonderful or utterly dreadful time in your life, but it is certainly the only time you will travel this path of exploring colleges together. We have heard stories of kids and parents who barely spoke a word on the entire journey; such is the way of a sullen teen. Yet other parents speak fondly of using this time as a way to grow closer to a teen who might be drifting away, and to talk about some of the dreams and plans they have for life after high school.

ASK FOR TEACHERS' RECOMMENDATIONS EARLY. Teacher recommendations need to be written by a teacher students have during junior or senior year. With early college-application deadlines falling in November of senior year, this may mean a junior-year teacher would be a better bet. Students should ask for this letter of recommendation before school ends in eleventh grade. Teachers are inundated with requests, and students should ask early, politely, and give the teacher the entire summer to address their request.

AVOID SIGNING UP FOR TOO MANY TESTS IN MAY. Standardized tests introduce an entirely new alphabet soup of terms to first-time junior parents. Help your teen plan where and when they will take all the standardized tests that occur this year. They could potentially face any combination of PSAT, SAT, Subject SATs, APs, ACT, and PLAN. Don't forget there will be classroom work and year-end exams to take as well, so avoid a May meltdown by looking to other months for the SAT, ACT, or Subject SAT tests.

Create a plan for testing. Use the results of the PSAT or PLAN to help recalibrate your student's studying. Make sure the Subject SATs (if they need them, and most students do not) are scheduled late enough in the year (and this is probably June for a regular course or May for an AP course) such that all the relevant coursework has been completed. There is a myriad of options to study for standardized exams, so plan ahead for what fits into your schedule and budget (and what seems most effective for your teen).

LEARN TO DRIVE IN THE SUMMER. Depending on your child's birthday, can they do any of the work for driver's education or training during the summer before junior year? This is not possible for all kids, but for those whose birthdays allow for it, summer is the best time to learn to drive, when they have more free time and foul weather is not an issue.

START THE YEAR RESTED. The most important thing to accomplish in the summer before this demanding year is to make sure your teen is rested. High school kids have summer jobs and perhaps, for the first time, are staying out a bit later. If they are studying for the SAT, learning to drive, or just staying up until all hours because they are teens, it is easy to not get the sleep they need. Beginning eleventh grade anything other than fully rested will only be a handicap in the year to come.

PARENTS: BE READY WITH AN EAR AND A SHOULDER. The most important thing a parent can do for their high school junior is continue to offer support and a listening ear. Even the calmest of teens will hit rough patches, and angry rants or tears of exhaustion will emerge. Being there to listen, console, and offer counsel is the single best thing a parent can do when guiding them through this tough year.

Start with What's Most Important

Sit down with an uninterrupted hour or two and no cell phones (we know, but this is important) sometime in the first semester of junior year. It will be very easy to get buried under the college admissions "process." In no time, your teen will be juggling applications, recommendations, college visits, meetings with her counselors, perhaps alumni interviews as well. Before this frenzy of activity takes on a life of its own, step back, paper or computer in hand, and have a long quiet chat with your teen.

This should be a very real look at your student and what is important to her. What are the most important things, listed in order, that she hopes her college experience will provide? Run through the list of questions from the "Do some soul-searching" section (page 165), and have your teen record her responses. The answers will change and evolve, but this is a document that she can refer to when creating her final list or when deciding between more than one acceptance. It is a useful guideline to keep in mind during college visits and for you to use for discussions. This list is hardly exhaustive, but it will let you start a discussion and get closer to finding the right fit.

A NEW PARENT-TEACHER RELATIONSHIP

As our kids work their way through high school, our relationship with their teachers changes profoundly from when they were younger. No longer can we send an email explaining why our child did or did not do something—that is now up to them. Despite the fact that this person has the best view into our teen's academic life, we may see them once at a back-to-school night and barely hear from them again after that. And while this may be as it should be, in the absence of any larger issues, there are many things we can learn and understand from our kid's high school teachers. Lori Stratton shares her experience:

> As the parent of three young adults and as a twenty-seven-year veteran high school English teacher, I understand how important it is for teachers and parents to maintain strong relationships. But I also know that sometimes these relationships can be confusing as we all try to find the best way to help teenagers navigate adolescence. So I've compiled a list of fifteen things high school teachers really want the parents of their students to know—things that might help encourage communication and understanding between the classroom and home.
>
> 1. I love it when you email me to tell me about your child. Given my college degrees and professional experience, I consider myself an expert on education, but you are the expert when it comes to your own child. And I want to know more about my students, so feel free to share anything that may help me work with your teenager more effectively.

2. I spend a lot of time planning lessons and assessments. If you are confused about why I am teaching something in a particular way, please ask. I work hard to meet the curriculum standards and still plan lessons that will be engaging and relevant to my students.

3. Grades are not as important as they may seem. In my experience, as both a teacher and a parent, so many parts of high school are more important than getting straight A's, including helping your teenagers discover lifelong interests and passions and teaching them how to get along with others. Learning to advocate for themselves and how to handle disappointment are likewise essential skills that students can learn and practice in high school.

4. On a related note: it really is okay if your child fails a test or assignment. It is much better for teenagers to experience this for the first time in high school, where there are many support systems in place, than when they are in college. Learning how to fail something and survive is an important life skill. I won't give up on your child, and a few poor grades do not define who your child is.

5. It's normal for your child to behave differently at school than at home. Remember that school is where teenagers practice being young adults and take on new roles and identities. At home, expect your teenager to still want to be treated like a child from time to time.

6. I care about your child, but I don't play favorites. That's why I won't discuss other students' behavior or achieve-

ment levels with you. However, I will always be willing to discuss any issues concerning your teenager.

7. I won't always assign homework, and that's okay. The research surrounding the effectiveness of homework on student achievement is mixed. School looks much different today than it did when we were in high school. Instead of worksheets and packets, your child may be working more on collaborative projects that use technology.

8. Please talk to your child about cell phone etiquette. I waste so much class time asking students to put their phones away. And please, don't text or call your teenager during my class. If it's a true emergency, call the school office.

9. Teenagers feel a lot of stress these days, and it's critical to watch for signs of stress and learn to recognize it. Try to remember what it's like to be sixteen. It isn't easy. And social media has added a whole new layer of stress that we didn't experience at their age. Please help your home be a safe haven from the world's stressors for your teenagers, even if that means consciously shelving discussions about grades, test scores, and college. Trust me, your children know these challenges are out there and must be addressed. But sometimes they just want to hang out with you without having to talk about their futures.

10. That said, the competition for college admissions and scholarship money is intense. Students know this, and I believe it is a major contributor to the rising stress levels those of us who work with teens have been seeing. In my experience, the majority of teenagers go on

to lead happy and productive lives no matter where they did or did not go to college. Try to help your relationship with your teenager by keeping the college and scholarship chase in perspective.

11. Help your child get enough sleep. A majority of the teenagers I see on any given day are sleep-deprived, and this affects their learning, their attitudes—even their tendency to experience anxiety and depression. Talk to them about the importance of sleep, and try to model a healthy sleep schedule yourself. They listen to what you say and watch what you do far more closely than you imagine.

12. It's just hair. Really. It will grow back. And I've seen it all—shaved, buzzed, pink, green, even mullets. It's normal for students at this age to experiment with their appearance. I promise not to make a moral or academic judgment about your child based on his or her appearance on any given day.

13. When I give my students a choice of writing topics, more often than not they will choose to write something about their families. They may not tell you or show you, but they still value time spent with their families. Traditions are important to them, as are grandparents, pets, vacations, shared hobbies, siblings, and even family jokes. Try to spend time with your teenagers, even when it seems like they don't want to spend time with you.

14. Teenagers speak their own language, and I don't just mean slang. When a teenager says, "This assignment is stupid," what he is really saying is "I don't get this, and I'm afraid I'm not smart enough to do it." When you are driving to drop her off at an activity and she

says, "I don't want to go. Nobody else is going," what she might really be saying is "I'm afraid I won't know anyone there, and I will feel embarrassed." Once you figure out what your teen is really saying, you can then address the anxiety behind the sullen statements.

15. And finally, I feel incredibly honored that you have entrusted me with your child. I will not take that trust for granted. It is such a privilege to walk for a while with these fun and interesting people on their path to adulthood.

HELPING YOUR STRUGGLING COLLEGE FRESHMAN

While we hope things go well for our kids in college, even the most able students sometimes find themselves struggling academically in their new environment. Freshman year is when some kids hit the academic wall, unable to adapt quickly enough to the changing pattern of their education as they transition from high school to college academics. Professors and parents Polly Diven and Michelle Miller-Adams of Grand Valley State University take a look at how college students can get back on track.

The high-stakes tests have been taken, senioritis conquered, graduation ceremonies attended, colleges chosen, housing arranged. It's time for parents to heave a sigh of relief as their children start college, right? Perhaps not. Nationally, almost a third of freshmen fail to return to college for their second year, although this rate varies widely by type of higher-ed institution. There are several reasons behind this statistic, but academic struggles are an important factor. Students who struggle academically their first semester of college may drop or fail classes, or even drop out. What can these students do to help themselves, and what can you as a parent do to help?

Without understanding the reasons for failure, it's hard to think about solutions. But before that, there is another challenge: you may not know that your child is struggling. Federal privacy protections (often referred to by their shorthand acronym FERPA) mean that parents—even those paying the tuition bills—do not have access to their children's grades unless that permission is expressly granted by the student. Parents also may not know if their student is seeking help from a counselor, has dropped a class, or is on academic probation. (We find that many students in our university who are in jeopardy of dismissal have not told their parents.) However close you and your children may be, don't count on hearing about their academic struggles.

You can't help unless you know what's going on, so keep the lines of communication open. Your children need to know that you want to hear about their college experience, good, bad, or otherwise. And consider asking your child to give you the right to view his or her grades by filing a FERPA waiver form. The point is not to engage in surveillance of your child's college experience but to be prepared to help if something goes wrong.

WHY SOME FRESHMEN FAIL

Many first-year college students have never experienced academic struggles or failure. After all, grade inflation is a fact of life and graduating high school seniors across the United

States in 2016 had an average GPA of 3.38 out of 4.0. High school grades such as these may have created unreasonable expectations for transitioning college students and their parents. But while it may be normal for students to see their GPAs dip, academic failure is less common and much more of a concern.

One reason for failure during freshman year is a lack of sufficient academic preparation for college. Students can end up in over their heads, facing a level of academic rigor and demands that high school didn't prepare them for.

In our experience, there are a few important adjustments that some incoming freshmen fail to make. Students have to be ready to read and review materials on their own with less guidance and less of the type of instructional support they had in high school. Although exam study guides have become commonplace in college courses, very few professors will use class time to review and college instructors rarely (if ever) provide "retakes" for tests.

College courses normally meet for three or four hours per week, and professors expect that students are spending many more hours each week reading and reviewing on their own. (According to national accreditation bodies, a three-credit course that meets three hours a week is supposed to require two to three times that much work outside of class.) At a college orientation one summer, we worked with an incoming student who scheduled all her classes on Tuesdays and Thursdays, noting with excitement that she would have "five days off." That student is poorly anticipating the workload outside of class hours.

Still, these sorts of adjustments do not normally result in academic failure. A typical college student who faces new expectations may receive a couple of poor grades the first semester, but her grades will improve as she adjusts. However, a student who has opted for a college or a course of study that is not a good match will see her grades continue to decline. We have found that many college students feel pressure to choose majors and career paths early on, often before they are prepared to do so. Most incoming students can identify only a handful of majors, and their career plans may not extend beyond doctor, lawyer, nurse, or teacher. After the first year, your child may be thinking about careers in policy analysis, supply-chain management, human resources, or urban planning.

It's true that some majors require students get on board early to complete their degree in four years. This is especially true for students who hope to be engineers and health professionals. But many students who enter STEM fields face hurdles in the introductory courses that we sometimes refer to as "weeder" classes. At this point, a student needs to reassess this career path. Some students will need to retake tough courses if they are committed to their original career choice. Students with doubts about these majors should start on a new path before too much time and money is wasted on a program that will undermine their academic progress.

Another challenge that can undermine students is spending too many hours earning money to pay for school. While work is a reality for many, students need to find a balance between paying for school and leaving time to complete papers and assignments. We encourage students in this situation to think of college as a job and schedule time to study.

Some academic challenges result from poor choices young people make when they first leave home and are socially or emotionally unprepared for college. They may spend too much time partying, playing video games, and socializing. Some of these poor choices are time-honored college traditions. But in some cases, students may find themselves on academic probation.

In other cases, life challenges like depression, anxiety, familial stresses, or substance abuse can cause academic collapse. Usually, students who experience such a collapse stop attending classes, stop submitting work, and fail most or all of their courses. This type of academic failure is much more worrisome. In these cases, students need professional help to address underlying issues.

Finally, it's possible that your child is at a college that doesn't suit his or her background, interests, or personality. An introverted student who is used to small classes may be overwhelmed and adrift at a large state university. A student who grew up in a large, diverse city may feel isolated and bored at a small, rural college. Transferring to a school that is a better fit is less difficult than you may imagine and can make all the difference. It strikes us as strange that parents often defer to their children, who are all of seventeen or eighteen, in deciding which college is best for them. Often these decisions are based on nothing more than what students hear from their friends or which college admissions officer comes calling. Parents can help by getting involved in their children's college research and weighing in on fit ahead of time.

HOW A STRUGGLING STUDENT CAN GET BACK ON TRACK

Parents can help their teens determine the best approach to academic struggles during freshman year. The good news is that many resources exist, some specific to the college and others available beyond its walls. The bad news is that these resources are usually offered buffet-style, without targeted outreach and with the responsibility resting on the student to find the help he or she needs. If your child can approach freshman year armed with the knowledge of the resources available, that potentially bumpy first year may be smoother.

Most of the professors we know care about student success and are willing to give students guidance about how to focus their studying, clarify a confusing point of a lecture, or point the way to other resources. Depending on the type of college, support may be available from a professor or teaching assistant. Peer support, such as study groups, can also be invaluable.

Colleges invest major resources in academic and other support services. While quality will vary, almost every college will offer advising and tutoring (sometimes both online and in person), as well as counseling resources and support programs for students with disabilities. Some may host programs geared toward disadvantaged students, while large institutions may offer cohort programs or specialized services for populations ranging from veterans to LGBTQ youth to students aging out of the foster system. Our university has centers devoted to helping students carry out research, use library materials, work with statistics, and improve their writing.

There are also more intensive support programs available to prevent or address academic failure. Students entering college with identified academic weaknesses may be asked or required to come early for a summer bridge program or take developmental coursework in a particular subject. First-year experience programs, optional precollege programs, or freshman seminars are popular; these seek to create affiliation and cohesion among an incoming group of students.

More help can be found outside the institution. Online tutoring resources, such as Khan Academy, have practice exercises, instructional videos, and personal diagnostics that provide free guided study. Participating in a "massive open online course" (or MOOC) offered by a high-quality, free provider can reinforce what students are learning on campus; among the largest of these are Coursera, Udacity, and edX. And many parents have found their children's universities' Facebook parents' pages a valuable source of advice and experience for dealing with issues their children are facing.

For students experiencing more severe academic challenges, withdrawing from a class (as long as students are aware of the economic penalties, including the potential loss of financial aid) is generally preferable to receiving a failing grade. Often, withdrawals can be arranged even after the formal deadline with documentation of specific health or life challenges that may have interfered with the semester. We are not big fans of the incomplete grade, and as professors we are encouraged to grant these only in very special circumstances. Adjusting a rigorous course schedule to combine easier with more challenging classes is a good move. Changing majors may also be called for, and dropping below a full course load may also be on the table.

Throughout our research, we heard from many parents about their children's—as well as their own—lack of readiness, lack of understanding of their own interests, and lack of a clear idea of why they were in college. The good news is that most of these kids went back to school (sometimes a different one) after a break and graduated. As society has increasingly emphasized the economic need for a college degree, it seems that many students attend college simply because it is expected of them. Parents need to listen to their children, let them take time off, and wait for them to be college ready, if needed. Struggles in the first year of college are increasingly recognized as a barrier to completion. The good news is that if you and your child can work through freshman year in a positive way, the journey ahead will be easier.

THE NEXT STEP IS NOT ALWAYS COLLEGE

While we have focused primarily on the process of getting our kids academically prepared for college, there are many other valuable and rewarding routes that kids can take. As Melissa Fenton, librarian, writer, and mother of four, sat through some of the classic year-end celebrations for her high school son, she considered some of these options.

Last week it was senior night at my son's regional cross-country meet. Before the girls' and boys' races began, every senior from participating schools lined up with their parents and were then introduced and thanked for their athletic participation. Each senior also received a hearty applause and well-wishes for their future.

And from what was said about these seniors, what amazing futures it appears they are all headed for! Proud and beaming parents held hands with their sons and daughters, while coaches read about each athlete's academic accolades and future college plans.

Things like *John will be attending Harvard in the fall, pur-*

suing a career in environmental law, and *Laura has accepted a full academic scholarship at Vanderbilt and hopes to one day be a cardiothoracic surgeon,* and *Rachel will be studying at Brown next year, double majoring in applied mathematics and Russian literature.*

I smiled along with their proud parents, clapping with the crowd and acknowledging these great accomplishments and all the hard work these kids have put in to get where they are.

Then, as one overachieving student after the other was introduced, I found my mind drifting to my to-do list at home. A list that included finding a plumber to come and fix our no-longer-functioning water softener.

And that's when it hit me. Among these forty or so wonderfully bright and dedicated young adults, there wasn't a single one seeking a career in a vocational or technical field. *Not ONE.*

There wasn't a senior who confidently announced that after graduation he would be seeking an apprenticeship in masonry or construction.

There wasn't one who shared that their future entailed training under an electrician for the next eighteen months to become licensed.

No one said they would be attending cosmetology or massage-therapy school.

Nobody walked proudly out into the crowd and said they would be seeking an associate degree or becoming a phlebotomist, a certified nursing assistant, or a licensed day-care worker.

No one boasted about joining the armed services to become a mechanic or was seeking to become a dental hygienist.

There wasn't one single student who shared anything other than going to a four-year university as their future plans and ultimate success story. And all, ironically, before they had even stepped one foot on a college campus as a freshman.

When did the success of our young people become solely and exclusively dependent on attending a four-year university? Well, for starters, when we started to stigmatize any other post-high-school options, career choices, armed forces, community college, and vocational/technical schools as "failures," or options only meant for those who "can't."

It started when high schools replaced vocational and in-house technical and transitional career programs, agriculture programs, and classes like shop, graphic design, and home economics with another set of classes—those with an AP prefix.

But what's possibly even scarier than how this "college only for success" mentality started and continues to be accepted is how scary our future is going to look without a skilled workforce. It's why in the middle of overachievement night, my only thought was *Where are all the plumbers?*

Is anyone in today's high schools offering other options and a different kind of future to students? Is anyone hosting or promoting vocational- and technical-school night with just as much verve and excitement as college night?

As senior night dragged on, I thought about what we can do as parents (and educators, if you are one), to encourage and inspire kids no matter what dreams they have for their future—but especially if they have one that doesn't fit the four-year-university mold.

I recall a time I was assisting students in a senior English class in the school library. They were doing career research and writing about their future plans. Among a table of future doctors, lawyers, and financial analysts sat a young lady who spoke up and said, "Honestly, I want to go to bartending school, and I already know what you're going to say about that. You're going to say it's an awful decision and I can do better."

The whole table was shocked by my reply. I told the young woman the following:

"I think that is a great decision and here's why: You will be gaining a learned skill that will most likely always be able to provide you with a job. It will offer you flexibility, and the option to work evenings and go to school during the day if you so choose. It will be lucrative and possibly keep you from going into huge college-loan debt. And if it is something you are truly passionate about and do to the best of your ability, then I don't want you to think about just working at the bar, I want you to think about one day *owning* the bar. Because guess what all the future doctors, lawyers, and financial analysts at this table need at the end of their workday? A *drink*."

I don't think I've ever seen a bigger smile come across the face of a teenage girl. In that moment, someone validated her dreams and made them seem not only possible but successful and stigma-free, not second-class.

Encouraging our high school students to tackle life and their futures as they see fit, and to especially do so when it's a path less taken, is something we all need to get behind. Besides, I can't think of one single household that has never needed a plumber, can you?

To Portal or Not to Portal

As high school students, long ago, our grades were largely confined to a discussion midsemester and at the end of the term. Our parents mostly lived in ignorant bliss of our grades until the term was over. At that point, there might have been a short but intense blowup (with maybe a bit of grounding) if things had gone really badly, but the grade was already in the books. And during our college years, it never even occurred to our parents to ask.

Enter the parent portal. Now parents can check their kids' grades online whenever they want. By simply logging on to the designated software, a parent can know the grade on a test or homework assignment before their teen is even home from school. And parents can certainly know their teen's grades before the teen knows themselves.

We asked the Grown and Flown community if this was a good thing and inquired how many times a week parents check their kids' grades. Many answered back, "Week? You mean how many times an hour?" Sadly, parents were not kidding, and more than one explained, "I am a recovering parent portal addict, especially after it started to affect my relationship with my kid."

So how should parents use the grade portal? The real answer is that, like so much else in parenting, it is particular to a student and family. Some parents check grades throughout the semester so that they don't get any surprises at the end, and so that they can help their kids with tutoring or urge them to speak to their teacher if their average begins to falter. Others tell their kids how often they will check, for example weekly or biweekly, and it acts as an incentive for their kids to stay on top of their work—or even the determinant if they are going out that weekend to parties or friends' houses. A common theme we hear from parents is that they checked more in ninth grade as their kids were adapting to high school and then eased off as they saw their teens could manage the workload unaided. Some parents even automated the grade portal and to get their information in a weekly email or automatic notification to their phone when a grade was entered.

As we queried more parents online, the responses came back in two camps. There were those who rarely or never checked the grade portal. They had the following reasons:

"We tried that and it was a disaster. Teachers don't always have the time (understandably) to enter things right away and that caused my kid to stress out. There were also times when 'pretests' were given and the grades were entered, but those grades were never intended to be counted in the final tally. I suppose it depends on the kid and a family's particular situation, but that level of tracking seemed to cause added tension and feed into a fear of failure in this household."

"Never. And that doesn't make me any less 'actively involved.' At some point, a student has to own their grades on their own."

"No! No! No! Step away from the portal! I check very occasionally, maybe 3–4 times a semester. School is my kids' job, not mine."

"I only check if it sends me an email that the grade is a C or below. Then I notify my kids to look into what happened."

"For my own sanity, I stopped checking. My daughter (a junior) has the app on her phone, and when she wants to do things on the weekend, I ask her to check her GPA and make sure all her assignments are done. I leave it up to her to keep track. It has reduced my stress level and the number of fights we have."

Parents on the other side, those who used the grade portal, argued:

"Parents need to be actively involved. These are teenagers learning responsibility, and parents need to be there for guidance—you need to know what is going on in their lives. Plus, teachers appreciate parents who are interested enough to check on their child's progress. And if your kids are doing great it is an opportune time to give them well-deserved praise; if not, perhaps that cell phone or the car needs to go for a while. Checking grades is definitely one way that tells your child that you care."

"Yes, absolutely. High school grades are too important to college admissions. Every grade matters, and sometimes an intervention such as tutoring or other assistance is needed."

"Yes, we do monitor. We get a notification each time a grade is posted. One, to see if there are any missing assignments. Two, we have found mistakes when teachers enter a grade. Three, school comes first . . . our kids are very good about studying, completing homework and projects on time, and they care about what their grades are. We, as parents, stay actively involved."

Finally, some parents argued that there is no one-size-fits-all approach:

"I no longer check my daughter's grades online. I do care, but my daughter is responsible and has straight A's. She's also open and honest with us, and I see her progress reports and report cards. She tells us what's going on with her grades and classes as well as with sports and friends on a daily basis. She's a senior, so she needs to learn to be independent too. Now, my son is only in eighth grade and isn't quite as responsible yet, so I check his grades online a few times a month. I suppose maybe there is no right or wrong way, and it isn't a reflection of how much parents care—it's just that each child is different and needs different levels of support."

While parents' views around checking the grade portal ranged from obsessively or not at all, many saw the short-term conflict it caused. But Jessica Lahey, mother, educator, and author of *The Gift of Failure: How the Best Parents Learn to Let Go So Their Children Can Succeed*, reminds us that there are larger issues at stake:

Portals are surveillance. When you put a program on your kid's phone that allows you to know where your kid is 24-7 and your kid knows they are being tracked, that's surveillance. And while I am not saying we can never use these things, I am saying we need to be really careful about what we do and how we use these things. Because if you want your kid to be intrinsically motivated, if you want your kid to do their schoolwork for the sake of their schoolwork, or if you want your kid to be honest with you and fess up where they have been, your chances of having that happen are better when you don't do surveillance on them. Studies show that kids who are more tightly controlled lie to their parents more. I am not a fan of the portal because it undermines parent-child relationships, it undermines parent-teacher relationships, it is a form of control, it reduces kids' feeling of autonomy, and it just makes us crazy.

We think this is a tough parenting question, but we come down on the side of not using the portal, except when you need to use it. Let us explain. As kids work their way through high school, we shift responsibility of most aspects of their lives from us and onto them. In most cases it is a gradual process, and the hand-off comes in fits and starts. In the realm of academics, kids from the ninth grade on can certainly monitor their own grades. We see a winning process where we express our expectations about their effort, and as long as they are working hard and their grades reflect their effort, the portal remains closed to us. However, in cases where students are underperforming, lying about their grades, or failing to try, the portal is opened. We are on the side of striking a bargain: they provide diligence and honesty, and in return we treat them like adults who don't need to be monitored.

Academics are about so much more than just what teens learn from books and the grades they receive. While most of us can't begin to help our students with many of their academic subjects, nor should we, there are places where we can help prepare our kids for the greater academic challenges they will find in college. A crucial step is for them to embrace the concept of their teachers as their partners in education. If they leave home understanding how to manage their time, how they best learn, and what the family's values and expectations are around education, we will have prepared them well.

CHAPTER SIX

College Admissions

While there are many worthy and important alternatives, college may still be the next step for many of our children. Almost 70 percent of 2018 high school graduates enrolled in higher education. And as the parents of five kids collectively who have gone or are going off to college, we know what a minefield the college admissions process can be.

I (Lisa) remember knowing next to nothing about college admissions when my older sons reached sophomore and junior year in high school. I had no idea what schools would be a good fit for them or what criteria they should use in deciding where to visit and later apply. I was unaware of the mountain of standardized tests they were going to have to scale and the breadth of information their applications would require. Even as a writer I struggled to judge their essays. More than a little blinded by love, I tend to think everything they write is great, even when it isn't.

The college admissions process is one of the biggest parenting challenges we face, and it comes at us just as we start to fully face the impending departure of our kids. As writer, teacher, and mother of three Gabby McCree explains, "It's ironic that we're required to do some of our best and most important parenting in the midst of so much stress, emotion (happy and sad), and nostalgia." This is a tall order. It's a moment when we need to bring our parenting A game, and yet it is also a moment when we can feel the furthest out of our depth. Our kids are looking to us for advice—life-changing, direction-setting advice—and we may not have many more answers than they do.

As parents, we need to cut ourselves a break during the college admissions process. We will have parenting triumphs—moments when our kids will need support, or wisdom, or merely a sympathetic ear, and we will nail it. But we should also anticipate utter failures—meltdowns where we find ourselves screaming threats or ultimatums through a closed bedroom door at a kid almost certainly wearing headphones on the other side.

One of the hardest and most important things to do in this process is to try to separate our very real frustrations or problems around the college process, including our own feelings about our kids leaving home. Trying to get your kid to focus on college choices or study for the SAT can be a battleground. But are you venting your anxiety because your kid is skating perilously close to the application deadline with his essay still incomplete, or does that tension have more to do with the prospect of "losing" your child to college? Are you really railing about a high school counselor who failed to send a promised transcript, or could it be you're rattled by the specter of an empty nest?

It's easy to feel anxious. There is the very real anxiety of paying a staggering amount of money for one or more kids to attend college. The admissions process can feel like a lottery where our teens have little control over the outcome. But these feelings are heightened and easily confused with the feelings we have about the impending changes in our families. We need to be honest with ourselves and tweeze these emotions apart.

This is not a college admissions guide; that would be far beyond our expertise. But we hope to examine the experience that parents and their teens have during this process and bring you some hard-won lessons from both parents and the experts. We are going to look at personal coping strategies and then we are going to zoom out and look at the broader admissions landscape with a *New York Times* columnist and university president.

One word of warning: feel free to peruse the following pages if your child is in ninth or tenth grade, but please heed our strong suggestion that your kid steer clear of the college process until eleventh grade.

Why such caution? Because our teens need to live in this moment and experience the entire spectrum of fun and learning and growing those midteen years have to offer. Thinking about college too early makes high school about college. It pushes them out of the stage they are currently in too soon and makes them live absorbed in their future. Don't let that happen. We have seen kids "miss" their high school years because their families were so focused on the outcome of their college search.

If that isn't a strong enough argument for you (and really, we hope it is), remember how much your kid will change between fifteen and eighteen and how much time and money you will have wasted looking at colleges with a too-young teen. No sooner will you have researched and visited every mechanical engineering program in the Midwest than your teen will announce they've decided to pursue computer science on the East Coast instead. So save yourself some aggravation; wait until they are ready.

Preparing for Applications

Keep a record.

Have your teen keep a file, paper or digital, that chronicles her accomplishments. High school is only four years, and it may seem like she won't possibly forget any of her activities or accolades, but you would be surprised. And even if she remembers everything she did, the list will make an easy place to start on this Common App section.

But, do things for the right reasons.

It would be dishonest and unrealistic to say that your kid should never do anything just for their college application. All through high school they will make decisions with that goal in mind, whether it is selecting a certain course or studying for the ACT. But kids also need to do what they genuinely care about—and colleges care that they do that. The MIT dean of admissions, Stu Schmill, tells students, "If you couldn't write about this on your college application, would you still do it? If the answer is no, then you shouldn't be doing it."

WHAT WE WISH WE HAD KNOWN

Lisa attended a large public university in California; with certain grades and SAT scores, admission was all but guaranteed. She wasn't required to write an essay or submit teacher recommendations. The notion of "reach" and "safety" schools was not yet known, and the college that admitted her was the only one to which she applied. Mary Dell attended an even larger public university that auto-admitted based on high school standings. Going into the admissions process with our kids decades later, the two of us knew almost nothing about the uncertainty that is embedded in applying to most colleges today.

Lisa reflects:

I felt as though I was losing my mind as I tried to help my sons with a college admissions process that I barely understood.

The experience of helping my kids apply to college taught me many things—most crucially, that my discomfort stemmed from my fear of the unknown. I didn't know where my kids would go to school or what they would study. I didn't know if they would find lifelong friends or move easily (or painfully) away from each other and our family. And I didn't know how they would handle the stings of rejection, although I did know that those would inevitably arrive.

But, the most excruciating uncertainty of all: How would I cope with them leaving home?

When your kid begins to study for the SAT, memories of your own junior year come rushing back. But the morning you drop him at the high school to take that test, it becomes more real. With each campus visit you begin to imagine her living there, with the tables turned and you now just a visitor in her life. Sure, there is pride and relief that you have arrived at the moment when your kid can consider college as their next step. There is gratitude that your teen has set themselves a goal and is heading toward it. And there is excitement for this momentous step your child is about to take.

But there is also pain, real pain.

The advice we offer now is how to calm down, reflect, enjoy this period, and put your teen's needs at the forefront of the process. So let's sit down, grab yet another cup of coffee, and try to focus in on how a parent is supposed to get through the college admissions process, perhaps more than once, without losing his or her mind.

Here are six essential sanity preservers we have learned along the way:

1. **Find a friend.** No, we mean a real friend—someone to whom you will reveal your inner panicked self. Make sure it's someone you trust implicitly. (If they are going through the college process now or have done so recently, so much the better.)

   Once you've found this friend, don't discuss the admissions process with anyone else. There is nothing to be gained by comparison, and there is your sanity to lose. We are human and need to share. You and your friend will offer each other just that. The two of you will support, commiserate, and celebrate with each other.

2. **Linger on your love.** Look at your kid long and hard as the process kicks off. This is a great kid and your love for her can bring you to tears. Let your mind wander through a montage of moments when your love for her has been at its fiercest. There will be tough moments (11:58 p.m. and the essay is not quite finished but the deadline is 120 seconds away) when that love will be, if not tested, at least tried. Hold on to those images of love, as you will need to pull them out from time to time. It may seem unlikely now, but you will know and love this kid even more by the end of this process. (And, hopefully, she will feel the same.)

3. **Plug your ears.** You are not raising every kid in town, so ignore other's college searches as much as you can for this process. Comparison is not just the thief of joy; it's the font of angst. There is too much mystery, too many unknowns to understand why this kid got accepted here and that one was wait-listed or denied. If you're a parent of a high school junior or senior, you can all too easily become mired in the swirling college admissions gossip all around you. Let it go before it ever takes hold of you, or misery is your only option.

4. **Chart the madness.** One of the challenging things about the long college process is the hamster wheel of your mind spinning through all that needs to be done by your kid and to a lesser extent by you. Make a spreadsheet or paper file or whatever it takes to keep from going over and over the seemingly endless list of tasks and decision points.

Plot out with your teen how they will meet deadlines and gather all the information they need to select a college that is best for them. This is one of life's best chances to teach your seventeen-year-old something about how adults make complex, life-changing decisions. We take the time required to weigh alternatives. We solicit information from both experts and those with direct experience. Finally, we narrow down our options and pick the best option for us.

And don't let any of the finger-waggers shame you into thinking that this is your kid's college search and you should just stand by and merely watch. First, unless your kid is getting a full ride and there is no money changing hands, this is a family decision. Sure, the college they will attend needs to be one they have chosen, but if and how that can happen involves parents.

Second, you don't want to let this great teaching moment slip by. Your kid is more than likely to get rejected from some, maybe even many schools. How quickly they are able to shake that off and move on to the good things happening in their lives will depend partly on you. One of the most important things about the college admission process is how we deal with the consequences of decisions and inevitable failure. Here is a chance to do some really good, essential parenting, by showing them how you take in the disappointment, let it sting a little, gather any lessons that are there to be learned, and then rebound.

5. **Plead the Fifth.** I wish someone had said this to me when my oldest son was entering eleventh grade: "You don't have to answer any questions about college and neither does your kid." Part of the way to take pressure off yourself is to have your teen endure less pressure. Well-meaning adults will pepper any high school junior or senior in their path with the usual cross-examination. *Do you know where you want to go? Have you applied early? How are your scores/grades/applications?* And so on. They will bring up information about colleges that is thirty or more years out of date. They will, unsolicited, weigh in with their opinions. I promise you, this will happen. No high school student needs this additional pressure. Explain to your child that they need not submit to collegiate cross-examination. In fact, give them specific ways to respond: "My parents and I plan to talk about this after we hear something definitive from the colleges. We're really just at the exploratory stage right now."

6. **It's going to be an emotional ride.** Your kid may transform into someone you barely recognize. They may become sentimental and caring, positively mushy when talking about how much they will miss the dog. They may become as unpleasant as they were during their second year of life with almost as many meltdowns and an equally unreasonable na-

ture. And they may vacillate between the two. If you are unprepared, it can feel like you have lost your kid even as they still live down the hall.

No one can protect you as a parent from the emotional roller coaster your kid will take you on during this process. But you can stand back and repeat this useful mantra about their behavior: "All normal, all normal, all normal."

THIS IS NOT YOUR REPORT CARD

Before our kids submit their first application or visit their first campus, it is important to get our heads around what goes into choosing a college. We will share some thoughts from experts on how to best gauge college fit, along with wise words from a college president on what parents and kids should look for—but before that let's have some honest talk.

Choosing a college should be about finding a place where your kid will thrive, end of story. But it is not. It is about so much more, and we won't put our heads in the sand and say it isn't. What we will say is that facing these things head-on will let you understand them and then move on to what is truly important.

Sadly, college admissions is viewed by many as the ultimate report card on parenting: a single, defining letter grade given at the end of eighteen long years of loving effort. If college was viewed as merely four years of a person's life, we might be able to gain some perspective, but rather it is as if we are all, parent and child, car rear windows with college decals forever affixed to our foreheads.

No one has ever asked Lisa if she raised three good men . . . three caring sons . . . three fine citizens. Nor has she ever met someone who, upon learning that she (or any other parent) has college-aged kids, has not asked which schools they attend. If you doubt for one minute how much college matters in some circles, stand in the middle of Bed Bath & Beyond and hold a package of twin XL sheets in one hand and a power strip or under-bed storage container in the other. Now wait to see how long it takes a perfect stranger to pop the unavoidable question: "Kid heading to college? What school?"

There seems to be no escape—everyone is a college expert. Grandparents share college insights that are half a century out of date. Friends enumerate the colleges their kids loved, failing to acknowledge their kid is nothing like yours. And when you make the mistake of telling people where your kid is thinking of applying, you will encounter one of three reactions: silence, word stumbles, or gushing. All three are strains of social pressure you and your kid can do without.

Remember that everyone has an opinion, that most of those opinions are based on an individual's *very* limited personal experience, and that the bulk of those opinions can be safely ignored. Here is what matters:

Your kid. What she needs. What works for your family.

It really is that simple.

In 2015, *New York Times* columnist Frank Bruni published a reassuring and important book entitled *Where You Go Is Not Who You'll Be: An Antidote to the College Admissions Mania*. Bruni, who chose to attend the University of North Carolina over Yale, takes an eye-opening look at the impact on people's lives of the college they attend. He talks about how the choice of college has come to be seen as an assessment of our parenting or a judgment on the worthiness of our teen's accomplishments, rather than a point of pride that your kid found an institution of higher learning where they will thrive. He explains how the search for colleges has been blown out of any reasonable proportion and has come to be "seen as the conclusive measure of a young person's worth, an uncontestable harbinger of the accomplishments or disappointments to come. Winner or loser: This is when the judgment is made. This is the great, brutal culling."

In his book, Bruni dismantles the edifice constructed over the twentieth century and fortified dramatically in the twenty-first that there are a few great universities and that through them leads the one true road to success. But that leaves the question of whether parents are unmoored from reality in caring as much as they do about their child's college admissions. This question breaks down into two parts: Does it matter at all where our kids attend college? And is there any damage we do to our kids from caring?

The answer to the first question is: it does not matter nearly as much as we think, but that is not the same as saying it does not matter at all. Parents are obsessed with well-regarded universities, not because they believe that there is no other route to their child's dreams but rather because they believe that finding a successful route is more likely from a more selective school. They are also obsessed with certain colleges in the face of evidence that teens thrive when there is a good fit between what a school offers (in every sense of that word) and what the student needs.

As parents, we are not crazy to care which university our children attend, but we are crazy to care as much as we do. And does our caring matter or in any way damage our kids? To this we would answer a resounding yes. As Bruni explains, "The climate of the college admissions process is overheated, in a way that un-necessarily addles kids, can be detrimental to their educations, and perverts the true point of learning, which isn't about the acquisition of badges. It's about the refinement of a mind, the cultivation of a soul. Let's focus on that."

In *Where You Go Is Not Who You'll Be*, Bruni lets parents off the hook a bit, and gives us a pass for our own crazy behavior. Part of what make us crazy is everyone around us going crazy. We could stand up and say, "I won't fall prey to this," but very few of us do. Even though we are equipped with a lifetime of experience in school and the workplace that shows how you can get almost anywhere from almost anywhere with some determination and effort, we fail to acknowledge what we see and instead focus on what we fear: that those who have graduated from certain institutions might have a permanent advantage.

Bruni makes his case, and it is a compelling one, that wherever our children's lives take them, whatever degree of professional success or personal happiness they might find is determined in large part by their own efforts, not their alma mater. "College has no monopoly," he reminds us, "on the ingredients for professional success or for a life well lived." Bruni was kind enough to answer a few of our questions about college admissions, and his responses reveal a very important reframing we should give to the college admissions process: the value of experience over admission.

Q: I come away from your book feeling like where my kid goes to college is less important than I thought, but not entirely irrelevant. It seems that for parents, the real danger comes from caring so much—that the parental investment in college, or worse a particular college, seeps into family life, damaging so much of what goes on between parent and child. By setting narrow expectations, parents give their kids plenty of room to fail. Would this be fair?

A: First off, "less important . . . but not entirely irrelevant" is precisely the right takeaway. Admission to an elite school involves a very particular script: these advanced-placement courses, that SAT score, this athletic triumph, that community service. Your child's distinction may not be accommodated by that script, so don't tether his or her self-worth to it. By setting less specific expectations, you give your kid plenty of room to succeed according to a less unforgiving metric.

Q: You say that an acceptance to a school like Duke or Northwestern is a "binding verdict on the life that [a student] has led up until that point." Do you think the same could be said of parents, or at least the job they did as parents? Isn't college admission perceived as a report card on our parenting?

A: Many parents see what happens during the college admissions juncture as a reflection on them. I say that not in a damning manner but in a sympathetic one: these parents are products of the culture we live in, and they're getting their cues from all they see around them. But, yes, admission to Stanford or Duke or Northwestern or Williams is the ultimate brag: the honor society and the athletic trophy and the lead in the school play all rolled into one. And kids pick up on how much what happens to them will mean to Mom and Dad.

Q: Don't parents just aspire to a small edge that will make our children's journey through life just a touch easier? Aren't we just looking for something that will tip the odds of professional success, however slightly, in our child's favor?

A: Parents, in the best possible sense, want to give kids as much of a leg up as possible in a competitive world, and they want to give them as much of a safety net. And they're right to. That's sort of their responsibility and job, if it falls within their powers. And parents indeed think that an elite school, with the connections and network that it can bring, falls into the categories of "leg up" and "safety net."

They're not entirely wrong. In many instances and in some ways, an elite school does confer advantages. My point is that those advantages are nullified, and maybe even reversed, if a child buys too fully into the idea of them and shortchanges the quality and energy of the work done in college. That's the danger of too much belief in, and talk about, the importance of a school's name.

The danger is that you think admission is all and experience is secondary. If you adopt that perspective, even without meaning to, and you act accordingly, your elite school isn't going to do much to increase your odds of professional success or ensure smooth sailing.

The Danger of College Rankings

College rankings are designed to mess with parents' heads. Really, they are. We live in a country with thousands of amazing colleges, and yet those who rank them try to reduce their rich complexity down to a single digit or two. Do not be fooled. First, there are dozens of rankings and they all disagree—so clearly, they are not all "right." Second, the ones that are best known are simply the oldest, not the most useful. Our thoughts? By and large ignore the rankings. They can be helpful when you want to find all the schools in Illinois that have bioengineering programs and you don't know where to start. But don't let them matter more than that.

Realize that applying to college is a process, and it will take time. It's a really important decision, but don't stress about it, because everyone ends up where they should. Give yourself time to narrow your choice, and it will all come together at the end. If you can afford it, give yourself some options so you have a choice. I'm not a fan of early decision, because you might not feel ready and able to make that kind of decision in the fall.

—MATT, 22

FINDING THE ONE THING
THAT DOES MATTER

One of the reasons we get tied up in knots about colleges is that we forget what every high school counselor and college admissions officer will tell you is the most important factor when picking a college: fit. But this can be a tough idea to get your head around. What is fit and why does it matter? How do I know my kid has found the right fit? Is it social fit? Academic fit? A fit with the family's finances? Like many important questions, it does not have an easy answer. Adam Weinberg, father of three and president of Denison University in Granville, Ohio, sheds some light:

> Let me start with an observation. The college search process has been heavily impacted by the state of the general economy. For many families, selecting a college is considered among the most important decisions they will make. Families are looking at a competitive job market and believe the college decision will impact their child's earning potential (and, hence, everything else) for the rest of their lives. They are searching for value.
>
> My first piece of advice is this: value comes largely from fit. There are many good colleges in this country where you can get a great education, but if the fit is wrong, it is nearly impossible to get a great education—no matter how good the college is.
>
> What does this mean? We don't have to guess—we have lots of data on what matters most about college. Students need to go to a college that provides the following:
>
> - Mentorship: It turns out that mentorship is one of the defining characteristics of a transformative college

experience. In particular, faculty mentorship is crucial.

- Student involvement: Students are more likely to succeed when they are able to participate in activities outside the classroom that supplement their learning (athletics, student organizations, the arts, etc.).
- Student-to-student engagement: Students learn a lot from one another. They need to be at a college where they are surrounded by peers who are in college for the right reasons and are pushing and prodding each other in the right ways.

The question is: How do you find a college where your son or daughter is likely to become immersed quickly, develop a close mentoring relationship with a faculty member, and get involved in sustained cocurricular activities that allow them to find good friends and develop strong life skills?

Now is the time to have a serious conversation with your son or daughter about where they are in their own personal development and what kind of college is going to be best for them. Are they more likely to thrive in a lecture hall or small classes? Will they be more comfortable in an urban or rural setting? What kinds of people do they tend to thrive around?

Make sure you understand the financial costs. The sticker price, meaning the listed tuition, is not altogether helpful. The financial aid letters you may have just received can be misleading. Make sure you understand: How many years does it take the average student to graduate? At Denison, like most private colleges, it is four years. At some public universities, it often takes five or even six years (therefore, an extra year or two of tuition). And will financial aid be in place for the entire time they are in college?

One of the mistakes prospective families make is selecting a college because of very small differences in price. Fit is most important. It does not make sense to go to a college that is slightly less expensive if the fit is not right. At the same time, debt does matter. My own view is that a manageable level of debt is worth it to get an education that is the right fit for the student, and families need to determine what that level is for them.

Too often, the rankings lead parents to imagine that choosing the right college is all about where it sits on a list. Nothing could be further from the truth. Choosing the right college is far more personal than that.

Choose a college where your son or daughter can pursue their passions. If your son or daughter plays a sport or has a passion for an artistic endeavor, choose a college where they will be able to nurture their interests and talents. This is really important—don't choose a college where they only will be able to watch others perform. Choose a college where they will be likely to make the team, be cast in a play, join a music ensemble, and have a chance to engage in their passions.

This is also true for students who want to major in the sciences. So much of the value of undergraduate work in the sciences comes from hands-on research. Choose a college where undergraduates get to conduct their own research and where it is built into courses. Be wary of places where graduate students replace professors in classrooms and knock undergraduates out of the labs.

Pay attention to the first-year program. Transitioning into college can be hard. Select a college where a lot of attention is paid to how students transition into college and the support they receive if and when they stumble. Once students get connected to courses, faculty, friends, and co-curricular activities, they will be fine.

Pay attention to location. You want to be on a campus that has a good vibe. I also think there is a huge advantage to being in a location that has a healthy community surrounding the college and easy access to an airport and city.

Visit the colleges one more time. Try to attend one of the April visit days; most colleges now offer these to admitted students. Let your son or daughter spend the night at their top two or three colleges, then tell them to go with their gut. Rather than making observations, ask questions: Where do they feel comfortable? Which place feels right?

(Editor's note: Some colleges will pay for accepted students to make visits to campus if their families cannot afford it. Don't let the cost of a revisit keep your teen from making an informed decision.)

Listen to the People Who Really Know

One of the very best places to learn about college admissions is from the people who actually admit students. Many colleges have excellent admissions blogs (go to the admissions part of a college's website, not the general website), which are written by the deans of admissions themselves. There, parents and students can learn much about admissions in general and that college in particular. We learned a great deal from the deans of admissions at UVA and Georgia Tech by reading their informative sites. And we read the websites of many schools to which our kids were not even applying to learn more about the process. Search social media for more information, and follow the colleges your teen is interested in—many have admissions-specific social media accounts. The Common Data Set is also an unrivaled source of unbiased college information. It is a great way to make apples to apples comparisons between two schools. Search the words "Common Data Set" with the name of the college.

IT IS UP TO THEM

Helene Wingens knew that the college decision was her son's to make, but when the process did not go exactly to plan, she found that hard to remember.

I went into my son's senior year in high school with a silent, steadfast vow that I would not partake in the insanity surrounding college applications. I would not allow my clear thinking to be muddied by the madness of the crowd. In the end, of course, that proved easier said than done.

After my son was deferred from his early decision school, we were on tenterhooks waiting to hear from the half-dozen or so schools to which he had applied. Even though my son is a kid who had never missed a deadline, and even though I was confident that he would get his college applications done, after his early action school did not pan out, I resorted to nagging, wheedling, and threatening until all other applications were completed. It was not my finest moment and it portended a series of "not so fine" moments.

Later when the acceptances and rejections were in, even though we had forcefully and repeatedly reiterated that the most important aspect of college selection was finding a school with the appropriate social and academic fit, and even though we had encouraged him to disregard the name and ranking of a school in favor of his *gestalt* feeling about the place, I could not resist the overwhelming urge to lean heavily on him to choose the college with the more prestigious name. In truth, the pressure I put on him was more about me than about him.

Because our face-to-face conversations became so fraught, we started to communicate by text. To my repeated entreaties to pick the higher-rated school, my son responded,

I know that you have more life experience and I trust you and Dad are always looking out for me and encouraging only what you believe is best and when you think I'm about to make a mistake, the only reaction you can logically have is to do whatever you can to stop me from falling off the edge. I get it and I appreciate it. But, sometimes you need to trust that I too am looking out for myself and that I need to make my own choices and live with my own consequences.

I see the wisdom of those sentiments now, but back then I could only see him making what I thought was a big life mistake.

I continued to push, accusing him of basing his decision on emotions and not on pragmatism, to which he responded,

Yes, part of this decision is driven by emotion. Over the last two months I have fallen in love with the idea of going to XX University. I have been captured by the people, the atmosphere, the campus and the institution itself.

In hindsight, my arguments were also steeped in emotion, so how could I fault him for making an emotional decision?

I don't believe the oft-heard platitude that kids end up "where they're supposed to be." I believe that if you teach them to be resilient, they will do well wherever they end up. I believe that you need to trust them to make the right decision for themselves. I believe that you need to be looking for the right fit rather than the right name, and I believe more than ever that what you do once you get to college matters far more than where you go to college.

To the parents who sit where I sat last year, take a deep breath and try to remove yourself emotionally from the process as much as possible. It really is your child's life, and it really is their decision to make and to live with. This process does not reflect your child's essence. It does not define the person they are, and it does not predict the success they will have in life, whatever your definition of success is.

Where your child goes to college matters, but (here's the conundrum) you will never know how things might have been different elsewhere, so embrace what is and hope that your child finds their unique place in the community in which they matriculate.

In a process steeped in uncertainty, there is one certainty. Before you can even clear your thoughts, your current high school senior will be registering for their sophomore year courses. And, about ten seconds after that they will be ordering their cap and gown. Hopefully.

READY OR NOT

Assuming our kids have successfully completed high school and they are college bound, we send them there with only a summer's break. When our kids are young we readily acknowledge that they walk, talk, or read at different ages. Yet we treat college-going as if it is a one-size-fits-all moment. Some eighteen-year-olds are not ready academically, socially, or in terms of their ability to live as independent adults, yet we make few allowances for this.

As parents, we watch our kids go through high school with their class, and we envision them starting college, or taking the next step in their lives, with their cohort. But thriving in college is our goal, not merely attending college. And, succeeding in college for your teen means beginning college when they are ready, not when their classmates are.

In the United States, just over 58 percent of freshmen returned to the same college for a second year. If parents want to make sure kids thrive in college, they need start with the question of whether they are ready. We sat down with a few experts on the topic of college readiness and distilled what parents might think about if they are concerned that a trip straight from high school to college might not yet be the right journey for their student.

Dr. Lisa Damour, who we met earlier, makes an impassioned case for not confusing college admission with college readiness from her years of working with teens as a psychologist. She says that when college students wind up in her office because of a disastrous first semester, "They spent their senior year of high school and usually several years before that hinting, if not skywriting, that they weren't ready to go to college."

How can parents distinguish between the normal stumbles and troubles of a high school teen and the deeper problems that may signal a rocky landing on campus? And what can—what should— parents do upon realizing their student is not quite ready to go? These nine questions can help you assess the college readiness of your teen, and (even with a teen who is completely ready) help you think through some of the milestones that will help him or her succeed.

1. **Who is applying to college (i.e., are you driving the whole process for your teen)?**

   Howard Greene, a well-known educational consultant and the author of many college guides, cautions that parents should become concerned when they find themselves dragging their teen through the college process. When parents are managing their kid's college applications and hauling along their passive or even resistant teen, they need to reflect on whether their student will thrive in college the following year.

2. **Can your teen cope with the "hard" feelings in life?**

   The emotional life of a teen is filled with turmoil. In high school and college, kids often deal with academic, social, or romantic setbacks. They will have times of triumph and exuberance as well as doubt and disappointment. All of this is normal, and even desirable as a way to prepare them for adult life.

   A close look at how your teen deals with these challenging moments sheds some light on their readiness for life on their own, explains Damour. When they perform poorly on an exam do they go for a run or a beer? When a love interest rebuffs them do they soothe themselves with music or drugs? When they are suffering from doubt do they turn to their parents looking for a compassionate listener or to someone to swoop down and solve their problems? Can they handle their problems without their parents' help at all? Students who struggle to deal independently and effectively with "hard" feelings in high school may feel overwhelmed in the college environment.

3. **Can your teen take full responsibility for self-care?**

   Self-care is one of the basic requirements for life in college. This skill set covers a wide range of issues, from sleep to eating to exercise to self-control, and Damour suggests that parents evaluate how able their teen is to manage each of these things on their own. High school kids who still need to be reminded to go to bed, who have no sense of the nutritional needs of their bodies, or who find it hard to exercise self-control in the presence of drugs, alcohol, or distractions may well struggle when they are on their own. Ask yourself if your teen can schedule an appointment, take care of themselves physically, or talk to a teacher about a problem they are having. If they cannot manage the practical aspects of their life, they might just need more time.

4. Can your teen manage his or her time?

While in theory, high school kids should be given more and more control over their time and learn to effectively manage it, in reality, their life is still highly structured. Once teens enter college, with more free time in their day and more flexibility around their activities, scheduling their time becomes a new, and for some, unwieldy responsibility.

The maturity required to do this depends, in part, on the development of a teen's brain, but students who repeatedly show in high school that they struggle to get their work in on time or to manage the competing demands of multiple classes and longer-term assignments may find college very challenging. Parents who constantly intervene with reminders for their high school student about academic and other responsibilities need to realize that their teen may not be able to manage their own obligations.

5. Does your teen know when and how to seek help?

When our kids live at home it is easy to tell them when they need to see a doctor or suggest to them that they seek extra help from a teacher. Once they are in college they will need to decide for themselves when to seek medical or psychological services or academic support. Teens who have not learned to both assess their own problems and then seek appropriate help may falter when faced with inevitable problems.

Dr. Julia Routbort, associate dean of student affairs for health and wellness at Skidmore College, emphasizes that freshmen need to have shown in high school that they can both learn and rebound from their failures and that they do not fall apart when they have setbacks. She notes that it is important that students going to college can recognize when they are in some sort of trouble (academic, emotional, or other), assess the severity of their problems, and that they are capable of reaching out for help on campus.

6. **Can your teen take responsibility for and learn from their poor decisions?**

Teens make mistakes. Their good judgment is still developing and their impulse control is a work in progress. Damour suggests that one of the signs of a teen who is ready to leave home is not that she doesn't make mistakes or show an occasional lapse judgment (as that is too high of a bar for most teens to clear), but rather that when misbehavior or misjudgment is uncovered, the teen owns up to their responsibility and alters their future behavior.

Teens are capable of changing much faster than adults, Damour notes, so if you find yourself threatening your teen, "Do that again and you are not going away to college next year," don't despair. Many teens are shaken at this thought and learn to change their behavior. However, concern might arise when parents make such a threat and their teen's behavior remains unchanged.

7. **Has your teen shown that they can manage themselves in a setting without their family?**

Not every teen has the opportunity to spend time away from their family. But if your teen has shown that at camp, away on a trip, or in the workplace they are able to manage their behavior, this is a very encouraging sign for their move away.

8. **Can your teen assess risk?**

College is a time of increased risky behavior. Teens and young adults need to constantly assess the risks of their actions. When your teen is making a decision involving sex, drugs, or alcohol, can they think through the implications of their actions? Damour suggests that teens who are showing the kind of maturity that is required for college have moved away from asking themselves, "What are the chances I could get caught?" to the important question "What could go wrong if I do this?"

9. **College is an (expensive) gift like none other. Will your teen take advantage of what it has to offer? Is it truly their decision to go?**

Routbort finds that some kids arrive as freshmen almost as a default. College was expected and at no point was there ever a question about their attending. The difficulty in this is that the decision, and thus the outcome, belongs to a student's parents and not to the student himself.

One of the solutions for a kid who is not quite ready for college is to push off the moment of departure for a year or two. Taking a gap year or spending some time locally in community college can do wonders for kids who need a bit more time before setting off on their own.

While taking some time to work, travel, and grow up is still not the norm in the United States, many experts suggest that a year away from studies after high school can have a remarkable maturing effect on a teen. Routbort believes that an "autonomous gap year," in other words a year in which the student makes plans and then carries out those plans and looks after themselves, leads to a qualitatively better college experience.

Greene points out that most colleges will allow students to defer admission for a year and take time to get themselves ready. He finds parents are often concerned about a gap year, fearing that their child will not end up matriculating at college. In his experience, this has not been the case. After a year working in the real world, most teens are eager and far more ready than they initially were to go to college.

EVEN AN EXPERT CAN FEEL LIKE AN AMATEUR

Jess Lahey is the author of *The Gift of Failure*, which is about the importance of getting your hands off your kid's life and letting them fail so they can learn independence and ultimately succeed. She writes and speaks to parents and educators all over the country about the perils of overparenting. Her book had become a national bestseller by the time her son reached twelfth grade, which was the year Lahey watched her real life diverge from the research. Read her story, and then go easy on yourself.

My shtick is calm, cool, and collected parenting. I've been one of those parenting writers reminding readers to let your child fail, to parent not for the moment but for the long haul, that middle school failures can lead to medical school success. My shtick became a bestselling book, a crammed speaking schedule, and a job writing articles that get lots of hits and shares because a calm, cool, and collected approach to parenting sounds so darn appealing, so reasonable, so commonsensical.

And then, this year, my son started looking ahead to college, and my shtick hit the fan.

I'd been warned this could happen. Older, wiser parents whose children had successfully grown and flown warned me about the perils of the college application process in graphic detail. The anxiety, the deadlines, the cost, the panic and stress, they lamented. I heard it all, and I really thought I understood.

But when the full impact of college application season hit our family, I became incapable of reason and forgot my own best advice.

My oldest son, Ben—my firstborn, my baby—is eighteen; a legal adult. He can go to war, he can vote, heck, he can purchase cigarettes if he is daft enough to do so. A nurse recently informed me that because he's eighteen, I don't have to sign his medical forms or accompany him when he has his wisdom teeth pulled. He will, however, need someone to drive him home when he's distracted by unicorns in the road, so I'm the designated driver. Plus, a sedated teen is a compliant teen, and I wouldn't miss a morning with compliant Ben for anything.

My point is, Ben does not need me for much anymore, and that includes the college application process. He researched schools based on his interests and strengths and made a solid list of candidates. He scheduled and sat for the tests he needed to take. He planned the visits and the interviews and the information sessions. My job, then, is that of support staff: to tag along on tours, listen, and try not to embarrass him.

Simple rules, and yet I have managed to fail miserably. I nagged him about his Common Application essay, even when I knew he had it well in hand. I nagged not because I thought it would help him, but because it made me feel better. I repeatedly pressured him to apply to schools he didn't love, not because they were right for him but because they were right for me. So when it came time to visit the schools he'd selected, I vowed to do better.

COLLEGE 1: OOPS. We arrived at the admissions office for our information session and subsequent tour on a beautiful spring morning, when New England is still gray but just beginning to thaw.

We were both anxious about the first visit, each for our own personal reasons. Ben couldn't wait to step foot on campus and envision his life at college, while I knew I'd be an emotional wreck; alternately mourning the loss of my baby and mooning over glimpses of the man he'd become. What I chose not to share with Ben, however, was the fact that College 1 was the college I wish I'd attended.

However, on the morning of the visit, I pushed down my impulse to use my child as a way to remediate my own personal regrets, secured a cup of coffee, and found a seat in the back of the information session.

I was quiet and unobtrusive for an entire hour, but when the student presenters introduced us to our tour guides, I realized our guide was one of my former students, a kid I adore.

I tried to keep my cool, I really did. But I was so proud of my former student for being so grown-up and capable of walking backward for an hour without tripping that I monopolized the tour, peppering him with questions and pointing out all the interests he had in common with my son.

I promised Ben I'd do better next time.

COLLEGE 2: DNF (DID NOT FINISH). I did, in fact, do better next time, but Ben says I'm not allowed to count this visit toward my score total because we did not finish the tour.

By the time our student tour guide finished enumerating her many, many academic and personal achievements, and the many, many reasons the applicants would be lucky to gain admission to attend College 2, Ben and I had formed a tacit agreement to escape. Ben did not want to make the tour guide feel bad by conspicuously fleeing the tour, so we hung back and found cover when the group turned a corner around a dorm.

We waited until her boasty voice faded into the distance, then we circled around the back of the building, past the dumpster, and toward our car. I am pretty sure our getaway went unnoticed.

COLLEGE 3: HORRIBLE. In my defense, I was trying to stay out of Ben's way.

Unfortunately, my method for staying out of Ben's way was to entertain myself by live-tweeting the college tour. This was a rollicking good time for me, but Ben said my obvious use of an iPhone when I was supposed to be oohing and aahing over the very impressive new library was, as he put it, "Horrible."

He has another interview scheduled in a couple of weeks, so I have time to reassess my behavior and find a way to keep myself occupied and out of trouble.

I may not have handled Ben's college search perfectly, but I have enjoyed every minute of it. Sure, I've had to watch my son endure rejection, self-doubt, and stress, but I have also watched him gain confidence, a sense of identity, and self-worth. As the college catalogs pile up on his desk, so too do the possibilities, adventures, and options.

The long drives on rural back roads and meals in roadside diners have given me what I yearn for in these last months of his childhood: time to scrape the bottom of the conversational barrel and talk about small things that don't usually rate a mention in the midst of our busy lives. When he drives, I sneak peeks at his face, looking for vestiges of the baby I raised and marveling at the man he's becoming.

On this next trip, I will have plenty of thinking to do, enough to keep me occupied and out of trouble. As Ben searches for his place in the world, I'm feeling out the newly redrawn borders of my role in his life. This is uncharted territory for both of us, but I'm grateful we are exploring it together.

> *Two things about college admissions. First, consider all options. Don't limit yourself to what you think you might like or what might look best on paper. Second, celebrate admission to "backup" schools. I got the admissions email to my current university while at work and called home to tell my family. We all, including myself, weren't very excited, as we were looking toward the decisions from my top choice. This still bothers me, that I didn't get that "celebration moment." When I decided to go to this school, it was more of an "okay, I guess this is where I land," instead of "I can't wait to live out my dream!" However, from the other side, past all the waiting and hand-wringing, I can say that I'm probably having a similar college experience at this school as I would most other places. Your mark of success is how you tailor your new place to foster your growth. You will flourish by seeking out people who support you and experiences that fuel and challenge you, no matter where you end up. Oh, and go to class!*
>
> *—AMANDA, 19*

WHEN THE NEWS IS NOT GOOD

Rejection stings. And a rejection from a college your teen loved and hoped to attend stings badly. College counselors, parents, and peers will all try to tell him not to take it personally. They will tell her the admissions office gets more applications than they can possibly accept and many well-qualified candidates are rejected. But there will still be anguish. College rejection feels personal, deeply personal.

We asked a few experts for their advice on ways to move past this letdown. Here are some things to consider.

FEEL THE PAIN. Experts suggest that teens (and, we would add, their parents) take a little time to feel sad. We have all been disappointed before. We know that pain usually fades with time. Give your teen and yourself permission to feel bad for a short period, to mourn something your teen wanted (and in turn you wanted for them) and will not have, and then get ready to move on.

TRY TO COME TO GRIPS WITH HOW MUCH OF THIS IS ABOUT YOU, THE PARENT. The excruciating truth is that we often take our kids' disappointments harder than they do. We have dreams for our kids' lives even as they live in the here and now. Life is about to take your teen on a different path than the one you might have envisioned. Yet, we have all lived long enough to know that it might just be a better one.

WHEN THE COLLEGE REJECTION LETTER ARRIVES, DON'T SECOND-GUESS DECISIONS YOU OR YOUR TEEN MADE. Do not beat yourself up. Good parents want the best for their kids. It is not time to change that formula but time to recognize that when it comes to college it is impossible to know what is "best." The best is a college at which our kids can thrive, find their intellectual home, make friends for life, and explore opportunities. There is not a single school where this can take place but rather many.

The sooner a parent moves on, the sooner their teen will be able to as well. Yes, this is easier said than done sometimes. But how a teen views the college they will be attending next fall may have everything to do with how their parents embraced that option this spring.

KNOW YOU'RE IN GOOD COMPANY. Yes, it sounds cliché, but discourage your kid from taking a college rejection personally. The admissions committee does not know your child. They have a list of facts, a few hundred words, and a handful of recommendations. Your kid is simply pieces of paper, and while most admissions officers are trying their best to see behind the application, this is a highly fallible process.

Many colleges reject 50 percent, 60 percent, 70 percent, 80 percent, 90 percent or more of their applicants. Anyone experiencing a college rejection from a school they set their sights on is in very good company. *The Wall Street Journal* notes that "teenagers who face rejection will be joining good company, including Nobel laureates, billionaire philanthropists, university presidents, constitutional scholars, bestselling authors and other leaders of business, media and the arts who once received college or graduate-school rejection letters of their own."

The painful truth is that there is always an element of chance in admissions.

HELP MAKE IT BETTER (NOT WORSE) FOR YOUR KIDS. Warren Buffett, the storied investor, has described being rejected from Harvard Business School as a pivotal moment in his life. He matriculated at Columbia Business School and worked with professors who helped form his approach to investing and set the course of his life.

One of his biggest fears when Harvard sent the seemingly bad news? Letting down his father. Getting rejected hurts, but getting rejected and disappointing your parents just makes the experience that much more painful. Buffet describes the relief he felt when his father showed "only this unconditional love . . . an unconditional belief in me."

A college rejection may be one of the best "teachable" moments in childhood. On the threshold of adult life, our kids may feel that they have suffered a setback. Parents know, and perhaps in this moment teens may learn, that the only way to escape setbacks, disappointments, and even failures is to never take a risk, to never try. In this moment, we can help them learn a new level of resilience.

TAKE ANOTHER LOOK AT THE OPTIONS. After receiving rejections, it is time to learn a lot more about the schools that accepted your teen. On reconsideration, it may be that another choice looks more attractive. Time to delve in with visits, emails to professors or admissions staff with any questions, plans for overnight stays, if possible, and querying any current students about their experience.

While your kid may have thought she knew exactly what she wanted to study and why that "school who cannot be named" was perfect for her, consider this: 80 percent of students change their major from what they anticipated studying when they were in high school. Your student may be setting off in a whole new direction at the school that will turn out to be the very best for her.

LET YOUR TEEN BE ROMANCED. Many schools, once they have accepted your teen, will fall all over themselves to get her. They will send materials by mail and email and even hold revisiting days or weekends where they try to romance the students they want to see on their campus the following fall. Give in to being wooed. Being wanted is nice, and when your student takes a good hard look at the colleges that have accepted her, she may discover a highly desirable option.

AVOID SOCIAL MEDIA. It is time to take a bit of a social media vacation. Step away from Facebook and have your kids tune out Snapchat. Social media will still be there when you return, but in the height of accept/reject/wait-list season it might be a good idea to take a break. Social media is a place to brag, and few people advertise deferrals and rejections. Once your child is settled, once she has looked at her options and found her new love, it is safe to return to social media.

REMEMBER THAT TRANSFERRING IS A POSSIBILITY. Remind yourself that few things are immutable. If it turns out that after your teen gives their second-choice school their best shot and they still long for that other school, most colleges accept transfers. But keep in mind that at many schools, it is even harder to transfer in, so it is essential that they have something to show from their time elsewhere.

CONSULT WITH OLDER KIDS AND THEIR PARENTS. Sometimes the college admissions process can feel like our own personal hell. But, in reality, it is a hell with lots of great company. When you or your teen are feeling the pains of rejection, find other students who, in previous years, had a similar experience and are now thriving. There is nothing as inspiring as listening to a college student talk about how they too were rejected from what they once thought was their first choice only to realize that now there is no place they would rather be than the college they attend.

BE OKAY WITH NOT KNOWING WHY IT HAPPENED. We can all speculate why some kids got into certain colleges and others didn't.

Why did a college take one kid and not another, who on the face of it look almost the same (or the rejected student seems even more qualified)? This is truly unknowable, and hours of speculation and wondering won't get you any closer to an answer. Stories abound of students who are accepted to schools that are more selective and rejected by seemingly less selective schools. It is one of the mysteries of the universe and it is best to just shake your head and walk away. Dwelling with your student on why they were not accepted keeps them, and you, from moving on to where your teen's future lies.

REALIZE THAT THIS IS THE BEGINNING OF ADULTHOOD. For many of us, a college rejection is the first time we will watch our kids experience a very real adult disappointment. We all know there will be more. But, if your teen handles this well, if they suffer their brief frustration, regroup, look at their options, and throw themselves headlong into the other opportunities offered, we can breathe a tiny sigh of relief knowing we have prepared them well for life.

As Julie Lythcott-Haims, former Dean of Freshmen at Stanford University and author of *How to Raise an Adult*, points out:

> Like it or not, unwanted, disappointing, and painful things happen in the normal course of life, starting in childhood. In our hearts, we want to shield our kids from all of these things. In reality, we can't. We need to help them learn to cope with difficulties and keep going; in other words, help them become resilient. Resilience isn't just useful in the moment—it's the gift that keeps on giving. The more

resilient your kid becomes, the better equipped they'll be to handle the next thing that happens. (And yes, the next thing will happen.)

We feel bad about ending this chapter on a low note, because in reality, the college process usually ends up well. Most kids get into a school they soon love, even if they don't go to what they once thought was their "dream school."

One final note: you will hear a lot of advice about how this is your kid's process, not yours. The argument runs that our budding adults need to manage this themselves, and that parents should take a check-writing back seat. But the college admissions process is not a single day or week or even, unfortunately, year. And it happens over a period when teens do an incredible, mind-blowing amount of growth. Your sixteen-year-old might not be able to effectively plan and book an early campus visit, but your eighteen-year-old may have no trouble scheduling everything he needs for an accepted students visit.

I (Lisa) viewed raising my boys as one long process of handing over more and more of their life responsibilities to them. I started in total control and over decades we transitioned that control. Your kid usually gets one shot at applying to college and they might gain the skills they are missing in the next six to twelve months. I had no problem with managing some of the clerical functions around college admissions. Some of these things my kids could manage, while some of the activities provided me with an opportunity to teach my boys life skills they hadn't needed until now.

The point here is that helping your kid is often just that—helping. And we help the people we love. So don't be afraid to find balance in the process—make sure your kids are driven in their own desire to attend college, and that they're taking initiative in the application process. But as parents, it's also okay to lend a helping hand through this pressure-filled process.

CHAPTER SEVEN

Separating and Letting Go

On a Sunday morning, a week after my (Lisa's) first son was born, my husband turned to me and said, "I can't believe he's 1/52nd of the way to his first birthday!"

Through a swirl of emotions—besotted with this new baby but exhausted and wondering what had just hit us—I recognized his words as prophetic: My son was a mere seven days old, yet I could already feel the wind of time whipping by my face.

Even back then, I should have known: parenting is and always will be about letting go, about preparing our kids for the road they will travel without us. And it starts on day one.

For a time, we fool ourselves; deep in the midst of parenting, it can feel like we have forever. But no one has that. And as we slog through the middle school years, it becomes all too clear that the years we have left with our kids in our homes—the day-to-day, I-will-annoy-you-and-you-can-annoy-me stage—can be counted on one hand. Then one day we realize it's a question of months, and suddenly, oh so suddenly, of weeks.

We started Grown and Flown because we found it so hard to let our own kids go. Some parents do this really well. They know this next step, be it college, work, or the military, will be a wonderful stage for their kids, and they take great pride in the accomplishment it represents. They know that simply being able to send a kid off to one of these next stages in life means the parents, too, did many things well. They rejoice in letting their kids go, confident that life has a natural, even wonderful, rhythm and this is how it plays out.

And then there are the parents who part ways in anguish: They pull over by the side of the road, sobbing their eyes out after drop-off at the dorm. Overcome with sadness, they cannot enter their kid's room at home for weeks afterward. They miss their kids so badly that they stare at their phones willing texts from their offspring to appear. We are not naming any names.

If we understood what's behind this hurt, could we better get our heads around it? Maybe we could work through the dislocation our families were experiencing a bit quicker? It has become clear that college drop-off is just one more episode of separation, something I had been experiencing with my kids since the first day I left them with a babysitter and went to work. We had been moving apart all the years of their lives; this step was simply more poignant.

Nothing drove home that realization more dramatically than my youngest son's high school graduation. Like every parent in the audience, I was bursting with pride—and more than a touch of regret. Weeks and months remained before he left, but experience had taught me he would begin to drift away once he crossed that stage, once he held that diploma in his hand.

The first time this happened with my eldest son, I wondered how I would survive.

The second time, with my middle son, I braced myself, knowing just how bad it would hurt—and it did.

The third and final time I was able to gird myself, fully aware how it feels to have a child move on. Yet still I wondered why the pain was so sharp.

Parents who mourn their children's departures are chided for their hovering ways, reminded that they should be proud of their offspring's achievements. Don't they know that clinging to their teens is both unhelpful and unseemly?

I have berated myself for being a wimpy mom—the parent who cannot walk away without tears, the mother who misses her kids every day. I have given myself the stern talking-to about being overly attached to my sons, and I have told myself a hundred times that it is not about me but about them. I have concluded there must be something wrong in my life, or missing from it, if saying goodbye is this hard.

In short, I have wondered—endlessly—why it hurts so much when they go.

Like so many aspects of parenting, this turned out to be a simple case of overthinking things. The reason it's so hard to let go of my kids is that the moment they walk out the door—be it for nursery school, middle school, college, or their "real life"—I will know them a little less.

I will never love anyone more than I love my sons, so why would I want to know them any less? And how is it possible that my life will not be diminished by their absence?

These are beings I loved even before they took their first breath. They have made my world bigger and brighter in every way. Being a parent has allowed me to see all of humanity through very different eyes. It has made me a better person.

If you asked me who in the world I know the best, my sons would be right at the top of the list. I have understood the rhythm of their lives from the time they were infants. I have known what would nourish their bodies, their minds, their souls. While my boys might not agree, at times I have felt I know them even better than they know themselves.

When they were tiny, they seemed to speak in a stream of consciousness, filtering almost nothing from my ears. By middle school they'd become more circumspect, sharing their world and their thoughts but starting to hold back. And high school? I'm not sure any high schooler could or should tell their parents everything. And so, the walling-off began—the natural and to-be-expected process of knowing them just a bit less.

And then they left home. They woke up one morning just like they had on thousands of other mornings, and by nightfall they were gone.

"Oh, this is just like camp," I told myself (my capacity for self-delusion apparently knows no bounds). After a few months, however, I had to let go of this pretense and contend with the fact that college means leaving home.

The ache of an empty nest is partly just a longing for their joyous presence—the way our lives are filled with our love for them. But there is real pain too, stemming from the knowledge that no matter how close we are to them, no matter how much we stay in touch, as their lives diverge from ours we will know them that tiny bit less.

Every year they will have more and more experiences that we know only from their photos and their retelling. And every year they will have more experiences we never hear about at all.

The love for my children remains untouched as my knowledge of them diminishes—not in the big meaningful ways, but around the edges: Have they ever tried paella? Whom did they study with last night? Is that a cold coming on, or just allergies? Did they work out this afternoon or blow it off and go out for a cheeseburger? They have professors I will never meet, friends I will never know. I try to content myself with sporadic dispatches from the front: a photo of something that strikes them as funny or strange; texts of random thoughts; phone calls to catch up. But the day-to-day rhythms of their lives are their own.

But here's the thing: nothing about them ever stopped being

fascinating to me. I never found their recounting of their day any less interesting, nor felt less concerned about their well-being. They may have outgrown telling, but I have never grown tired of listening.

So why is it so hard to let them go? It isn't that I wanted to hold them back or to play the role in their lives that I once did. It wasn't that I needed them to need me. These are the three people I have loved beyond reason, have loved more than I ever knew was possible to love, and I just don't want to know them even a little bit less.

THE WORDS WE WANT TO SAY

The summer before freshman year, as we prepare to send our kids off to college, it is all too easy to get caught up in the whirlwind of graduation, dorm shopping, packing, and moving. Our teens try to squeeze in every last second with their friends before they go, and even though they are technically still living at home, it may no longer feel that way as they are out the door early to their summer job and home late after socializing. But parenthood is always about looking forward and preparing for life's next stage. The summer before going to college is a time to talk, really truly talk, about some of the most important things in life. We are not talking about teaching kids to do their own laundry and sign up for classes but instead helping them look to the real challenges ahead.

TALK TO THEM ABOUT THE MAGNITUDE OF GOING TO COLLEGE. While going to college may well have been expected in your family, that doesn't diminish the magnitude of this step. This is the talk where we remind our teens of their true good fortune to be offered this unparalleled opportunity. This is when we ask them to step back and think about the fact that in any other time and place, they would be going to work or even war. Now is the moment to discuss the bounty a college campus has to offer with its speakers, concerts, athletics, and courses. There is truly no place else like this, and they need to be reminded that it would be tragic to waste four years playing video games, getting drunk, or shopping online.

TALK ABOUT SEXUAL MISCONDUCT. No matter your teen's gender or sexual orientation, talk about how sexual misconduct happens, what it is, why it happens, and what to do if it happens. Talk about doing the right thing, being a real friend to those in need, and the emotional, physical, and legal consequences of bad or simply careless behavior. Talk to them about what real relationships are based upon and what they feel like and why we value them so much. Define consent in the clearest of terms and how each party can be assured that it has been exchanged. This conversation needs to be serious, lengthy, and explicit. It is a conversation that will cover some very uncomfortable ground. It may not happen in one night, but instead over a period of time. Steel yourself, if you need to, and then sit down and talk.

TALK ABOUT MENTAL HEALTH. We need to tell our teens about any mental health risks in our families. They need to know warning signs of mental illness so that they recognize them. College is a time of stress, and a time when emotional and mental struggles may emerge. Freshmen need to know when and how to reach out for help for themselves or a friend.

ASK THEM TO ENVISION GRADUATING. At eighteen it may be hard to see themselves at twenty-two, but ask them anyway. College is ending, graduation is at hand, what will they want to have accomplished? What will they regret having missed? Maybe it is time for a college bucket list. By looking backward, they may have a clearer view of looking forward.

TELL THEM YOUR EXPECTATIONS. College is a new stage of life, and with it there may be new expectations. Don't wait until you have a misunderstanding with your kid, until you are feeling let down and they are feeling that they have messed up. If you have expectations around grades, working, or any other aspect of college life, speak up. Among other things, Lisa expected her kids to join up and get involved. To her, watching Netflix all afternoon did not fit with paying their tuition. Did she always get what she expected? No. But when the conflict came they couldn't say they had not been warned.

TALK ABOUT TAKING CARE OF OTHERS. Bad things will happen in college. Hopefully, the unfortunate events will confine themselves to broken laptops, missed classes, and some evenings of being overserved. But whether the bad news is big or small, college is where we learn to be there for our friends. Before college, families were at hand to help out. From college onward, our closest friends begin to feel like family. This is the time to tell your kids the importance of being there when they are needed, and of being the kind of friend they hope to have.

TALK ABOUT SLEEP. Before Lisa's boys left for college, she nagged them to get into bed every night. It was perhaps an inelegant solution, but her high schoolers got eight-plus hours of sleep a night whether they wanted it or not. As this was not a long-term strategy, it was important to teach them about the wonders of sleep and how our brains, bodies, and moods suffer without it, before they left for college. She can report that they all ignored her and learned their lessons the hard way . . . but at least when things started to fall apart, they knew why. Sleep is the elixir of the gods, alleviating so many ills, and our kids cannot hear that too many times. But the other value of this talk about sleep is that it can be part of a much larger discussion about self-care and personal responsibility—one that has been hopefully going on for years but heats up as the point of departure draws near.

THE IMPORTANCE OF LETTING GO

How we learn to let go is influenced by so many factors, beginning with how we were let go of. Leaving our own parents was exciting and scary, and now that the tables have turned, so much of what they did or didn't do seems much clearer. As we took our kids to college, the memory of the first days of our own freshman years came flooding back to us. We don't know anyone who loved college more than writer, journalist, and mother of four Allison Slater Tate, so it is no surprise that as her son begins to look at colleges, she wants him to feel the same way. What makes her college hopes for her son different is she has removed the rose-tinted glasses and remembers what goodbye truly felt like.

> In the dark hotel room, the crisp cotton sheets felt cool against my arms, and the churn of the air conditioner under the window muffled the occasional street noise below. My mom rustled in the twin bed on the other side of the nightstand. I couldn't see her face.
>
> She was leaving in the morning to go home to Florida, a thousand miles away, and I was going to walk to my one-room double in a squat, brown brick, '60s-style dorm to live with a girl I had just met and share a bathroom with two hallways of strangers from all over the world. There was

no air-conditioning in the dorm to help quell New Jersey's muggy, wool-blanket-style September heat.

We had spent that last day checking off all the boxes: my parents opened a local checking account for me, and I now had a debit card tucked next to my brand-new college ID in a bright orange plastic lanyard. My XL twin mattress was swathed in a blue-and-green Laura Ashley quilt from Bed Bath & Beyond, and pictures of my high school friends at homecoming last year were propped on my desk.

My dad, who knew how unprepared I was for a real winter, had bought me a barn jacket with a plaid flannel lining and brown duck boots before he had left a few days before. He would later send me what I suspect was meant to be a men's navy blue wool peacoat that still hangs in my closet today.

All my possessions were squished into a few milk crates under my bed and a single wooden armoire. My roommate and I had wooden loft beds built by upperclassmen that were so sketchy that if she sneezed, my bed swayed back and forth. I had a dining plan in place, and I knew how to find the infirmary and the Wawa without getting lost. I had all the essentials.

It was a no-brainer to stay with my mom for one last night at the hotel; it felt like I was getting away with something, basking in the relative lap of luxury compared to the sweltering room that waited for me just a few hundreds of yards away. As I lay in the bed—swimming in an over-size T-shirt and plaid flannel boxer shorts, because it was the early '90s and that is what we wore for some reason—I could not turn off my brain.

It felt like a moment. It felt like *the* moment. I knew that in the morning, there wouldn't be time for long goodbyes or conversations; there would be planes to catch and meetings with freshman advisers. So this was kind of it—this was my last real moment to just be my mom's kid.

As a mother myself now, I know that my mom had been preparing me for that night for eighteen years. But then, in that dark hotel room, I felt only a little bit of breathless panic as I realized that after we hugged goodbye in the hotel lobby the next morning amid the dark wood paneling and age-old emerald carpet, I would have to go be brave and figure out who I was going to be in the world, separate from her and my dad. I would sleep in a bed she made and wear the barn jacket my dad bought me, but I would never truly be theirs again.

Before we both let ourselves dissolve into our own exhaustion, I wanted to ask my mom everything else I needed to know about . . . everything. I needed to tell her that the lacrosse players next door were cute, that all the boarding school kids talked to only each other, that I felt like a hopeless rube. I wanted to tell her that I had been thinking about it, and that maybe I would try drinking in college. I had very little experience with alcohol, and the thought of getting drunk scared me to death. But it seemed like it might be required now, like my philosophy textbook.

"Mom?" The words tumbled out of me before I could think better of them. "Everyone drinks here. I'm probably going to have to drink a little. Just to fit in." I held my breath.

She told me, maybe a little too stridently, that I didn't *have* to drink. She told me I could just hold a beer, that people wouldn't notice if I wasn't drinking it. I could hear a bit of fear in her own voice then, as if she was trying to reassure us both. She didn't convince me, but I didn't tell her so. We were both quiet then, and the distance between our beds seemed a little wider as we drifted off to sleep.

My first few months of college were not easy. My roommate, who had a smart, popular older sister a few years above us, was impossibly cooler than I was. I was at the same time intimidated, awed, and baffled by her, and I think she felt the opposite way about me. It would take months for us to warm up to each other.

I was similarly stumped by the boys—really, men—on campus too. With very little dating experience and exactly zero confidence about my ability to flirt effectively, I felt suddenly like everyone's sidekick little sister trying hard to walk straight in heels that were way too high for her.

I decided to try to take French for the first time as a college freshman—a bad idea, apparently. When the weather turned, my native Floridian feet slipped and fell on black ice. Repeatedly. Without parents to tell me what to eat or when to go to bed, I settled into a diet that consisted solely of Rice Krispies topped with vanilla frozen yogurt and bagels from university-sponsored study breaks. I stayed up until 4:00 and 5:00 a.m. every night of the week just because I could.

In January, I got sick—really sick—and I didn't take myself to a doctor as soon as I should have. I ended up in the infirmary for a week, where I took my Psych 101 final in my hospital bed and watched Bill Clinton's presidential inauguration alone from a recliner in the infirmary lounge, the snow stacked up on the Gothic glass windowpanes behind me, my parents still a thousand miles away.

I formed crushes and had my heart broken more than

once. I held dozens of plastic cups of beer and, eventually, I drank them. I danced in dark taprooms to Meat Loaf and the Spin Doctors and Blondie.

I sat in the library and stared at words swimming on pages and stressed myself out, sure I was going to fail everything. I learned how to write an art paper. For French class, I baked in the dorm kitchen a bûche de noël that looked nothing like a bûche de noël.

I never washed my sheets and just slept on top of that Laura Ashley comforter. At times, I was lonely, I felt left out, and I had my feelings hurt. At times, I said the wrong thing, I was selfish, and I hurt other people's feelings.

In fact, all four years of college were packed with firsts and lasts, good decisions and judgment calls, and sometimes spectacularly bad ones. I failed an exam for the first time in my life. I jumped off a roof into a pile of what I thought was snow—but was actually ice—after one too many Pete's Wicked Winter Brews. Perhaps Mom was right to try to convince me not to drink after all.

I made out with boys. I went to Times Square for New Year's Eve in the pouring rain. I pulled all-nighters. I fought with my friends, I wrote papers about books I never read, and I skipped class. I suffered hangovers that made me proclaim, "I'll never drink again!"

But: I also made the very best friends of my life—the women who would carry me—sometimes literally, cheer for me, love me, and believe in me for the rest of my life, the same women who stood beside me on my wedding day and held my firstborn when he was weeks old and declared him the most beautiful baby ever.

One of the boys I made out with turned out to be my soul mate, my boyfriend, my husband, and the father of my four children, someone who knows me, understands me, and somehow loves me anyway.

I figured out how to take care of myself, how to speak up for myself, and how to course correct when I choose the wrong fork in the road. I learned how to be brave enough to pick the fork in the road in the first place. I decided to ask myself, "Why not me?"

And for all of it, my parents were not there. They bought me futons and calling cards; they paid for parking tickets and French tutors and about a million cups of Thomas Sweet frozen yogurt with chocolate sprinkles on the top and the bottom. I talked to my mom on the phone several times a week, venting my frustration about anything and everyone, but aside from a few visits for parents' weekend or dorm moves, my parents let me figure it out.

There were a few times when they would have had every reason to swoop in and rescue me. The night I rear-ended someone and had to figure out the insurance and take my car to an auto body shop, for example, or when I got a speeding ticket that required a court appearance. There was the time I woke them up at 3:00 a.m. with a broken heart, crying so hard I could barely speak. It must have scared the crap out of them; I know it would if one of my children did the same to me. But they didn't complain about the time or book a flight to New Jersey the next day. They just let me weep until I didn't need to weep anymore, and as it turns out—that is all I needed them to do.

I went to college to study and earn an academic degree, but college turned out to be a lot more about studying who I am and earning degrees in subjects I never imagined. College was my work to do. I told my parents all about it, but I did it myself.

I had the time of my life.

I realize now that the last night I spent with my mom in that hotel room, she was probably the one who was terrified. We had talked for months about the day I would leave home for college, but we didn't think about the fact that at the last minute, it would be her who would have to leave me. She had the harder job.

Now, that job is mine. Soon, I will have to leave my own child to walk to a dorm on a campus far from home. He has his parents' sense of independence; I don't expect him to ever really be home again once he leaves. He'll be off to break hearts and have his heart broken, to try and to fail and to achieve dreams he hasn't even dreamed yet, to fumble his way through the final laps of adolescence, to figure out just who the heck he is going to be now that he won't be our kid anymore.

I can't wait to hear all about it from a thousand miles away.

PARTING SHOTS: TEN TRUTHS GLEANED FROM A THOUSAND SEPARATIONS

Letting go of our kids has become an almost contentious issue. On one side of the philosophical spectrum are parents who argue that clinging to your teens is a selfish act that impedes their progress toward adulthood. On the other side are parents who argue that we cannot love our kids too much. Teens who know that their parents are there for them benefit from a solid foundation that lets them go out and face the adult world.

Not surprisingly, both sides have a point. Equally commonsensical, the wisest approach may lie somewhere between the two.

As we have watched literally thousands of parents in real life and in our online communities getting their kids ready for college, ten hard truths have emerged:

1. Parents are not trying to hold their kids back, by and large, and they are not even clinging. Most parents just want to retain the unique intimacy between parent and child. They want to hold on to not their kid, per se, but one of the most important relationships in all of our lives. It is an important and consequential distinction.

2. Families give us psychological nourishment and are one of life's greatest joys. When we see our kids moving away we fear this web of connections weakening. This is not just about the parent and teen but the interconnectedness that includes siblings, grandparents, aunts and uncles and cousins. Sure, there is a lot of talk about parents missing kids, but much of the truth is larger than that and includes the whole family.

3. Most parents are beyond grateful and proud that their teen has figured out their next step and is going to college, a job, or the military. They are thrilled that they are taking this positive move forward in their lives. But in the same way there was a tug when we weaned our kids or dropped them at nursery school or middle school, feelings of happiness and pride can easily coexist with those of wistfulness. This is one in a series of partings; we should not feel surprised or dismayed to feel the same way we did during those other leave-takings.

4. Parents often feel let down because they are no longer needed. Feeling needed by our kids was one of life's great gifts. But wanting to feel needed is not the same thing as wanting your kid to be needy.

5. We are sad because they are leaving and taking a chapter of our lives with them. We liked nothing more than complaining about our kids' overscheduled lives, but that does not mean we didn't miss the old hectic pattern of our lives as soon as it was gone. And as they moved on, we had to move on. So, if this juncture feels scary, messy, and a little complicated, that's because in so many ways we also are starting anew.

6. Because the traffic patterns of our lives change when our teens leave, some of our own relationships will wither. Other parents and community members, those we saw regularly around our kids and with whom we shared so much, will drift away. Any parent whose child has been on a sports team, in a band, or onstage will tell you there is great joy in watching our kids play and in bonding with other parents on the sidelines or in the audience. As this chapter closes it is the end of an era for us. Feeling sad or at least wistful is a natural response.

7. Some of our kids are anxious and scared about taking the next step. Not all kids blithely go off to college, make friends right away, jump into their activities, and hum along in their courses. This is a big life-altering transition, and for many teens it is one riddled with fear and anxiety. Some kids will have social or academic problems, and most kids will be homesick. In its annual Your First College Year survey for 2016, the Higher Education Research Institute at UCLA found that "almost three-quarters (71.4 percent) [of first-year students] reported that they 'occasionally' or 'frequently' felt lonely or homesick and over half (56.7 percent) said that they 'occasionally' or 'frequently' felt isolated from campus life."

8. We are also scared. Some of our kids have never been out on their own—and, truth to tell, some of them have not yet

shown the ability to care for themselves. Sure, they will get there. And sure, you can point the finger at us parents for not making them college-ready. But here is the truth: there is no buzzer that goes off the summer after senior year declaring all kids are ready to go. Some of us send kids off to college who are not quite prepared for independence, and parents have a very good reason to be concerned. And when looking at the data on freshmen, parents' concerns do not seem overblown but rather realistic; there will be substantial bumps in this road. Yes, we may trust them and know that they will cope, but that isn't the same as not having some concern.

9. Many parents are reduced to tears and a wrenching feeling as if something has been torn away. And then they are fine, if their kid is fine. Sure, they count the days to Thanksgiving break, and some of the pain starts all over again, albeit less intense, with each drop-off, but most parents rebound if their kid is thriving.

10. At some point in your student's college career, maybe even their first visit home for Thanksgiving, they will call school "home." Home. You will hear that word and feel the breath knocked out of you. You will want to shout or argue or leave the room in a puddle of tears. You will wonder how they can call a place with mattresses as hard as stone and food that borders on inedible, home. But then you will pause and recognize your good fortune. Through the stress, joy, and hard work, and the long, long road to get to college, your teen has a place they love so much it feels like home. They have found roommates or friends or professors who care about them and the things that matter to them. They have found a place that makes them feel they are exactly where they should be. With this one word, you will know all is well.

For all these reasons, you can see why we think that getting emotional when you have to say goodbye to someone who's been underfoot for the last eighteen years does not make you a helicopter parent or, worse still, a snowplow parent. It's simply a sign of how intensely you'll miss this person you love when they're suddenly no longer around.

But each parting is different, even within the same family. Best-selling author and mother of three Deborah Copaken explains:

The day after I packed up the family station wagon to move to college, the car stuffed with what now fits into the palms of my kids' hands, I was essentially gone from my parents' lives. Long-distance phone calls were too expensive. Digital bread crumbs had yet to be baked. Summer internships were far from home. I don't recall feeling homesick at the time, or at least not in any way that has left an impression. I felt elated. I had friends to meet; papers to write; tailgates to attend; spending money to make; causes to embrace; a new self to invent; boys to kiss; and a stint at the school paper that kept me busier than I would have thought.

My daughter, twenty-one, is equally busy at college. Busier, in fact, as she works ten hours a week to fulfill the requirements of her financial aid, plus she's premed. And yet her face pops up on my computer screen at work at least once a day via FaceTime. That's on top of sending me texts throughout the day: aperçus about life or her classes; videos of puppies; funny memes; and the occasional "Ugh, I'm so stressed." When she's not reaching out to talk or text with me, I can scroll through my Instagram feed and see what she's seen or visit Snapchat to watch her rocking out at a dance marathon or login to Facebook to check out the photos in which she's been tagged by friends. She even allowed

me to follow her short-lived finstagram (fake Instagram account), containing laugh-out-loud photos and videos you
wouldn't want a job recruiter to see. When she spent her
junior fall abroad in Madrid, she created short music videos
of her weekend jaunts throughout Europe and shared them
online, allowing me to feel as if I'd been there with her.

These digital missives continue to thrill me, and yet I
also grew to appreciate how her older brother, twenty-two,
went through college: ghostlike. His father and I split up
the day he left, so there was legitimate hurt, sadness, and
anger to process, but he, like me, vanished. He's not a tex-
ter. Or a poster. Or a caller. Or a sharer. What little I knew
of his college life I had to glean during parents' weekends
or when one of his a cappella buddies or roommates would
show up for dinner with us during school breaks. Did this
upset me at first, even though it echoed my own separation
from my parents? Of course, it did. There's a *New Yorker*
cartoon with two women standing by a headstone marked
"RIP James Frost, 1969–2014, Loving Son." James's mother
carries flowers and her grief; the other woman has her arm
around her in sympathy. The caption reads, "He finally
called, and it did kill him." I showed it to my son, and we
both cracked up. Every joke has its origins in pain.

And yet now that my son is out of college and working his first adult job, we're growing closer again. I get to
see him many mornings at breakfast, thanks to an economy
that puts the average city rent far out of reach for most college graduates. He helps me take care of his much younger
brother. He even joins my boyfriend and me for dinner now
and then.

All this to say, there are many ways to separate from
one's parents, and none is better than another. Eventually,

your children will come back on their terms. In fact, I would go so far to say that it is our job to follow our kids' leads and embrace whichever version of separation they choose, without imposing our own parameters. That separation from us is not only necessary for our children's maturation into adulthood, it's crucial for the emotional health and well-being of that adulthood.

I happen to be writing this essay in the wee hours of the morning from my childhood bedroom, having returned home for the funeral of my beloved uncle, who took over as patriarch of our extended family after the too-early demise of my father from pancreatic cancer. Death, of course, is the ultimate separation. The one for which all others are both rehearsal and reminder: we must separate from our parents in order to embrace the rest of our time here together as adults who come together by choice, not because a parent tells us we have to. If we've poured enough love into the cup of our relationships, it'll always be there to slake, even when we're apart.

My daughter is asleep in the bed next to mine. She's missing an important bio lab tomorrow, and I told her she didn't have to fly in from school to attend the funeral, but she insisted. She's spent every summer with my uncle, loving him like a grandchild loves a grandfather, and wants to be here to mourn him. Her brothers are asleep on air mattresses on the floor of my father's art studio, long since cleared of its canvases and paints. But Dad's spirit and face and curiosity and artistic leanings live on in them. My three sisters are scattered throughout the rest of the house, over which grief now hangs like a lead X-ray apron. And yet last night we had a three-generational dance party in the kitchen to celebrate my twin sisters' birthday. As we shucked off our sadness for this small window of release, we were as close and as joyful as a family can be. But that closeness, on an everyday basis, is neither sustainable nor desirable. Which is why separation, no matter how it's done—like a yanked-off Band-Aid or at the slower pace of the healing wound underneath—is imperative: as a means of bringing us back together, on our own volition, when it counts.

In a few hours, we will bury my uncle. Tomorrow we will head back to the cities we each call home, separate but forever bound while we still have breath to dance.

SOILING THE NEST

It sounds so, well, disgusting and in its own way, it is. The expression, soiling the nest, has come to describe the miserable, oppositional, deliberately difficult behavior our teens often engage in during the weeks (okay, it can be months) before they move away from home for school, the military, or possibly a job. Not every kid puts their parents through this and the ones who do each exhibit their own personal brand of soiling.

How do you know if your teen has soiled the nest? If you or your child's other parent has uttered or thought the words "it is time for him/her to *go*," you can be pretty sure that you are living this well-documented practice. Each teen takes their own approach to soiling, but some of the most popular methods include: wanting to spend every last minute with their high school friends despite the fact that the family wants to be with them as well, refusing to get ready for college as if their parents are going to make this magically happen (filling out forms, dorm shopping, registering for important events), acting like a self-absorbed irresponsible teen while insisting they should be treated like an adult, arguing about *everything*, treating siblings with disdain, only having the time of day for the family dog. Are any of these high crimes and misdemeanors? Of course not. But each is a tiny dagger to the heart of a parent who knows that time is winding down and wants to make the most of the remaining weeks with their new high school graduate.

Why do they do this, and how can we best deal with our beloved but annoying teen?

Psychologists tell us our teens display this behavior because of their own ambivalence about the next stage in their lives. They are excited and can't wait to begin college, but they are also scared to leave everyone and everything they have ever known and fearful of how their new life will unfold. While leaving us, their siblings, and their home is hard, they try to make it easier by pushing us away and reminding themselves how awful it is to be with us. If they can get annoyed enough at the family that has bathed them in love and support, the argument runs, it becomes a whole lot easier to walk out the door.

"As if their wanting to leave our homes isn't painful enough, they sometimes make it feel worse because they act as if they hate us," explains Kenneth Ginsburg, MD, an adolescent medicine specialist at the Children's Hospital of Philadelphia and a professor at the University of Pennsylvania's Perelman School of Medicine. "Think about it though, why would they want to leave a warm and comfortable nest? If they are going to exercise their wings and ultimately fly—as their instincts say they must—they need to view the nest as practically uninhabitable, prickly at the least."

What can we do when we see the last weeks and days of our teen's life at home sullied by this negative behavior? Recognize it for what it is. It feels almost impossible not to engage in the emotional struggle our teens are having (you will not see your friends for the tenth time this week, you will see your grandparents), but deescalating, stepping back, and reminding ourselves that this is but a brief moment in time, one that will almost certainly have faded by fall break or at least Thanksgiving or whatever is the first milestone at which we will see them again. Our relationship will not necessarily be a bed of roses months hence, but their need to prove that they can live without us (ironically while they are still living with us) will soon become a moot point. Our off-to-college kids, or teens who are leaving for work or the military, are setting us up for a trap, trying to bait us into engaging with them in the most unpleasant ways so that they can remind themselves how horrible we really are. If we bring understanding and kindness instead, reminding them we will always be there for them, we may not make saying goodbye any easier, but we will leave ourselves with far better memories of those parting weeks.

THE LAWN-MOWER PARENTS

Many of us are finding our footing in the process of letting our kids go—figuring out which lines not to cross, learning the right balance between staying close to those we love and supporting them as fully independent adults. That's the view from the parenting trenches, but what does this dynamic look like to those who deal with our kids on an everyday basis? Dr. Karen Fancher, a professor of oncology in Duquesne University's School of Pharmacy (and the mother of two), shared the insights she has gained in eight years of watching parents successfully launch their college-aged children:

> Although I'm a university professor, campus visitors often mistake me for the department secretary: my office sits directly opposite the elevators, and I maintain a literal open-door policy for my students. This makes for a recurring drama each spring:

I'm concentrating on something, when out of the corner of my eye I see the elevator doors slide open. It's a teenage girl and a middle-aged woman, presumably her mother. The parent walks into my office, the girl trailing sheepishly behind, and announces, "My daughter will be starting here in the fall. We want to change one of her elective classes."

I try to make eye contact and address the girl as I politely give them directions to the Office of Student Services down the hall, but it's the mother who apologizes for interrupting me. They leave my office, Mom leading the way with the class schedule in her hand.

Do you see the issue here? The child has been accepted into a major university and is weeks away from starting a difficult area of study, but her parent is doing all of the talking to get her problem corrected, while she says nothing and appears to be dragged along against her will.

You're probably familiar with the term "helicopter parents," where parents hover over their children and swoop down to rescue them at the first sign of trouble. At the college level, the physical presence required to hover may be limited, so we are now observing a different parenting style: "lawn-mower parents." These are the parents who rush ahead to intervene, saving the child from any potential inconvenience, problem, or discomfort.

Other practitioners of this parenting style include snowplow parents, bulldozer parents, and—my personal favorite—curling parents, so named for their similarity to the Olympic athletes who scurry ahead of a stone gently shoved across a sheet of ice, frantically smoothing its course toward a predetermined location.

Facetious labels aside, this kind of parental behavior can

have long-lasting, detrimental effects on your child. Some of these include:

- It leaves a teen ill-equipped to deal with routine growing and learning experiences. This includes everything from asking for directions and dealing with an annoying roommate to communicating with superiors, negotiating for a desired item, and coping with disappointment.
- Conditioned to follow only the path prepared by the lawn-mower parent, the teen is deprived of the opportunity to develop a sense of personal motivation or drive.
- Making a decision, big or small, becomes difficult without the guidance of others.
- The student can't help gleaning the negative message implicit in lawn-mower parenting: the child cannot be trusted to accomplish things on her own.

The modern style of overly present parenting has also forced college administrators to clarify certain boundaries:

- Spurred by the blatantly abusive behavior of some parents, many universities maintain a policy that all contact from a parent be referred to the administration office. A parent's request to "keep this conversation just between us" or "not tell my daughter that I called you" is unlikely to be honored; instead it may single your child out to the administration—and not in a flattering way.
- The Family Educational Rights and Privacy Act of

1974 (FERPA) bars faculty members and administrators from revealing certain information to the parents of a student who is over eighteen and has not authorized its release. This creates scenarios in which the university cannot share the student's grades with the parents, regardless of who is paying the tuition. Professors must contact the school administration to find out what they are permitted to disclose.

- If the behavior of a student's parent is threatening, outlandish, repetitive, or otherwise inappropriate, there's a good chance it will wind up being discussed among the instructors. The student may then quickly gain a reputation within the faculty that is the exact opposite of that which the parent hoped to achieve.

- Faculty members are heavily involved in job searches, recommendations, referrals, and the like. If a parent has been contacting me to "help" her child through my class, how can I honestly rate that student highly on communication, motivation, and maturity to a future employer?

Train yourself to break the lawn-mower habit:

School-aged kids: Let your child do the talking as often as possible. This includes ordering at restaurants, asking for directions, or calling a friend on the phone to ask for a playdate instead of arranging it yourself via text message.

High school kids: Although there is still room for parental involvement at this age, insist that your child attempt all communication on her own first. If she misses a quiz and needs to take it later on, have her make the arrangements with the teacher; intervene only after she has made the first attempt on her own. If she has a conflict between track practice and music lessons, for example, have her discuss the possibility of a schedule adjustment with the involved groups; she will then be more invested in making the decision—and dealing with the potential consequences—herself.

Kids of all ages: Trust your child to do well. Let her know you believe she can make good decisions on her own. Give her room to make mistakes—even major ones, sometimes—and learn from them together.

As parents, we cannot escape watching our kids struggle, feel uncomfortable, and even fail. Painful? No question. But you're doing your child no favors by trying to shield her from this part of life or solve her problems for her. Instead, give her opportunities to learn strength and self-confidence. These tools will equip her to handle future challenges with grace.

THE TEARS

Even when we tell ourselves that we will not cry, that there is no reason to cry, that it's simply humiliating to fall apart at our age, the tears somehow find a way of coming. Helene Wingens, managing editor at Grown and Flown, was a practicing lawyer before she took a break to raise her three children. When Wingens returned to work, it was as a writer; and now, in a few hundred words, she captures the essence of our tears as we face letting go of our kids. We'll leave you with her words:

This weekend we dropped off son number two at college. This is not my first rodeo, so I was somewhat prepared for the flood of emotion that comes with the process. Despite the fact that I've been feeling weepy for the last week or two, the actual separation went surprisingly well—even though I did feel that familiar lump rise in my throat as we watched him walk away.

Pondering my reaction later, I came up with half a dozen perfectly sound reasons for why parents tear up as their kids tear off:

- My heart is so full of love for you that it aches like a physical pain; it's that almost unbearable fullness that brings tears to my eyes.
- I will miss the way we were. Things will change between us now. We will always be mother and son, but I will become an increasingly less important person to you—as it should be.
- I will miss almost everything about you: your sense of humor; your long, rambling diatribes; even your closed bedroom door. But it's not just you I'll miss; it's the light and life you brought into this home, as well as your close friends who became dear to me too, over the years.
- I will worry about you because I desperately don't want you to ever feel lost or alone. Still, I am certain you will experience those "lost and alone" days—everyone has them. Thinking about the times that you will not be okay (and the fact that I can't make you okay) makes me terribly sad.
- I am not worried that you will not succeed. In fact, just the opposite: I have no doubt that you will succeed,

and that success will lead you further from me. Again, all this is as it should be, but it is sad nonetheless.

- That moment when you walked away from us on campus, we went one way and you went the other. You walked into a bright new chapter of your life where the possibilities are almost endless. I was walking away from a piece of my heart, and the poignancy of that moment is not lost on me.

I know that we will all soon adjust, enabling me to see this moment for what it truly is: a beginning, not an end, for both of us. As we drive away, I look back and hope I've done most things right (or right enough), that you make wise choices, and that fortune goes your way.

CHAPTER EIGHT

College Move-in

> *I was on an adrenaline high and busy exploring my new college, so it didn't hit me until a few days later. Oh, wow! I realized I needed my parents a lot more than I thought I did. You miss your parents when they are gone. What hurt me the most was realizing I was not in the same zip code as them any longer.*
>
> —ANNA, 21

We founded Grown and Flown partly because we handled freshman drop-off day with each of our oldest sons so badly.

Nothing we had read, and no conversation we had held, prepared us for the sharp pain of ripping off this emotional Band-Aid. No one told us that the feeling of loss would be so great. No one said that the pride we would feel about sending our teens to school would be the phoenix that would only later rise from the ashes of this pain. We felt we should have been warned, or at least had a shoulder to cry on once it happened. We wished that someone had told us that it was unsafe to drop and drive, as no one should be allowed behind the wheel of a car when crying that hard.

Even now, writing these words years after our first freshman drop-offs, we could be reduced to tears just thinking about move-in day. A mother in our Facebook group said it simply and best: "If you Ugly Cried in the last forty-eight hours, raise your hand." Another responded, "Can anyone tell me how long it takes for this terribly empty feeling to pass, after dropping your child off at college six hundred miles away? This is the hardest thing I have ever had to do! I didn't know I had so many tears."

Some offered encouragement: "It does get better and the new normal can be wonderful! Just think of all the adventures and exciting times your child is having . . . this is what they are supposed to do . . . grow up and have a life that they get to tell you all about when they talk to you! It is very, very hard and very sad, but if you think about it as the start of a new 'grown-up' relationship with your kid, it makes it a little easier."

Many parents noted that even their pets were depressed.

But then we looked around. Not every parent was acting like they had a limb severed. Many were sharing in the excitement their kids were feeling and were pretty happy to lighten up on some of those parenting duties (car pools anyone?). Some shared their teen's joy and knew that parenting had just shifted to a new stage, as it had many times over the previous eighteen years—and that it was far from over. They knew that parenting was something that would never end, and that their kids were exactly where they should be.

Said one parent: "Am I the only mom that, when dropping our children (three) off at their selected universities, didn't cry? I'm reading how people wear dark sunglasses, have to turn around so the kiddos don't see the tears, call them the following day . . . I sort of feel like this is our job well done and it is a privilege to see them off to spread their wings. It's what we raised them to do, knowing this special day would come. Instead, we celebrated with each of them, helped them with the setup and organizing of their dorms, left their 'pride letter' that I wrote for each of them, along with some hidden money, and said, 'See you later.'"

And another: "All of these posts about being sad to see your kids go back to school make me feel like a terrible mother. I haven't cried once since mine left in the fall. I am so happy for him and love seeing him enjoying his college experience and growing. I'm not saying there's anything wrong with being sad, I'm just wondering if there are others who also aren't sad?"

While many volumes have been written and seemingly millions of websites have explored the process of our babies arriving in our lives and all that followed in childhood, very little has addressed their transition to separate lives as young adults. As parents, this change felt as monumental as the day we brought them home from the hospital, but no one was really talking about it.

The process of moving a kid to college starts the summer before senior year in high school. That summer is the kickoff to the year of lasts. For 365 days, the calendar and our senior remind us that this is the last time that we will ever [fill in the blank], and in our hearts and minds we begin the process of advancing our kids to the next stage in their lives.

We begin to imagine them living someplace else, although, as no college applications have yet been sent, we don't know where that place may be. Over the year, at family milestones and traditions, we are aware that in fewer than twelve months we will be celebrating or gathering without them. When they find out where they will be continuing their education, we begin to imagine them in their new "home." Then the physical signs emerge. It starts with the college sweatshirt. Then the piles of XL sheets, towels, and a new laundry basket appear over the summer. And then one day the boxes are packed and it is really happening.

Whatever reaction you have to your teen's send-off is the right reaction. It is all normal. The parents who rejoice also miss their kids. The parents who sit crying helplessly on the shoulder of I-95 will soon recover.

In this chapter, we are going to talk about move-in strategies, freshman transition, and later discuss with the dean of the College of Liberal Arts at the University of Texas at Austin some of the ways freshmen can get off on the right foot as they start their college journey. But first, the goodbye.

Wise Words from Drop-off Veterans

Here are some thoughts to keep in mind after drop-off:

That white-hot pain will not last.

Your child is already a big success. She or he has learned something about hard work and deferred gratification—two sure markers of future achievement.

Feel proud of yourself. You were handed a baby and you created a young adult who is now a college student. That's no small feat.

Your kid is a good person. This should give you great joy. It's also a testament to your parenting.

This is college. This is not war or jail.

We have always learned from our teens. As their world expands, so will ours.

This being the twenty-first century, you will hear from your kid in a number of ways—perhaps even more than you want.

Rejoice for your child; this is one of life's triumphant moments.

A college semester hardly lasts forever; in fact, you may be surprised at how much time your student spends at home.

Parenting, by contrast, never ends. This is the first step along the path of the longest relationship we will have with our kids—the one between two adults.

> *I was terrified moving in. I had been anxiously awaiting finally leaving and moving to college since my junior year of high school. My mom and I waited in the car line to unload my things into my dorm and it hit me. I was really going to be alone, with my family across the country. As soon as I met my roommate, who would quickly become my best friend, I instantly felt a wave of relief and affirmation that I was ready for this big transition.*
>
> —MAYA, 20

A LETTER IS FOREVER

Our kids know we are proud of them. They have bathed in our love for eighteen years. But no one ever tires of hearing how valued they are.

Lisa reflects:

When my kids were going off to college, I failed to write them the kind of goodbye letter that they would want to save forever. Instead, I made due with a series of texts that have long since been deleted or left on discarded phones.

This moment, when you are dropping your kids off at college, is the moment to pour your heart out, to share the love you have felt since you wrapped them up as babies and brought them home from the hospital. This is the moment to tell them that you have loved them more than you ever believed possible and are bursting with pride as you watch them go. This is the moment to share whatever last bits of wisdom we need to impress one more time and to remind them that we will always be here when they need us.

As our kids can see the finish line, the process of leaving may be exciting, but also daunting. It can be scary for anyone, particularly a teen, to move away from all they have ever known and loved, including parents, siblings, and even pets. They may be worried about whether they will make friends as close as the ones they have at home, or if they can handle the work or make the team or join the club. They may be worried about living on their own for the first time and having to adult for real.

If they weren't teens, they might spend lots of time with us and tell us how much they love, appreciate, and will miss us. But because they are teens, they very occasionally express their gratitude (thanks, Mom, for spending $700 to outfit my dorm room) and the rest of the time they may make themselves incredibly unpleasant. Because if they sow dissent, if they create disharmony in our homes, it makes it easy to push us away. As Dr. Lisa Damour explains, "Home life can become so unpleasant that those who once dreaded their graduate's departure can't wait to pack his or her bags. There's a hidden function to this friction: it's easier to part from people whose company we can hardly stand."

One of the most painful aspects of this is their need to spend every last minute with their friends, forsaking their family. We are grateful for their close ties, happy that they have bonds with friends or even romances that make their departure more poignant, but it can be deeply frustrating for parents. Damour urges parents to look beyond the difficult behavior: "Adults don't need to take a teenager's consuming social life as a personal rejection. The intense focus on peer relationships is often connected to the psychological strain of parting with family. A teenager who preoccupies himself with saying goodbye to his friends often manages to distract himself from difficult feelings about leaving his family." By being horrible to us, casting us in the role of villain (we won't let them stay out every night, we insist they get packed and ready, we want them to have dinner with their grandparents), we are easier to leave.

Is it any wonder, then, that when we finally arrive on campus for drop-off, we can be a bundle of mixed emotions after a sometimes turbulent summer? For parents, this goodbye can feel deep and immediate and profound, even if this isn't our first rodeo. And so we turned to someone who has watched this ritual play out for decades to help us put words to this momentous event.

Why was this leaving, the very day of departure, so momentous? If all summer we had been barreling toward this day, surely, we should be prepared for it? Why did the day feel so big and then suddenly so small? The answer, according to Professor Marshall Duke at Emory University, is that there are only a few days in life that are like none other. Those days, in their poignancy, are forever seared into our memory, and we cannot, must not, treat them like days of lesser consequence. Duke has watched this process through the generations, and he explains:

In the opening paragraphs of his novel *White Noise*, the amazing Don DeLillo evokes an image that plays out across America every year—the return or first arrival of college students on college campuses:

I've witnessed this spectacle every September for twenty-one years. It is a brilliant event, invariably. The students greet each other with comic cries. . . . The parents stand sun-dazed near their automobiles, seeing images of themselves in every direction. . . . They feel a sense of renewal, of communal recognition. . . . This assembly . . . as much as anything they might do in the course of the year, more than formal liturgies or laws, tells the parents they are a collection of the like-minded and the spiritually akin, a people, a nation.

Like the narrator in DeLillo's novel, I, too, have witnessed this spectacle, in my case for forty-two years at Emory University, and it truly is a "brilliant event." It has not only been my thrill to witness the arrival of new freshmen, but my privilege and honor to have been afforded the opportunity to talk with parents bringing their children to Emory.

I began an annual "Talk to Parents" when I was director of the Emory University Psychological Student Counseling Center, in an effort to help them and their children deal with the transitions they were all about to experience. I am no longer director of the counseling center, but I have continued to talk with the parents of our new students as more than three decades have slipped by.

There are many things I tell the parents in the hour that they sit with me on one of the most emotional days of their lives. Here are some of the key things that I want them to know.

1. This is one of the most emotional times in the lives of parents, especially if they are bringing their oldest or youngest child to school. Bringing their first

child represents the culmination of one phase of their family's life and the beginning of another; they are moving from a period of stability as a family with children into a transition, at the other end of which they will be a family whose children have grown. For parents with more than one child, this "launching" of the first child is a "shot across the bow," a notice served that the empty nest is slowly beginning to take shape somewhere up ahead. For the parents of a single child or for those bringing their youngest, the empty nest awaits them upon their return home. I tell the first-time college parents that it will take them several months to adjust to their newly patterned family at home. I tell the empty nesters that the adjustment will take several years. It will. But it is not all, or even mostly, bad. This is an exciting time, indeed.

2. I tell the parents that just because their children are at college, it does not mean that they are "college students." The best description I have found is to say they are "high school students at college." This is because it takes time to learn how to be a college student—how to study, how to eat, how to do laundry, how to play, how to handle money, etc. My best estimate is that this process requires about one semester, by which time the students will have studied for and taken major exams, written papers, given in-class reports, messed up, done well, fended off the "freshman fifteen" weight gain, drunk gallons of coffee or other stimulating beverages, eaten uncountable pizzas, and attended a variety of college events, some noteworthy, some forgettable. I urge the parents to await the emergence of their college student with patience. This brings me to number three.

3. Waiting patiently for the "college student" to emerge means not doing what seems to come naturally to modern parents. They are problem solvers, they are action-oriented, they are capable. They want their children to succeed in their lives and they want to be sure to help as much as they can. Here's what I tell them: During the course of normal events at college, your children will face problems that need solving. Roommate problems, social problems, registration problems, problems with specific subjects or professors. And there are two ways for these problems to get solved.

- *Number one*: Parents call the school and talk to the Office of the Dean, or the director of residence life, or even the president. What happens? The problem gets solved. Oh, but there's one other thing that happens— their children are weakened. Not only are the children not given the chance to learn how to solve the problem and to grow in self-confidence from doing so, they are also "told" by their parents' interventions that Mom and Dad do not believe that they can take care of themselves, increasing the likelihood that they will remain dependent on their parents to solve their problems, which results in parents continuing to intervene, which tells the students they can't take care of themselves . . . you get the picture.

- *Number two*: Your children figure out how to solve the problem on their own. The bottom line is this: either way the problems get solved. But if parents solve them, the kids are weakened or prevented from growing. If the kids do it, the problem is still solved, but they are stronger and moving toward a readiness to live their lives independently.

One thing I add to drive home my urging that parents let kids deal with problems on their own: someday these children will be adults and their parents (you) will be elderly and in need of being cared for. What sort of people do you want taking care of you? Unsure adults who are afraid to make good decisions and reach solutions with confidence? Or adults who have grown in strength and wisdom and will know how to weigh the best options for your care?

4. As I said, the day that parents leave their children at college—or send them off if they are traveling there alone—is among the most emotional days of parents' and children's lives. It is a moment that comes along once in a lifetime. Each child only starts college once. Given the uniqueness of the day, it falls into the category that includes wedding days, special anniversaries, even days on which family losses occurred—big days, days that stick in our memories throughout life. Such moments are rare. They have power. They give us as parents one-time opportunities to say things to our children that will stick with them not only because of what is said but because of when it is said.

Think of what you want to tell your children when you finally take leave of them and they go off to their dorm and the beginning of their new chapter in life. What thoughts, feelings, and advice do you want to stick? "Always make your bed!"? "Don't wear your hair that way!"? Surely not. This is a moment to tell them the big things. Things you feel about them as children, as people. Wise things. Things that have guided you in your life. Ways that you hope they will live. Ways that you hope they will be. Life-level things.

I, myself, was never able to do this, because I was too emotional and couldn't quite say what I wanted without crying. But all is not lost if this happens to you too. As soon as you can after you leave the campus, write your child a letter—with a pen, on real paper, in your own hand. The first sentence can be something like, "When I left you at the campus today (or at the airport, etc.), I could not tell you what I wanted to say, so I've written it all down . . ." Mail the letter to your child. It can't be deleted like an email can; it will not be tossed away; it will be kept. Its message will stick. Always.

With this last bit of advice, I bid the parents well and assure them that the admissions committee did not make a mistake and that their children really do belong at college. I will urge them to stand back and let these talented young people begin to grow. I will tell them that being the parent of a college student is one of the most prideful things that they will ever experience. I thank them for working so hard, so that college professors like me can have the joy of working with the children that they have so carefully nurtured. I then tell them to go home. The kids will be okay.

The professor is right: the kids will be okay, and many of them know viscerally the meaning of this moment. If your kids do not say anything profound or more consequential than "Why did you buy me this, I am never going to use it," do not fret. As much as we wish it were, this is not the moment that most kids choose to thank us for a lifetime of love and caring. They are teens, they are caught between excitement and nerves for this next monumental step in their lives, and that is probably as it should be. But if your kid is the kind who reflects deeply, who can step outside of themselves in this auspicious moment, here is what they might say, as imagined by college senior Mac Stiles:

There I was, two nights before move-in day, relaxing in bed and about to fall asleep, when the soft and fuzzy feeling previously associated with leaving for college suddenly disappeared. My mind flooded with all the change I was about to encounter as a college freshman and the people who would be left behind. No one warned me about this strong and overpowering sensation. It hit me like a tidal wave, drowning me in thoughts and memories. I found it easiest to grasp and process it all by putting my feelings into these letters:

Dear Mom and Dad,

Today must be one of the hardest days of your lives. I promise you everything will be okay. You've spent seventeen years, ten months, and twenty-nine days instilling values in me that I will never forget. The time you spent repeating yourself over and over has paid off. I am taking your lessons with me to college to mold myself into a better person, the person you raised me to be.

But it's time to let go.

You have to trust that I can hold my own. It's no different than learning to walk or ride a bike. You held my hand and showed me the way. The first couple of times, I may have come back bruised and bloodied, with tears streaming down my cheeks, but I learned. And today is no different. You're sending me off knowing that I'll hit some bumps in the road and face obstacles that seem impossible to overcome. I will still need you to show me the way every once in a while, even if it's through a phone call or text. I value your input. Eventually, just like walking or biking, I will learn and find my way myself.

I love you both more than words can describe and will be forever indebted to you for what you have given me physically, mentally, and emotionally. All of my achievements root back to the two of you, and even if I might not show it at the time, I'm extremely grateful. I may be moving out from under your roof at home, but I will always be under the roof of your heart.

Drew and Reed,

I will miss you both more than I can convey. You are my two best friends in the world and I'll never forget the memories we've made growing up with each other. It's never a dull moment when the three of us are together, and I cherish that. Whether it's walking Murphy at night, blaring music all over the neighborhood as we drive, or just playing PS3 and laughing, I always have a blast.

Take your schoolwork seriously but allow time for fun in high school too. Both of you are incredibly gifted, and you'll soon learn what those gifts are and be able to truly embrace them. Try not to worry too much either. Worrying is a waste of time. If it already happened, you can't change it. Just forget about it and use your mistakes to grow and learn. You know my favorite saying: "Let the past drive the present."

Look out and care for one another. It's important for both of you to know that I am so incredibly proud to call you my brothers and I wouldn't trade you for anything in the world. Sometimes we bicker and fight, but we're always able to laugh it off right away and get back to normal. You both are exceeding expectations left and right and nothing makes me happier. I love you both immensely and can't wait to hear about your adventures while I'm gone.

Murphy,

I think you're going to take this the hardest. It's easy for the rest of us to understand what's going on because we can talk to each other. But you will just see us pack up the car with a lot of my stuff, then have everyone else come home but me. I don't know what I'm going to do without you running in and jumping on my bed to lie with me. I always felt that you understood me and we were pretty similar, even though you're a dog and I'm human.

Orhan Pamuk once said, "Dogs do speak, but only to those who know how to listen." I find that pretty accurate. I'm always listening, buddy. I'll be back soon and I can't wait to see you in my bed, tail wagging a hundred miles per hour, exactly how I left you.

Love, Mac

50 Questions to Ask Before You Go Dorm Shopping

BEDROOM

1. Are the room dimensions available for the specific dorm room to plan how to use the space?
2. Are there closets or wardrobes, and how much rail/hanger space is available?
3. How much floor space is there in the closet and will a shoe rack be useful or fit?
4. Are the beds elevated or bunk or traditional?
5. Are desks and desk chairs provided?
6. Does the dorm room come with a dresser?
7. Does the room come equipped with lamp or trash can/recycling bin? Is there overhead lighting? Is a lamp by the bed something that your student could use in addition to a desk lamp?

8. Is there a bookcase or is an over-the-desk hutch for book storage needed?

9. Will your student have roommates and, if so, how many? Will they coordinate on decor or sharing things like a mini fridge, TV, computer printer?

10. How cold/drafty are the rooms and how much extra bedding is needed for the winter?

11. Is there air-conditioning and, if not, will it be hot and how big of a fan would work best?

12. How much room is there for under-bed storage and what size plastic storage units will fit best?

13. Is there any room for suitcases, or will they need to be brought back home? Can you use duffel bags that can be slid under the bed or will black garbage bags be the easiest way to transport things?

14. How heavy a sleeper is your student? Does he have an alarm clock he depends upon or will a cell phone alarm suffice?

15. Will your teen be taking valuables (passport, jewelry, money, credit cards, prescription drugs) from home that could require a lockbox?

16. Does your child have allergies that necessitate allergy-free bedding encasements for mattresses and pillows?

17. Is the college mattress provided the typical paper-thin one or does it look (and feel) like a brick? Will your student sleep better on an egg crate or mattress topper?

18. How much wall space does your student have and will he want to decorate it?

19. Does the school allow decorations to be hammered into the wall or just stuck on? Are there any wall hangings outlawed?

20. Do the windows have blinds or do they need to be provided?

21. How many outlets does the room have and what power strips or surge protectors will be useful? Are regular extension cords allowed?

22. Does the weather turn cold early such that winter clothes go with your student in September, or will they have a chance to switch out shorts for a heavy coat during fall break?

23. What bits of home does your student want to take with them?

24. Is the bathroom shared by a suite of rooms or is it down the hall or nearby?

25. Does your student need a robe or towel wrap for modesty when walking to the bathroom from her dorm room?

26. Can toiletries be stored in the bath or carried back and forth?

27. Where can a wet towel be hung to dry?

28. Does your student already have flip-flops that can be worn in the shower?

29. Are you sending towels from home or buying new?

30. Would adding a monogram to new towels keep them from walking off?

COMMON ROOM

31. Are any appliances forbidden by the school as fire hazards or for other reasons?

32. Is the floor carpeted or would an area rug be useful/desirable?

33. What is the square footage of the floor for the best rug size?

34. Does the common room have furniture or are students expected to provide it?

35. Will your student have siblings/out-of-town friends visiting and do they need extra sheets and blankets?

36. What rentals, if any, does the campus provide, such as microwaves, watercoolers, mini refrigerators?

37. Are there kitchen facilities and does your student need to bring pots, pans, plates, silverware, etc.?

LAUNDRY AND CLEANING

38. Will your student drop off her laundry and will she be given a bag for that?

39. If he does his own laundry, how far away are the machines from his dorm room and is it easier to carry a bag or basket with handles?

40. Is there a vacuum cleaner that can be borrowed on occasion?

41. What cleaning are students expected to do in their room, bathroom, kitchen, and/or common room and do they need their own supplies?

SHOPPING

42. When and where are the dorm room shopping sales in your area?

43. Is there a big-box or online store where your student can place an order online and later pick up all the items at a store near campus in the fall?

44. What are the relative costs of shipping or using a store's "buy here/deliver there" programs?

45. Is it easy to get to a drugstore or campus store or should your student bring extra toiletry supplies?

46. Is there a package-delivery location close enough to receive packages, and can your student carry heavy ones back to their room?

47. Will the student have access to a car or public transport to be able to buy additional items he might need after moving in?
48. What are your student's electronic needs and does his college offer any discounts for computers purchased through the school?

MOVE-IN DAY
49. Is there an elevator or only stairs in the building?
50. Are you driving or flying with your student on the big day?

WHY WE SHOP

One of the big rites of passage for parents of soon-to-be college kids is buying stuff. We think we are doing this because our kids need us to help them get organized for their new life. They don't. Most of them are eighteen, and with a debit card and a driver's license in hand they can get this job done on their own. They have grown up in the age of Amazon and could probably outfit their dorm from the safe confines of their childhood bedroom.

We have a different and ultimately more important reason we make the lists, ask other parents for suggestions, and then, on the hottest days of summer, run our kids around buying things we are not even sure they will need. Writer and mom Katie Collins explains:

There are few things that feel as satisfying to me as a good organizational project. For a few weeks now, our finished basement has been command central for operation "get the girl ready for college." The floor next to the now empty storage unit that once held Barbies, Polly Pockets, and later, sheet music and notebooks and binders from each passing school year, is lined with a succession of plastic tubs, each bearing the essentials of college life.

One tub holds laundry detergent and cleaning supplies; another toiletries, a first aid kit, cold medicine for the sore throats that plague actors, and Benadryl for the mosquito bites she's so allergic to; a third holds pens, highlighters, a dry-erase board; and the final, a laundry basket, itself home to nests of hangers and Command hooks. Amazon Prime Day recently added a hair dryer to the mix, and as I deposited this newest addition to the stash, I surveyed the contents with satisfaction. *We're really making progress on that list!* I thought to myself, carefully avoiding the fact that the ultimate end to this progress will mean her leaving.

Having a dorm shopping list has brought out things in me I didn't know were there. Who knew that I would get so excited over a desk lamp with a USB charging port? It's overwhelming, it's silly, it's monumental, it's exciting . . . and it's taking everything I have not to cry every time we darken Target's door. Recently I decided that since dorm fridges now come with a built-in microwave on top (*kids today!*), it stood to reason the girl would need at the least a bowl, a mug, a plate, and some utensils for late night dorm munchies. Friends, the search for the perfect affordable and microwave-safe dish set has turned me into Indiana Jones looking for the Ark of the Covenant.

On a recent excursion, the girl turned to me and asked, partly laughing, partly mocking (the Force runs deep with this one, what can I say), "Why are you so *obsessed* with this plate/bowl/mug thing?" I couldn't answer, not there in the middle of Walmart, that it was because this felt like one of the only ways I can still actively mother her. All the other college preparations, the course selection, the *plus* loans (sigh), the health forms, are bureaucratic and removed. But the care and feeding of the girl—that's my turf—and it's fast slipping from my fingers.

Recently, a longtime friend in an online mom's group good-naturedly ribbed me about my "Great Big Dorm Shopping List." Cool in her "slacker mom of a teenage boy" identity, she poked fun at things like stain sticks and antibacterial wipes that nest securely in their bins waiting for move-in day. And I get it. Some of us deal with this looming separation by hyperfocusing on the list, and some of us deal with it by distancing themselves from it. But neither approach covers the fact that these birds are flying their respective nests very, very soon.

I won't be there when the girl gets her first bad grade, has her first spat with a friend or roommate, experiences her first off-campus party, or has to go to the infirmary the first time. I won't be there as she starts her campus job or auditions for her first college show or pulls her first all-nighter. I won't be there when she navigates her first campus romance, sits outside a professor's door during office hours, or makes her first 2:00 a.m. Denny's run. Nor should I be.

This path with all its highs and lows is hers alone to journey. So, I focus on what I can do, and sit with her over the Bed Bath & Beyond catalog to find the perfect comforter, remind her she'll need a rack to dry all those cotton dresses that tall girls never throw in the dryer, and agree that yes, that desk lamp *is* perfect. And when she's not looking, I add some Advil to the bins . . . after all, that first hangover is out there too.

It's easy to make fun of us college freshman moms. We get it; we can be a bit much. We know they're not leaving for good, and we know they "all come back." We know the four years will fly by. But we also know this is the beginning of the big separation; we're not just saying goodbye to our kids, we're saying goodbye to the hands-on role we play. Saying goodbye to a pretty significant part of ourselves. So, give us a break and, instead of asking if we're excited to be empty nesters, ask us what we've crossed off the list lately.

WHAT TO PACK

Let's cut to the chase: things have changed. We could almost send our kids to college with their clothes, electronics, and our Amazon password. While dorm shopping is a rite of passage, in a world with overnight delivery, two-day free shipping, and well-stocked campus stores, we suggest you risk *underbuying* for your kid. This is hard, really hard. The urge to buy comes not from avaricious overconsumption but from wanting to take care of them one last time and ease them on their way. It is all about love and caring for someone to whom you gave life and not the least about buying stuff. Once you come face-to-face with this reality, it becomes a whole lot easier not to waste money. Your kid knows you love them; they don't need a receipt from a store to prove that.

So, what do college students *need*? The answer can be summed up in a single sentence. *Less than you think.* There is a massive industry that has grown up around getting kids off to college. The number one most popular post on Grown and Flown is entitled "Top 12 Dorm Shopping Mistakes." Intuitively, we know that the piles of stuff on offer are far more than our kids need. So without further ado, here are the necessities:

XL Sheets and comforter
Towels

Mattress topper (most college mattresses are like concrete)

Mattress protector (because, yuck)

A multiport surge protector (dorms have notoriously few outlets and extension cords are often forbidden)

Laundry hamper (though they may just use the floor in the center of their room)

Some plastic storage bins (for many kids, not all)

Pillows (plural, they are probably going to use their bed like a couch to study on)

Hangers

Toiletries

Some first aid/pharmacy supplies/prescription meds (see the health section on page 86 for suggestions)

Flip-flops (because shared bathrooms are gross)

With this relatively short list, and the ability to order the extras they may need, they are set. We are not saying they shouldn't get wall hangings and shoe racks and a mini fridge, but this is what they *need* in their dorm along with their clothes, backpack, any prescription meds, phone, and laptop. College is expensive, so give your budget a break by getting what your kid needs and waiting to see about the rest. The number one mistake that parents tell us they made dorm shopping was overbuying. It is disheartening to come back in May and move out the dust-covered items your kid never touched.

Outside of the stuff you pack for your kid, there are a few extra things you might want to bring along just for move-in day, to make things easier:

1. Four-wheel folding platform cart or a dolly. This can be very helpful if you are moving things a long distance or carrying heavy items like refrigerators or furniture.

2. Snacks. You're going to be hungry and thirsty, and at some point you may want to stop for a meal, but in the meantime you'll want cold water and some munchies to get you through. We recommend bringing a small cooler with drinks and snacks.

3. A fan. It's August or September, and many dorms are not air-conditioned.

4. A tool set, including a screwdriver, rubber mallet, tape measure, hammer, scissors, and duct tape. Leave this behind for your student who will use it moving in and out of dorms and apartments over the next four years.

5. Door stopper. As soon as you get to your teen's room, prop the door open and it will make your life much easier. The room will be cooler, it will be faster to get in and out, and, most important, other families moving in are more likely to stop by and say hi.

6. Command strips. These come in all shapes and sizes and are perfect for "hanging" things on walls—they peel off easily without ruining the walls (depending on the school or the type of walls, you may not be able to/be allowed to make holes in the walls).

7. Cleaning supplies. Fill a bucket with a few cleaning supplies, such as disinfectant wipes, trash bags, and paper towels. You may want to wipe everything down, but know that it will never be this clean again. As much as we wish otherwise, kids in college don't clean their cramped dorm rooms very well or very often, so these basics can be left behind with them.

8. A roll of toilet paper. It might not be there . . . need we say more?

Finally, the most popular answer parents gave us by far when we asked what they needed was to bring your smile, your sense of humor, and your patience. In fact, bring an overabundance of patience because you'll need it. And follow your student's lead—it's not your room; it's theirs. You are there to help but not to dictate. It's a long day. It's a hot day. It's a difficult day. But it's also a tremendously exciting day. As Professor Marshall reminded us, this is one of "those" days, the days we remember forever.

I was very, very grateful that my parents were there to help me move in to college. My mom had a better idea of what I needed than I did and there were lots of things she got me that I would have never thought of. I didn't have a clue.

I do wish my parents had let me and my roommate set up the room the way we wanted it to be. After they left we ended up moving things around. I understand why they wanted to help—I am the eldest child and I know they still wanted to be a part of my life. They still wanted to feel like I was their little girl.

My advice to freshmen is to remember that they will be excited to get all moved in and meet their roommates, but they should be patient and not rush their parents out. This is the first time they are living on their own, and it will be hard on the kids and hard on the parents.

Let's be honest here. For many parents this is, as it should be, a moment of triumph. Being a good parent is hard work, and after eighteen years if you are sending your kid off to college, there is much to rejoice about. These parents are looking forward to the next stage in their lives, knowing that some of the best is yet to come.

—ANNA, 21

MOVING IN: THE SUM OF PARENT WISDOM

So, we've dealt with the sullen, largely absent teen. We've shopped until we cannot look at one more fan or shower caddy. We have come to grips with the fact that this is *really* happening, and all that is left is move-in day. The college has been sending your kid emails, which you may or may not be seeing, with a series of instructions that seem to offer more questions than answers. When you ask your kid for details, you get a shrug—or perhaps you realize you are only increasing their anxiety about the big day, and that seems inadvisable. Where to start? Gathered here is the collective wisdom of many parents who have gone before you. We are going to get into the nitty-gritty here, sharing solutions to their mistakes so that you can begin a step ahead.

1. How is your family getting to campus?

   - Are you close enough to drive to your teen's new college? Can you fit everything into your car, or will you need to make multiple trips or ship some of the bedding or bulkier items?
   - Do you plan to fly, and have you looked into how expensive it is for each checked bag and compared it to shipping?
   - If you still have dorm shopping to do, many retailers will ship for free or hold items at their closest store to campus. You can select the items online or in the nearest store. On move-in day, you and your teen will have an even better idea of what is needed, and you can go to the local store where your items will have been set aside.

2. Do some early reconnaissance.

- Have your student pick up her swipe card/key/ID card and make that her first stop. Don't unload her belongings only to discover that you cannot get into the building and key pickup is across campus, thereby forcing you to reload and move your car. It seems funny writing about it now, less so on a steamy August afternoon when everyone's stressed.
- Will there be student helpers with move-in? At many schools older students are waiting to lend a hand.
- Is there an elevator in the building or will you be walking up (endless) flights of stairs?
- Where is the closest parking, and is there a time limit on how long you can keep your car there? Schools often allow a very limited time for unloading, so don't assume you will be able to park near the dorm.
- Check the college website to see if there is any parent programming on move-in weekend and what time it begins.
- Check online to see what the rental costs are at the university for items like mini refrigerators and microwaves, so that you can decide between buying and renting.
- Would a small pushcart help this move-in (and move-out)? Your freshman will move more frequently during the next four years than you can ever imagine, and this is unlikely to be the last move she needs your help with.
- Make sure your teen has read the list of forbidden dorm items (these are usually fire hazards) and what can and cannot be hung on dorm room walls.

- Don't take all the luggage home. They will be returning at fall break or Thanksgiving. Leave a small bag for travel.

3. College move-in day will be a long day, so take care of yourself.

- Parents who show up with coffees, bagels, or doughnuts cannot help but win over a few fans.
- Wear clothing that is both comfortable and can get dirty. Forget the cute white jeans! Dorms can be filthy, even on move-in day.
- Family weekend may be a better time to bring the extended family, rather than move-in weekend. Dorm rooms are small, hot, and strewn with packing debris and stuff. There is no place for family members to sit, and your child barely knows their school or their roommate. They will have far more to show and tell grandparents and siblings by October.

4. Suggest that your student packs in the reverse order that they will unpack, with the things they will need first packed last. When you get to campus, your kid's dorm will be crowded. Their hall will be filled with empty cardboard boxes and their room will be covered with their roommate's belongings. The more they organize their packing ahead of time, the easier it will be to unpack upon arrival.

- Pack hanging items on their hangers in tall garbage bags. That way putting them in the closet is as simple as tearing away the bags. No wrinkles, no packing of hangers, and no suitcases required.

- Pack bedding all in one place (duffel bag or, even better, large black garbage bags or blue IKEA bags), so that it can easily be accessed all at once. It is best to wash it before you leave home.
- Get rid of as much packing material as possible at home. The dorm will be piled high with cardboard boxes and plastic wrapping and the trash cans overflowing.
- Pack the under-bed storage containers with the items your student will keep in them during the year. Bulky sweaters and extra sheets and towels are often good items. Use one storage drawer as a "medicine cabinet" with extra toiletries and over-the-counter remedies. Tape the drawers shut before you leave for move-in.

5. Have a plan for getting the room ready.

- Make your child's bed. It is a timeworn parental prerogative and completes the circle from when you first made their crib.
- Tell them why it makes sense to put underwear in the top drawer and sweaters in the bottom, but then step back and repeat to yourself, "This is not my room. I am not going to live here. This is not my room. I am not going to live here," as many times as necessary.
- Cleaning wipes are not a bad idea. On many campuses dorm rooms are used over the summer and may not have been well cleaned.
- Take away anything they don't think they will use. Bring heavy winter things to the family weekend that usually takes place in the fall or let them return with them after fall or Thanksgiving break.

6. Get ready to bid farewell.

- Slip a letter or short note with words of love and good luck into something that you are not going to unpack.
- Have a hard stop, the hour that you are going to walk away and leave them to begin their new life. Like taking off a Band-Aid, saying goodbye may need to be done quickly.
- Think about your college move-in-day goodbye before it happens, as it will take you by surprise. All the tears you may have shed in the previous weeks won't save you from today. Know in advance how you want to say goodbye.
- Plan for your final alone time before you reach campus, even if it is a quick family meal at a roadside diner or breakfast at the hotel. Once your child finds their room, meets their roommate, is introduced to their RA and their classmates on their hall . . . their new life has begun.
- Try to remember, through the quivering lip and the boulder in your throat, that even if it doesn't feel that way, this is one of our finest parenting moments.

Finally, we leave you with one of our favorite drop-off stories. This day will not go as planned, but then neither did any of the other big days in our lives. Still, writer and mother of three Alexandra Rosas thought she had it all planned out:

I had memorized every word the night before and it would be perfect. By 2:19 a.m., I knew exactly what I was going to say and do when we dropped off our oldest son at college the following day.

I would stand before my child, offering gentle, outstretched hands, and I would pull my son in close. Reaching up to smooth his hair, his trusting eyes would search out mine. I would smile with peaceful restraint and sigh, "My beautiful baby boy. How proud we are of you, how well you will do this year. We love you so!"

Then we would share a brief but meaningful hug, with the goal being that it lasts just long enough to cement the moment forever. His arms over mine, I would whisper, "Goodbye, son!" I would then turn, no looking back, and walk to our minivan, on firm—not Jell-O—legs. And then, it would be over. Goodbye, with a noble chin up like Margaret Thatcher.

Ha!

Wednesday's college drop-off went like this: Our son walked us to the car. We both knew it was the goodbye. My resolve was to gift him with the reassuring calm of our love and wisdom. What sprang forth instead, was:

Use single-ply for toilet paper because double-ply plugs. Make sure you smile back so you look happy to be here. Never put your drinking cups mouth-side down on counters because of the germs. You have to sleep or you'll start to feel depressed. Wash your hands because other people wipe their butts and they never wash their hands. I've seen it.

He tried to step away for air as I made his neck into a lifesaver.

Did that stop my brilliance? Nope. I was giving instructions like I did that night nearly two decades ago when we left him with a babysitter for the first time.

Clenching him by his shirt, I continued:

Don't lend money. Eat protein or you'll feel depressed. Always take a shower because it's like a miracle. So is a new shirt, so let me know and I'll send you some. Look over your shoulder when you walk home alone at night and do not walk home with earbuds in so you can hear if someone is following you. Good posture and a good haircut save many a day.

Then I fell full-face into my son, in the same desperate way that he clutched my arms when he was four months old, trying to crawl back up to me and out of his small plastic bathtub.

My voice muffled by his chest, I couldn't stop:

In your white plastic bin are three bottles of vitamins and calcium each, take them. Change your toothbrush when it's splayed. Drink water. Keep a hat—earmuffs aren't the same—in your backpack. And an umbrella—because chills and rain come out of nowhere in Wisconsin. Read labels so you know what you're eating. Move five minutes for every hour of sitting. If you think you need to go to the health clinic, don't think, go.

I forced down the lump rising in my throat. I don't know why I was on this mission, but I was. I cawed:

Purell. Wet socks are bad. Be sure and see some blue and green every day, because scurvy is real.

I knew it was now or never for the final goodbye, so I squared my shoulders and stepped back. I opened my mouth to bestow my practiced pearls of love and wisdom upon my son, and I heard a crackled vocal fry worse than a Kardashian's fill the air.

All the while I was spouting verses that sounded like Mother Goose, the real message was yet to happen. My beautifully rehearsed golden college send-off speech that I was determined to carry out wasn't materializing.

Suddenly, streams. No—rivers. Waterfalls. I lunged for my son and a flood of tears soaked his shirt and would not stop, all while I was back to swinging from his neck like a weighted pendulum. I tried to break through but the moment swallowed me up and I was croaking like a frog.

Never had my voice eluded me more.

"Mom," my son asked, sounding genuinely puzzled. "Why are you crying?"

He asked me so simply, as if words could answer. I squeezed my eyes and hid my face in his neck.

I can't be there anymore to make sure he does everything so I need him to do it. I need him to listen to my manual on how to care for himself because all these things I've thrown at him will keep him safe, sound, healthy, happy.

I pulled on both his shoulders and wanted him to know that I just needed him to do all these things I've sputtered at him like someone who has five minutes to blow up fifty balloons.

I have taken care of him his entire life, and now, I won't be there to do it. He has to be the one to make sure he arrives home every night. Without earbuds in.

Because this beautiful baby boy, the one who is going to do so well, the one we are so proud of, we love him so much.

And if there were a Google translator that he could plug in to make sense of my, "Wash your hands because others don't, and earmuffs are not the same as a hat," it would tell him with 100 percent accuracy, "Your mama loves you so much it leaves her stupid."

After You Drive Away

We asked hundreds of parents how they best dealt with their kids going off to college. The number one response was focusing on how happy their kid was in their new environment. The second most popular way to adapt was to focus on the kids who were still living at home. That was followed by throwing yourself into work and other activities, and taking up a new activity (including a new gym membership, regularly scheduled dinners with friends, and a renewed focus on an existing career or a new one).

Other suggestions from parents included:

- **If your budget and time allow for it, go away for a few days after drop-off.** After the buildup to that pivotal event, it's nice to get accustomed to the new normal before heading back home.
- **Make plans for the next time you will see your college kid.** This may be during their fall break, over a three-day weekend, or not until Thanksgiving, but the certainty of knowing when you'll see them next can give you something to look forward to.
- **Figure out how you will communicate.** We have so many ways to communicate with our kids, but that doesn't mean we will hear from them. Make a plan that works for your family and then try really hard not to abuse it. Some kids love to chat on the phone, others are happier to text, so find what works for yours. Best tactic for coaxing your kid to FaceTime or Skype? Ask them if they would like to say hello to the family dog . . . they will not be able to resist.
- **Be good to yourself.** If you feel like you have just suffered a loss, give into it for a brief while and just let yourself feel sad. One of the common things parents do is tell themselves they have nothing to feel sad about, that what happened is

a good thing. Yes, but . . . you can still leave yourself some time to feel sad if you need it. One mom of four pointed out that it was important to acknowledge the feelings and to talk about them: "Sharing how I felt helped me—being honest that it hurts to let them go and are anxious that they are okay, even while both you and they are enjoying a new freedom." Many parents find the worst of it is shorter than they anticipate.

- **Parenting is not over because your kid has a new address.** You just sent a kid out into the world who has much to learn, and you still have a big role to play as sounding board, most-concerned listener, and adviser to this still-forming adult.
- **Seek out others who feel the same.** As our kids grow older we lose some of the community that surrounded them. We no longer have that crew of other parents that we sat with at their events when they were younger. Find a friend, another parent who can understand what you're going through. A change this big calls for the buddy system.
- **Talk about the future of your relationship with your college kid.** What do they need? How will the two of you stay close? Make clear how much you value family closeness even when you're apart. Get some guidance on how your teen hopes your relationship evolves in this next stage.

Words We Wish We Had Said

We love lists. There has been some research that explains why we take in information and retain it better when someone has already organized it for us. We don't have to do the hard work of extracting the highlights, we just have to take them in. So here are our parting shots. The thirty-five short but utterly essential notions we wanted to share with our kids as they slipped out of our homes. Some of them we said, others we hope went without saying, and still others were delivered in a flurry of texts over freshmen year.

1. You got this. I have had a front-row seat at your life and I know with every fiber of my being that you are ready for this moment.
2. When I cry as I walk away, know those are good tears, the tears we shed when life has given us a gift. You have been a true gift.
3. Seek help when you need it. Academic, psychological, medical. There is no shame in asking for what you need.
4. There is never another time like the first weeks in college, so take advantage of this opportunity.
5. You will be homesick. It would be a sad commentary on the last eighteen years if you weren't. Call us and we will remind you that it will pass.
6. It is okay to call when you are sad. It's just not okay to call only when you are sad.
7. College is hard; add a social life, sports, and activities and it can seem overwhelming. But don't give up what you love. Run, listen to music, watch good movies. It is what keeps you sane.
8. Pregnancy, STDs . . . use condoms. There is a reason they call it protection.
9. Take one small class every semester if you can.
10. I am here, I will always be here.

11. Meet your professor, and if you can't or won't do that, get to know your TA.

12. When something you are learning really excites and interests you, pay attention, you are going to college to find just that.

13. Take at least one computer science class. It is an almost inescapable aspect of modern life.

14. The only way to have good friends is to be a good friend.

15. If your siblings are some of your very best friends, everything about the rest of your life will be better. Don't ignore them just because you moved away.

16. Saving money is a habit. Start now.

17. If you treat your body badly it will return the favor. Eat well, exercise often, worship at the altar of a good night's sleep.

18. Time management is one of the most important skills you learn in college.

19. But the most important thing you will learn is the ability to think critically and deeply. Intellectually, do not skate on the surface for four years. Dig deep.

20. You will never need to be able to fold a fitted sheet. Never.

21. Whatever is happening in front of your face is usually more consequential, more real, and more long-lasting than whatever is happening on your phone. Look up.

22. If something seems like a bad idea sober, but then, after a few drinks seems like a better idea, it was always a bad idea.

24. Unless you are studying culinary arts, stop photographing your food. No one cares.

25. Study something you have never heard of.

25. Know where the closest urgent-care center and emergency room are. When you need this information, it will be

2:00 a.m., your phone will be dead, and the student health center will be closed.

26. Join something. Anything. But, join.

27. You will feel scared and anxious and even defeated at times. Everybody does. How you deal with these feelings is all that matters.

28. You are at that unique moment in life where you can stretch your arms in one direction and already feel your adult life and stretch them in another and still feel your childhood. Enjoy this moment, it comes but once.

29. Over-the-counter medications are still medicine, so read the label. Or call me.

30. Do your laundry while you still have two pairs of clean underwear. Don't back yourself into a corner.

31. Have $10 you can always lay your hands on. Credit cards get denied.

32. Remember how high school seemed to go on forever? College is not like that.

33. Manners matter and they always will.

34. Your grandparents have adored you and your siblings since you took your first breath. Pick up the phone and call them. Give them glimpses into your college life.

35. Your dog saw you through your childhood and will be there as we pack up the car to drive you to college. Hug him tight before you go.

For all the years we have had children at home, we have mastered back to school shopping like pros. Crayons, rounded scissors, multicolored folders, laptops, check, check, check, check. Outfitting a teen for college and arranging the logistics of packing and moving into the dorm are the grand finale of school shopping (but hardly the last of helping your teen move in or out). In many ways, this business is the perfect distraction we need—for it is far easier to focus on endless checklists than the seismic change in our families. We hope that these more practical tasks of getting ready will help you and your teen connect, and that this type of tangible preparation for their departure will spill over to preparedness on the emotional side as well—or will at least serve as an easy distraction!

CHAPTER NINE

College Life

> Constant communication is probably the easiest way to push your child away. When you give us some space, it makes the calls we do have that much more meaningful for both of us. I find myself more excited to fill you in on the big things I'm doing, tell you funny stories about my friends, or complain about my mean professor. This year my parents let me decide when to call. That way I can set aside time to devote myself to the conversation instead of trying to squeeze it in between classes or when I'm exhausted after a long day. It works for both of us and I find myself dialing home every two to three days, much more often than I did last year.
>
> **—KALEIGH, COLLEGE SOPHOMORE**

We spent so much time focused on college admission and our kids' transition to college that we failed to focus on the most important thing: their time *in* college. While move-in was an emotional whirlwind (for parents and kids), the truth is that the early days of college can be both an exciting and scary time for teens. And, let's be totally honest here, many times it is also a period of sadness or letdown.

As we mentioned, one of the largest and longest running surveys of freshmen, conducted by UCLA, found that over 70 percent of all first-year college students find themselves feeling homesick or lonely. For many this is an unpleasant surprise. They have worked so hard to get into college, they have said their goodbyes, and they *know* from social media that all of their high school friends are having the time of their lives. One of Lisa's sons, who ended up loving his college experience, described his time there as, "the best three and a half years of your life." Going to a new school away from parents and siblings and everyone your kid has ever known or loved is not the easiest or most joyful moment, and it is something both parents and kids are loath to admit.

The college experience can be impacted by expectations adults set for their teens. When we share our own rose-tinted college recollections—when we insist that the next four years will be some kind of idealized existence—we do our kids a great disservice. And then the reality of college life can differ so radically from the fantasy version our teens start imagining the day they receive their acceptance letters.

We asked a clinical psychologist, Dr. Sharon Jacques, to suggest some ways that rising freshmen can better understand this disconnect. Jacques identifies six common college myths and then proceeds to debunk each one in turn. Talking about these fables with your freshman before they ever hit campus, she suggested, can go a long way toward reducing their power.

THE MYTHS

1. **Everyone is thrilled to be starting college.**

    Sure, there usually *is* excitement, but just as intense and common are feelings of nervousness, anxiety, or sadness. Maybe you're well aware of such feelings, or maybe you're just noticing physical signs of those feelings, such as unease, a racing heart, nausea, dizziness, trouble sleeping, or headaches.

These are possible signs of distress and anxiety, but they are quite typical when facing a big life change. You may feel ashamed having such feelings or worries. Actually, most kids heading off to college don't share these reactions with each other since it's hard to admit even to oneself, let alone to someone else. But sharing these concerns with someone you trust is often a huge relief, even if it doesn't change the reality.

Other things that help include reminding yourself of all the ways you've coped well with past challenges, new situations and stressors, and hopefully what you gained or how you grew as a result. With all the worry you are feeling now, you may fail to notice the ways that you are resilient, so take stock. Notice what helps you feel stronger under stress and keep these in mind to use now and throughout college.

2. **Everyone parties at college, so that's what I should be doing too, or I'll feel like an outcast.**

Sometimes, in a flurry of activity to distract themselves from feeling nervous, homesick, or sad, kids throw themselves into activities that aren't so adaptive—like partying too much. At many colleges, it's the freshmen who tend to do this much more than the older students, and being homesick is one reason why. The other reason is that it can feel liberating (at first) to do what you want without concern about parents supervising you or restricting your drinking and late-night hours. Just know that many freshmen have no real desire to party a lot and are hoping to meet other kids like them.

To help make that happen, go to activities on

weekends that don't revolve around drinking. When you're at a party, look for the kids who are consuming moderately or not at all; they do exist. Something as simple as your choice of which party to attend can govern how much you'll feel like you fit in.

3. Everyone adjusts easily to college.

Again, what you see on the surface is not always the true picture. Most freshmen struggle with the adjustment to campus life but are not eager to talk about it. The more outgoing you are by nature, of course, the less stressed you may feel when faced with the prospect of having to make new friends, manage unknown roommates, and navigate a new and bigger setting. But even extroverts are discomfited by leaving old friends and familiar turf behind. So with every new person you meet, keep in mind that they are feeling some degree of this too. This dovetails into the next, related myth . . .

4. Friends abound almost immediately on campus.

This is absolutely false. Many kids take a full year or two to find good friends. You may make acquaintances early on that you meet up with here and there, but we all know the difference between simply passing time in the company of others and feeling like you've found a true friend.

Connecting with people on a deeper level is by its very nature special, so it cannot happen easily. Even if you're the outgoing type, prepare for it to take some time to find that close circle of friends.

If you're an introvert, remind yourself that your capacity for close friendship is equally strong, but that you may have to push yourself to get out of your room. (Organized activities provide a great "excuse" to socialize.)

5. Most kids don't get homesick.

How homesick you feel in the beginning is no indication of how much you'll end up liking college or how many friendships you'll form. Homesickness is normal. Expect it especially at vulnerable moments: when you're drifting off to sleep at night, walking to class in the morning, or during downtime. That's why so many kids throw themselves into activities: to divert their attention from feelings of homesickness or anxiety. Activities also constitute a good coping tool. They let you make connections with other people and find your niche that much sooner. Rather than frequently calling home, also try confiding in someone at college; this, too, helps you form bonds where you are.

6. If I don't pick a major ASAP, my future career is in jeopardy.

Unless you're going to a specialty school (engineering or the arts, for example), it's a fact that college students often have no clue which career path or major they're going to end up with—and many change midstream. So relax; you got into college and have nothing more to prove on that front. But do seek out a college adviser early on and lay out your situation. Ask them to help you keep an eye on the bigger academic picture—and key decision points along the way.

Even when you've busted these six myths, college adjustment may not be easy. Every college has a counseling center, so reach out if your moods, anxiety, sadness, or actions worry you. Tell your parents, ideally, or your health provider. The objective is to let an adult help sooner rather than later.

> *Be true to yourself and utilize everything around you. The campus is chock-full of resources so it's good to familiarize yourself with them early in the year. And if all else fails, Mom knows best. I never hesitated to call my mom if I was stuck on something. Our parents know way more than you give them credit for, so don't be afraid to ask for help. I think it secretly makes them happy anyway.*
>
> —MAC, 21

THE LATE-NIGHT CALLS
YOUR FRESHMAN WILL MAKE

When college is not the experience teens hope for, parents are often the first to hear. If your new college student is calling you to complain, don't despair. First, it's normal for them to "dump their emotional trash" on you, in the words of psychologist Lisa Damour. By expressing their challenges to you—the safest person at a distance from their daily life—they may be seeking nothing more than a sympathetic ear. Second, it's a good sign that they are focused on any issues they might have (as opposed to ignoring their problems) and feel close enough to you to confess that all is not perfect. Finally, sometimes your teen is simply looking for confirmation that their problem is not unusual—and that practical solutions to it can be discussed together and later implemented by them.

Dr. Roger Martin is a retired college president, former Harvard dean, and father who has many years of experience with college students. He offers us some suggestions on how to handle the classic late-night calls that parents can expect from their college freshmen.

"Mom and Dad, I can't stand my roommate."

Nearly half of all roommate situations are problematic, according to UCLA's Higher Education Research Institute. But a big part of growing up is learning how to live with someone they might not initially get along with. This is a skill they will use the rest of their lives.

That said, certain roommate situations are unbearable. When this happens, says Sheri Hineman, assistant director of financial aid at Morningside College in Sioux City, Iowa, your student—not you—should contact someone in Student Affairs for help in resolving the problem. (To which "there's almost always a solution," notes Hineman.) If things are not resolved at this level, have your child appeal to the next rung up in the chain of command—perhaps the dean of students. Parents should intervene only when the situation is very serious (a roommate dealing drugs, for instance) and it is not being properly addressed by those in charge.

"Coach isn't playing me."

Almost every athlete sits on the bench in the beginning, so first-year students shouldn't expect to be starters. However, if for no apparent reason they're always sitting on the bench, even during practice, Andy Jennings, men's soccer coach at Vassar College, advises freshmen to first talk to the team captain and then to the coach. Of course, the coach must be able to determine who is to play, but having these conversations could provide some insight into their decision making. Parents can also discuss other athletic options with their student, as many find intramural and club teams very rewarding.

"There's nothing to do on campus. Can I come home for the weekend?"

It is not healthy when your child comes home every weekend. The usual excuse given is that there is nothing to do on campus. Shari Benson, assistant director of residence life at Morningside College, suggests that there is typically plenty of activity on campus and that, if first-year students are always going home, they will never establish friendships.

"I'm running out of money."

First-year students never seem to have enough money and sometimes for good reason. Colleges and universities are expensive, and many parents are doing everything they can just to pay for tuition, room, and board, let alone providing extra funds for things like concert tickets or Frappuccinos. So what about encouraging your child to take on a campus job to pay for these extras—or even help out with tuition?

Natalie Story, the associate director of financial aid at Washington College in Chestertown, Maryland, points out that not only do first-year students who work tend to complete their college education, but studies show that students who work twenty hours or less per week fare better academically than students who don't work at all. Having a college job on their résumé will also help them get a job after graduation.

"I can't get my assignments done on time."

There are several possible causes of this problem. One is faulty time management, perhaps the single biggest challenge that first-year students face. Freshmen who are struggling to complete their assignments on time should consider visiting the campus writing or academic center, suggests Nicole Anderson, assistant director of Career Services at Tufts University. There are people who can help your student with useful ideas for better managing their time and responsibilities.

Days Like No Others

Dr. Nicholas A. Christakis, a physician, sociologist, and professor who directs the Human Nature Lab at Yale, argues that freshman year is "critical," but not for the reasons most parents think. He explains that students have plenty of time to figure out their major and get situated academically, but that the beginning of freshman year is a time like no other. He describes it as a "window of opportunity."

While later in the year it will seem odd or at least awkward to just walk up to a classmate and begin a conversation, in those first heady weeks, it is perfectly normal. Christakis explains that "social inhibitions tend to dissolve when a group of strangers enters a new environment. Think of adults on a cruise, teenagers at a summer camp, or Chaucer's garrulous pilgrims, chatting and revealing volumes about themselves. The bond is all the more guaranteed when facing a shared hardship—say, the boredom of freshman orientation sessions or the stress of placement exams. But after that critical opportunity, a curtain begins to fall on the welcoming social scene. In my experience, which includes serving as the head of a residential college at both Yale and Harvard, this tends to occur about three weeks in. Attitudes begin to solidify. Friendships become fixed. And behaviors that initially seemed open and generous might come to feel forced, or even a little creepy."

This does not mean that students don't make their most important and meaningful connections with others after the start of freshman year, but it does mean that in those first whirl-wind weeks all social conventions are temporarily suspended, and meeting classmates is easier than ever.

FOUR-YEAR COLLEGE IS NOT THE ONLY OPTION

There is much written about the challenges of getting into and graduating from a four-year college. Facebook feeds are full of giddy and proud parents declaring where their kids will be matriculating. It is the happy culmination of years of study, work, and dedication, and it is a well-deserved accolade. But, Melissa Fenton explains that for many teens, it's simply not an option.

For a multitude of reasons and familial situations, many students will not be decorating a new dorm room in the fall; instead, they will be headed to study at a local community college. And yet, we don't boast and brag that our kids are headed to a community college. Why? Or better yet, why not? There is absolutely zero shame in your student staying home and attending community college.

Don't believe me? What do you think these successful people all have in common? Author Amy Tan, director George Lucas, NASA astronaut Eileen Collins, first Hispanic female congresswoman Ileana Ros-Lehtinen, PBS News Hour host Jim Lehrer, Costco CEO James Sinegal, and Pulitzer Prize–winner Oscar Hijuelos. They all went to community college.

If you haven't been on the campus of a community college lately, you may hold a skewed view of its environment.

Today's community college campuses have grown and developed significantly from what they once were. So what can a community college offer your student and why is it a good choice for so many now?

Lower costs: Earning your AA degree at a community college and then transferring to a four-year university can save tens of thousands of dollars. Students attending community college borrow far less than those at four-year institutions. And when/if you do decide to transfer, you have the potential to earn merit-based scholarships if you've received excellent grades during your first two years.

Speaking of scholarships: People are often unaware that community colleges offer merit-based academic scholarships. Those with higher grades and college entrance exam test scores stand a good chance of being awarded some type of financial (non-loan based) help.

Four-year degrees: It is common now for many community colleges to offer some type of four-year degree or transitional program where you can earn your four-year degree at the community college, but within the larger state university system.

Vocational, technical, certified professional programs: Not only is a community college an attractive option, it's often the only one for training and licensing in a long list of technical professions, among them emergency medical technician, firefighter, police officer, certified nursing assistant, software manager, physical therapist, cosmetologist, esthetician, child-care worker, and an abundance of jobs in horticulture, welding, plumbing, electrical trades, carpentry, and automotive technologies. These are professions that remain in high demand. They boast living wages. And the training can often be completed in the span of two years.

Athletics: Play a sport competitively but not well enough for Division I, II, or III schools? For many athletes, playing first at the community-college level may be their ticket to playing at the larger NCAA level.

Small classes, more attention: The average first-year biology class at a university can be sizable, with many hundreds of students in a single classroom. At the community-college level, class size is considerably smaller. This means more attention, instructors who are actually accessible and know your name, and more opportunities for tutoring and one-on-one academic help. As many community college students are working professionals, there is always an abundance of online classes offered, so you can keep working full- or part-time while earning your degree.

Diverse students: While most large universities claim to be diverse, when looking at the student body, the majority of students will still be between the ages of eighteen and twenty-four, and have little life experience. The average community college classroom will have students of all ages, backgrounds, demographics, and with a variety of life experiences.

Midlife career changers with twenty years of work experience will be sitting next to eighteen-year-olds fresh out of high school. This creates plenty of peer-to-peer learning experiences, and beneficial exposure of young people to older people who have been out in the "real world" and know the importance of education.

Community: Community college campuses are just as alive and thriving as larger four-year institutions, and have a variety of student special interest groups and clubs, multicultural-student organizations, student government, intramural athletic programs, work-study programs, and career centers and job placement assistance.

Networking: Staying local gives you access to local working professionals, many of whom are your instructors and even classmates. Career contacts and networking opportunities for a job in the local area may therefore be right under your nose upon graduation.

ADVICE FROM PEERS CAN BE BEST

Advising our kids on college life, or even just answering their questions when called upon, can be a painful reminder of how out of date we really are. Some of the best advice on college life comes not from us, but from recent grads. So we asked for advice from those who've recently "been there, studied that." They offered us the wisdom they wished someone had shared with them when they were still in college.

FRESHMEN. Put yourself out there at the beginning of your first year and meet as many classmates as you can. It's a unique time where everyone's in the same boat—no one knows anybody else, yet everyone wants to make friends. It can be a challenging transition from a high school where you knew practically everyone to a college where you know practically no one, so we won't sugarcoat it: the early days can be tough. If you're feeling lonely or homesick, know that you are not alone. You plan for college for years, yet it's still a huge adjustment when you arrive. All of the freshmen around you are making the same adjustment—even if they don't show it.

Ignore the social media accounts of your high school friends; no matter what they post publicly, they're feeling just as lost as you are.

Find a group to join early. Even if it doesn't last, even if it isn't something you are passionate about, join a club or a team because it will give you an activity, and foster friendships, right from the beginning. The earlier you meet people and find a place to belong, the sooner you will start enjoying school. And even if you think you hate your school and want to transfer, give it your all until at least winter break—things get better once you're settled and have found a good crew of friends.

Don't be shy about getting academic help (especially if you've never needed it before). Many schools make academic support easily available, so take advantage of it. And don't try to go it alone: group work, study sessions, and other academic collaborations are the norm in college—a big change from high school. Not only is it expected that you will work together academically, it's a great way to meet new people. Find a study group early in the year, before the midterm rush. (To stave off the "freshman fifteen," a workout buddy is not a bad idea either.)

When in doubt, go out. Sometimes you just need to push yourself to join that singing club or jump into the Ultimate Frisbee game. At home, your mom might have nagged you; hear her voice now, and follow that advice.

SOPHOMORES. As a first-year, you made a core group of friends—and that's awesome. Now it's time to broaden your horizons.

Push yourself outside your nucleus and stay open to meeting new people. You'll always stay close to some of your original friends, but you'll also be glad you met a wider circle of people—especially in the event you wind up in a new city or country one day. And you never know when someone on the periphery of your circle will become your new best friend!

Now that the newness has worn off, find a constant. You'll continue to encounter an extraordinary amount of change as you transition to this second year, so find something to hold on to— something you can carry with you throughout college as you adapt to new living situations, schedules, groups of friends, and academic expectations. Your constant might be an activity you've done your whole life, a new hobby, a book series you reread for comfort at bedtime, a new or old TV show, a once-a-week splurge at the local coffee shop, or something else altogether.

Regardless of what your constant is, practice making it as routine as brushing your teeth. Exercise, for example, is a good constant because it's a different kind of hard work—something that will not be graded or judged by teachers or peers but allows you to set and attain goals for yourself (plus, it's healthy and it feels good).

In the end, finding a constant is a gift that keeps on giving; even after you graduate—or whenever you encounter intimidating transitions as you move forward in your career—you'll have it in your back pocket to keep you grounded.

JUNIORS AND SENIORS. As upperclassmen, you may have decided that you are comfortable with the friends you've made and the activities you've become involved in. You've got your constant to fall back on and you've settled into an easy rhythm. You may be tempted to coast, but these final years of college should continue to be years of stretching and growth, so continue to reach out to new people and continue to engage in new opportunities with your remaining time.

Hit the job or internship market hard to engineer a relatively stress-free year. If you can manage to have a real job lined up by the time second semester senior year rolls around, you can actually—finally—just enjoy these last months on campus. Set up a LinkedIn account and work your networks. Don't be afraid to use whatever connections you have; relationships are critical to success in the real world. And, of course, take full advantage of any career-counseling services your school offers.

Don't worry too much if that first job you land is not perfection incarnate, though; a few years on you will probably have left it for something more interesting or promising. Also, don't become paralyzed with indecision; while taking a certain job may involve closing some options, it will open others.

Get a credit card in your name, then use it sparingly and pay off the balance promptly each month; the resulting good credit rating will come in handy when it's time to buy a car or rent an apartment. Prospective employers are increasingly checking credit scores as a way to assess your level of responsibility.

If you are thinking about graduate school, now is the time to decide which standardized test to take—and start preparing for it while your brain is still set to study mode. Find a friend to study with, and keep each other accountable. Even if you're working on a senior thesis, you'll have more time now than you will once you're working full-time. And most test scores can be banked for a number of years, allowing you to take your time deciding whether to continue your education.

With the time left at school, take a class that interests you but has no relationship to your career aspirations. Better yet, take a class that terrifies you: if you're a math major, take an art history class (and vice versa). Take whatever class has always intrigued you, even if it means getting yourself out of bed at the crack of dawn.

Seek out professors you've never met and ask about their research over coffee. This may be one of the last times for a while that you have the luxury of learning about something completely outside your comfort zone. By senior year make sure you have forged a close enough relationship with a faculty member that even when you are a couple of years out of college they still know who you are and would be happy to write you a work or graduate school recommendation. You need to get to know this person well enough that you will be comfortable emailing after graduation.

While all of college is not about preparing for the years afterward, by senior year it is useful to think about what you will want to have done in college come graduation. Are there shows or speakers you will want to have seen, research you would have loved to have done, or just long quiet walks in a part of campus you never visit? Senior year goes quickly, faster than the other three, so make sure when you don your cap and gown you have checked off as much of your college bucket list as possible.

Visiting Campus

The first time parents visit their new college student it can be awkward and uncomfortable. If there is one subject about which there is parental consensus, it is that kids will not want to spend as much time with their parents as their parents might hope when we visit. It might be family weekend or just an impromptu visit for some sorely missed family time. And while on the phone they seemed enthusiastic, once we arrive on campus, their excitement sometimes dims. College kids have friends, sports, activities, and academics to squeeze in during our visits. They will be nice about it, but at the first sign of a good party or an a cappella practice, parents will be dumped—and we know in truth that this is entirely as it should be. Here are a few things this experience has taught us:

DO show up bearing gifts. Nothing makes a parent more endearing than showing up with local treats, homemade goodies, or fun and foolish items that can be shared with roommates or new friends up and down the hall.

DON'T visit the actual dorm room or risk being overcome with the urge to straighten, clean, and restore the surroundings to their move-in-day condition. If you do foolishly visit the dorm room, stay away from the bathroom. Just a word to the wise.

DO use this face-to-face visit as a chance to tell your almost adult child how proud you are of the journey she has taken and the initiative she has shown. No child tires of hearing of their parent's pride. This may also be a good chance to say some of the heartfelt things that were swept away on a sea of tears at drop-off a few months earlier.

DON'T assume that everything is going perfectly well. College life is complex, and as one of our kids put it, "a time of high highs and low lows." It is all too common for college students to be swayed by the overpowering influence of social media into believing everyone else is managing their life better.

DO make hotel and restaurant reservations early. Small college towns have limited offerings, so plan accordingly.

DO invite roommates and friends to join you for a meal, even if it is just a slice of pizza. Nothing will give you a better window into your teen's new life than their new friends.

DON'T be surprised if your freshman wants to stay with you in the hotel. They are just getting used to the crowds, noise, and chaos of their dorms (which may include a roommate's siblings on visiting weekends), making those clean towels and rollaway bed in your hotel look mighty nice by comparison.

DO listen, without interruptions, to the challenges of academic life and the pressure of social life in college. This concentrated time, without the many distractions of home, is a chance to hear how your college student is really faring.

DON'T offer platitudes and say that it will all be fine and everyone goes through this process of adjustment.

DO offer constructive advice, compassion, and parental support. We are not here to help our kids solve their problems but rather to help them figure out their own solutions.

DON'T show up without a plan for spending time on campus. Your teen may think you will just "hang out." You do not want to hang out in that dorm room.

DO plan something your family loves to do together, that reminds everyone of your shared interests and attachment. It can be movies, museums, special food, religious services, or sporting or cultural events.

DON'T draw out the visit. It is always best to leave our kids before they tire of us and have them wanting us to return.

DO leave a little something when you go. A simple token like a note, a gift card to treat the roommates to a taco or frozen yogurt, or a new pair of gloves will remind your child that he is loved long after you are on the interstate heading back home.

DO plan to attend an on-campus event, show, or game as it will give you a better sense of college life.

DON'T let your college student act like they are still in middle school and embarrassed that they have parents. If they want to be treated like a grown-up, now would be a good time to start acting like one.

DO remember that this departure will sting a bit, too, as you drive away. This is not the big, bad punch in the gut that drop-off might have been. But walking away from those we love is never easy.

DON'T use this as an opportunity to nag about not calling or spending too much money; there is time for that later, and it may be better addressed on a phone call.

DO take selfies, okay, maybe just photos. Although it might make you feel like a tourist, these will give you many happy moments starting from the day after your visit.

DON'T let your kid make faces about the photos. Remind them that you put a ton of effort and an inconceivable amount of money into getting them to this moment and that all you are asking for is a nice photo in return.

We are not going to sugarcoat this. There may be a moment during the visit when you ask yourself, was this visit really worth it? Maybe your kid had not one activity planned for parents' weekend and seemed to stare at his phone the entire time. Or maybe he couldn't wait to dash out of the restaurant (that you spent hours making sure was the perfect spot for your first family dinner in months) to attend a dance concert. Maybe he said hello to a dozen different people you passed on that walk across campus, yet he introduced you to none of them. Meanwhile, you spent a fortune getting here, you're breaking the bank to cover tuition, and there were no gushing expressions of gratitude that you took the time to visit.

All very true. But then maybe when it came time to say good-bye, when that familiar lump appeared in your throat and it felt for a minute like drop-off all over again, there was that moment when he hugged you a bit tighter and held on a minute longer as you said goodbye—and that gesture says more than words ever can.

WHO THRIVES IN COLLEGE?

While there is a great deal of value in anecdotal advice on how to thrive in college, we took a look at what the research shows about the behaviors and practices that cause students to one day line up in their caps and gowns. And as it turns out, students are likelier to have a successful sojourn on campus when they involve themselves in the life of the college—academically, socially, athletically, or in any other constructive manner.

ENGAGEMENT. "Students who choose at least one small course each semester have, on the average, a significantly better overall experience than those who do not," writes Harvard professor Richard J. Light in *Strengthening Colleges and Universities: The Harvard Assessment Seminars*. Light found that students who took one small class, defined as fewer than sixteen students, had a higher level of engagement, worked harder, and thus were less likely to drop out of school. "[They] are noticeably more engaged, by their own rating, than students who take only larger classes," he explained. "Either small classes demand more time or students choose to invest more."

BELONGING. Not all students get offered or can afford on-campus housing their first year, yet multiple studies show that living in freshman housing increases social engagement and sense of belonging. Students living on campus are more likely to join study groups and get involved in extracurricular activities, both signposts toward success.

A meta-analysis of college-success studies found that students who thrived felt they belonged at their institution; they fit in well and were socially integrated. Eighty-five percent of these studies likewise turned up evidence that a sense of belonging has a positive impact on a student's grade point average.

COLLABORATION. In high school, the emphasis is on individual work—inadequate training for the premium that colleges place on academic cooperation. The students who flourish in a university setting are those who actively seek out study groups that let them connect with their peers over academic content. Indeed, this group not only performs better but feels better: "[S]tudents who work in small study groups outside of class commit more time to their coursework, feel more challenged by their work, and express a much higher level of personal interest in it," observes Light. "They are also much less likely to hesitate to seek help. The critical point is that the relationships are not merely social. They are organized to accomplish some work—a substantive exploration that students describe as 'stretching' themselves. And almost without exception, students who feel they have not yet found themselves, or fully hit their stride, report that they have not developed such relationships."

CONNECTIVITY. Forging a bond with a faculty member or a mentor such as a teaching assistant, a coach, or an academic adviser pays off long after graduation. A 2014 Gallup-Purdue University study of college graduates found that for students who recalled having a professor "who cared about them as a person, made them excited about learning, and encouraged them to pursue their dreams, their odds of being engaged at work more than doubled."

This mentor relationship did not necessarily need to be focused on the formal curriculum but could be formed around a research project, a committee, or even just in conversation. But that relationship has been shown to improve college experience with lasting benefits.

Yet this relationship is not always simple to establish. As parents, we found that our students often had to be encouraged, okay, nagged, to approach their instructors. In high school, they did not hold back from speaking to teachers who seemed accessible and interested, yet in college this seemed far more intimidating. "As a professor, I really enjoy engaging with students in a one-on-one fashion after class or in office hours," says Ben Y. Zhao, professor of computer science at UC Santa Barbara. "Yet I often find that many students come in with a preconceived notion that professors want to have nothing to do with them. Some see faculty as 'too busy to bother,' while others see faculty as aloof or antisocial. They're afraid to come in to office hours, and often hold back questions in class for fear of being rebuked or ignored.

There are numerous opportunities available at a university that do not present themselves in an obvious way," Zhao continues, "but require some initiative from the student. Whether it's after-class discussions with faculty on a topic related to class, undergraduate research positions, or other part-time jobs, students should be more proactive in asking for what they want."

MOTIVATION. The students who fare best on campus are inspired by a genuine desire to learn. Crucially, they believe their intelligence is not fixed, but rather within their power to expand. In his book *What the Best College Students Do*, Ken Bain, president of the Best Teachers Institute and a former history professor at Vanderbilt

University, said the best students "also learned that nothing is easy. Growth requires hard work. To learn is to strip away those deeply ingrained habits of the mind. To do so requires that we push ourselves, that we keep building and rebuilding, questioning, struggling, and seeking. . . . All had learned the power of intrinsic motivation over working for rewards like grades and honors. 'Grades never mattered,' they told us. Everything stemmed from an internal desire to learn, to create, and to grow."

SUPPORT. Two final markers for academic success are, not surprisingly, friends and family. Both can continue to exert a positive influence on a student and improve her college experience long after she leaves home.

Social interaction with peers is so critical that one study revealed that "institutions with higher levels of student social interaction also have higher levels of student educational aspirations." And finally, even as our kids move on with their lives, it appears that our influence remains highly relevant. College can be a daunting and far more challenging experience than high school. Research shows that undergrads, from freshmen to seniors, get a boost from reminders that our confidence in them is undimmed and our support unreserved.

WHAT LEADS TO A CAP AND GOWN

As our kids start college, it is hard to think about it not all going to plan. They were admitted because they were qualified, and in our excitement we give barely a thought to what could go wrong. But graduating college takes planning, and graduating on time takes careful planning. We took a look at why students fail to graduate in four years and then sat down with Dr. Randy Diehl, dean of the College of Liberal Arts at the University of Texas at Austin, to find out how parents can help their students achieve this goal.

Let's start with the problem:

- At non-flagship public universities, only 19 percent of full-time students graduate in four years.
- At flagship or research universities, only 36 percent of full-time students graduate in four years.
- Each additional year of college costs $22,826 for tuition (in state), room, board, and fees, plus an additional $45,327 in lost wages bringing the total to $68,153.
- Only 50 out of 580 public four-year colleges and universities report that the majority of full-time students graduate in four years.

Failing in college can stunt a student's academic and professional progress at the inception of their young adult lives and create substantial financial and emotional obstacles. For students who struggle, their challenges are both intensely personal and also contribute to a national social problem.

Student debt now totals $1.5 trillion, a gigantic sum, inflated by the extra year or two of classes added by so many students. It is no wonder that state governments and college administrators have targeted low graduation rates as a grave risk to the education and well-being of their populations. Retired chancellor of the University of Texas System, William H. McRaven, could not have been more emphatic:

> To me, the smartest, most effective thing we can do to reduce our students' debt burden is to increase our four-year graduation rates. Common sense tells us that earning a

degree in five years is going to cost you roughly 25 percent more than earning it in four. Imagine the uproar if any UT System school increased tuition by 25 percent! But the effect is the same.

So, why do kids take longer to graduate? And how can parents help? We'll answer these important questions in the following two sections, starting with common reasons why it may take longer than four years to graduate.

LACK OF PLANNING. Have you looked at a college course catalog recently? It is easy to get lost as you toggle between hundreds of individual courses in dozens of subjects. With the absence of a game plan for a major or lack of strategy for completing core course requirements, it is a common pitfall to sign up for superfluous classes that won't count toward the required coursework for a degree. In fact, the average graduate earns up to 134 credits when only 120 are required.

LACK OF ADVISING. Meeting with a college adviser before registration can be a safety net for students to help them fully understand the implications of their choices. The learning curve for course selection is a steep one and freshmen can easily get thrown off from the beginning and not end up meeting their requirements in time.

BOTTLENECK OF KEY COURSES. At some colleges, certain degrees are so popular that the number of seats in the gateway course(s) for the majors do not match the demand. Students who are unable to secure space in the classroom cannot create an optimal schedule to accumulate the required major courses in four years.

PART-TIME OR REDUCED LOAD. To graduate in four years, students need to take fifteen hours each semester for eight semesters, adding up to the 120 hours that result in a diploma. Some students have work or family responsibilities that make it impossible to attend school full-time, almost guaranteeing that they will need to tack on extra semesters to get their diploma.

TRANSFERRING SCHOOLS AND LOSING CREDITS. Unfortunately, even after long months of work leading up to a college admission decision, a student may decide they need to transfer to a different school. Schools have their own policies about accepting transfer credits and some may not be accepted when a student moves from one college to another.

REMEDIAL, NONCREDIT COURSES. Some students are not ready to tackle the academic demands of college coursework and may be placed into remedial classes that offer no course credit.

To learn more about what was succeeding at UT and other public universities, Diehl shared some important lessons for parents of high school and college students on how to focus on graduating in four years.

Q: What are the most strategic things that students should do to graduate in four years?

A:

1. Top of the list is to meet regularly with an academic adviser and to develop a plan. There is nothing wrong with changing your mind or in coming to college undecided. But there should be a plan about how you move toward choosing a

major and it involves discovering what your interests are and what courses are appropriate to take to explore those interests. At many institutions, there are peer mentors who are juniors and seniors and who can provide some good guidance in an informal way that the student may find less intimidating than meeting with a professor.

2. It starts in high school when students are able to choose advanced placement or international baccalaureate classes. These can make a huge difference because students can come in with quite a lot of college credit and it gives them a bit more flexibility in choosing a major. It is a great way to get ahead of the game and helps prepare students to choose a major because you are already being exposed to college-type courses.

3. If you pick a major second year, take core courses during freshman year to keep on track so that when you choose a major you have already covered the basic requirements.

4. Every college has a career services center, which is a very important office, but most students don't take advantage of it. By visiting and getting to know the staff you begin to know what kind of skills they can help you with. Visit there early and often!

Q: When families are looking at colleges with their high school juniors, are there services or programs that they should seek out that could help their student graduate on time? Conversely, what are some red flags?

A: It is important that students have a reasonably realistic understanding of what is expected to succeed at any given college or university. If students can visit colleges, it would be good to try to visit the office of admissions and talk to one of the staff people. Most colleges and universities do not post their four-year graduation rates on their websites if they have relatively low numbers to report. But the office of admissions will have that information. You want to know how committed an institution is to student success. And of course, student success is not just the four-year graduation rate. A lot of things go into it. You want to look at various indicators such as the number of credit hours students are taking each semester. If they are not high, it suggests there are a lot of part-time students and that is not a healthy indicator.

Q: Are there ways that parents can and should get involved to help their college student stay on track?

A: It is excellent for parents to be interested in their kids' higher education and to project that interest. If they care about the college experience for their kids, the kids are more likely to care too. I don't advocate extreme behavior of parents doing what the students should be doing for themselves, because an important part of the college education is growing up and taking responsibility. But parents can be there when it is time to visit colleges and give advice about visiting the career services center. And parents can recommend that kids take an extra AP course in high school and set the tone. When parents are supportive of their student's career and college aspirations, it is a positive and powerful thing.

Q: Do students have time to take internships and/or study abroad and still graduate in four years?

A: Yes! We did studies of graduation rates for both UT and nationally and the data are consistent in showing that students are more likely to graduate in four years if they study abroad, take internships, and/or get involved in undergraduate research. There is no doubt that there is a correlation with these activities and stronger students. In addition to having higher four-year graduation rates, their GPAs were higher and individual students did better after study abroad than before. The idea is that the more a student feels that she belongs to group and to the college, the better she will do academically. Social and academic integration are powerful predictors of success.

MOVING ON TO OUR NEWEST AND LONGEST RELATIONSHIP

The college years mark the beginning of the longest stage of our relationship with our kids, that of two adults. We move from the starting block, a teen who is often champing at the bit to get out of our homes and start their college life, to the road we will travel for decades. Every day we talk to parents who have made this journey and experts who have studied it, and a few key themes emerge.

Your teen has undergone a major life experience just by starting college, so prepare yourself from the very beginning for some possibly uncomfortable (or merely subtle) ways in which your relationship has shifted. There may be ink, piercings, or new political or other views. Tom Dingman, the long-serving former dean of freshmen at Harvard College, assures parents that this is all good and healthy, and part of our college student's "trying out of different postures, different viewpoints and that is part of developing your individuality and figuring out who you are apart from your family." He reminds parents that our teens "need our support and to know that we still believe in them."

Each year you will be less and less involved with the mechanics of their lives, but that is not the same thing as being less involved in their lives. At first the changes seem small, almost indiscernible, but by senior year it will become clear how far you both have traveled. Freshman year our kids texted us their symptoms of any illness and sent a picture of every medication they wondered if they should take. Four years later we simply heard they had been sick and how they took care of themselves. In their first year away we spent time urging them to get involved on their campuses; in the last year we just heard stories of that involvement.

Our eighteen-year-olds were monosyllabic at times and often had to be coaxed to fill us in on the details their freshman life. Our twenty-two-year-olds want to talk about every detail of their job search and ask us to proofread their résumés. Our eighteen-year-olds scoffed at dorm shopping, dismissing our concerns that they start college life with the right provisions as simply moms worrying too much. Our twenty-two-year-olds want us to come furniture shopping with them (and not just because our credit cards have higher limits).

Our eighteen-year-olds came home from school, dumped their laundry on the floor, and flew out the door with their high school friends. Our twenty-two-year-olds follow us into the kitchen and help make dinner. Our eighteen-year-olds wanted to be treated as adults, they insisted upon it, even as they acted like children. Our twenty-two-year-olds call us up and use words like "IRA," "tax filing date," "jury duty," and "voting."

On reflection, it surprises us to see that in so many instances their journey toward adulthood only improved their relationship with us. It turns out we had little to fear in the journey our families would travel. Our kids, and yours, are members of a generation that likes their parents, wants to spend time with them, and sees that relationship as a source of ongoing support and joy in their lives.

While over these years it is important that our kids establish their independence, and become the adults they choose to be, that is in no way at odds with the family closeness we all cherish. It took us living through these years to understand that, and we hope these pages have made this clear to you too.

Things That Surprised Us the Most

We don't know about you, but in winding our way through this parenting journey we have swung wildly between feelings that we had no idea what we were doing and were virtually flying blind, and that fist-pumping sensation that can only be described as "I got this." Sometimes we experienced both of these things on the same day. But as our kids cross the two-decade mark, it seems a good time to look back with a little more reflection on what surprised us the most.

These are the things we could not have imagined when we first launched our parenting journeys:

Our job is not done; it has just changed.

Our kids are physically separate but are always in touch with us and each other.

They reach out for help all the time, because they can.

We still nag; old habits die hard.

Watching your kids find their way never ceases to be a joy, whether it is learning to walk or starting a new job.

There is a pang every time they leave. Every time.

We never stop learning from our kids, and this is one of the most joyous, satisfying, and unexpected aspects of parenthood.

Parents always need community and so little is available to help us through this most challenging stage of parenthood.

Our children's joys give us greater joy than our own, and it's the same for their disappointments and setbacks.

If we are lucky enough to take this parenting journey with another adult, a partner in parenting, it is one of the greatest shared experiences in life.

This generation of kids still want to be with their parents. They enjoy many of the same things and look to their parents to have an active role in their lives. They have not cast off the older generation the way we did when we were their age.

There is no feeling more isolating than the one that comes when your teen is not moving forward with their lives as parents all around you crow about their kids' successes.

Having our kids leave for college is the definition of bittersweet, and it was a change as big in our lives as they day they arrived.

That standing at the sidelines, watching your kid both literally and metaphorically can be one of the great joys in life.

So much we knew about adolescence from having been teens ourselves was obsolete and of no use to us when our kids hit that age.

It's hard to gain perspective in the midst of any meltdown: an infant in the middle of the night or the teen in the middle of an argument.

Despite thinking we could not love our babies any more than we did, we love our sons and daughters more every day. Our kids may have grown less "cute," but they are no less amazing to us.

Our impulse to protect them will never abate; we just get it under control.

We will wage the battle between helping them too little and helping them too much all of our lives.

When we began Grown and Flown, we had no notion of where it would take us or how important it would become to us. From the time our children enter high school until they are truly flown, the stakes in parenting only seem to rise. Our teens are setting the direction for their lives and future happiness, and their problems and decisions become more consequential. As they leave childhood behind, the waters of parenting become murkier than ever. Do we advise or help them? Do we jump in, or do we move silently to the sidelines? Through their teen and young adult years we wrestle with the complex and persistent question of when to step up and when to step back.

Navigating this new terrain, we often wondered if any of the parent monikers—tiger, snowplow, lawn mower, helicopter, or (perhaps our favorite) drone—applied to us. We were bombarded by tales of rampant overparenting, but it seemed to us that the stories always highlight the egregious actions of a few zealous outliers. A recent survey by *The New York Times* showed that somewhere between 4 and 16 percent of parents helped their young adult with contacts to get a job or internship, helped them do a school assignment, or called their employers or college deans. We can cast aspersions, and start throwing labels around, or we can turn this notion on its head and realize that this also means that roughly 90 percent of us are getting this right. We are not ruining an entire generation with our overactive parenting.

However, we are raising a fundamentally different generation, and that has called for a fundamentally different way of parenting. Many of the norms of our own college and teen years no longer apply. This generation is not pushing their parents away, rejecting their familys' values and curtailing their contact with us as they leave home. Those who study family dynamics see a close intertwining of the lives of parents and their older offspring and a desire on both sides for more shared time and a profound connection. As we listened to thousands, and then tens of thousands, of parents describing their most intractable parenting dilemmas, we saw a pattern. Parents are overwhelmingly just trying to find their way, looking for a path that will lead their kids to independence and yet allow them to maintain a deep, loving, enduring closeness with their families.

In setting a course to find answers to our own parenting challenges, along the way we found millions of other parents who were charting a similar path. As we were trying to figure out what our relationships would look like with our teens and young adults, the stories of our community illuminated our path. Parents told us that the teen years are some of the loneliest and most isolated years in parenthood. They felt the keen loss of community that comes with having teens. The kind of support and advice they so valued when their children were younger had faded, just when they needed it most.

Whether your supportive group is two close friends in real life, thousands of friends online, or anything in between, we need counsel, differing opinions, shared wisdom, and the insight that comes from others' experiences. There is nothing more reassuring than hearing someone mention a challenge that your family faces and then watching one parent or hundreds of parents jump into the conversation admitting they too are wrestling with the same issue. Finding that community is a gift and we are grateful for it every day.

Acknowledgments

There are not enough words to adequately thank the contributors to this book. Some of them are well-known writers and experts and may already be familiar to you. Others are wise parents or educators who have much insight to offer. Many have become dear and valued friends. To all, we offer our profound thanks. They have improved *Grown and Flown* beyond measure and made this book possible.

We leaned heavily on Dr. Lisa Damour's friendship and expertise and feel strongly that anyone raising teenage girls should read both of her books, *Untangled* and *Under Pressure*, cover to cover. Her wisdom has helped guide us in writing about some of the most confounding parenting questions, and we could not have done this without her.

We want to thank the educators who have offered so much from their vantage point at the front of the classroom and, in many cases, also as parents of teens or college kids themselves. Dr. Adam Weinberg offers the experience of someone running a top university with the care and understanding we hope all our kids find at their colleges. Others from academia offered their invaluable insights in articles or interviews, and we are grateful to Dr. Randy Diehl (ret., University of Texas, Austin), Dr. Michelle Miller Adams and

Dr. Polly Diven (Grand Valley), Dr. Frances E. Jensen (University of Pennsylvania Medical School), Dr. Alan Schlechter and Daniel Lerner (New York University), Dr. Karen Fingerman (University of Texas, Austin), Dr. Marcy Ferdschneider (Columbia University), Dr. Kenneth Ginsburg (University of Pennsylvania Medical School), Dr. Marshall Duke (Emory University), Dr. Karen Fancher (Duquesne University, Pittsburgh Moms), Dr. Roger Martin (ret., Randolph-Macon College), Dr. Sharon Jacques (ret., psychologist), and three of our beloved high school teachers, Emily Genser, Lori Stratton, and Jess Burnquist.

Among our favorite authors who grace these pages and to whom we offer our heartfelt thanks are Frank Bruni (*New York Times* columnist and author of *Where You Go Is Not Who You'll Be*), Jessica Lahey (educator and author of *The Gift of Failure*), Deborah Copaken (*Ladyparts*, forthcoming), and Rachel Simmons (*Enough As She Is*).

Dr. Adina Keller shared her years of experience caring for teens and young women in her busy medical practice, and we are grateful for her insight.

When we started the Grown and Flown community we met so many wonderful writers who soon became friends. It all started with Sharon Greenthal, who really gave us our first helping hand. Allison Slater Tate has been a huge supporter, advocate, and friend, and we could not be more grateful. Jennifer Breheny Wallace has been the best writing partner, bar none, and a wonderful friend and collaborator. Her journalism truly sets the standard (her essay is adapted from her article in *The Wall Street Journal*).

Many others who we became friends with along the way shared their incredible parenting wisdom and insights on the pages of *Grown and Flown*. We love the words of Melissa Fenton, Marybeth Bock, Tracy Hargen, Christine Burke, Alexandra Rosas, Susan Bonifant, Katie Collins, Marlene Fischer, Marianne Lonsdale, Elizabeth

Spencer, Kari O'Driscoll, Lori Smith, Gretchen Sionkiewicz, and our two youngest writers, Sophie Burton and Mac Stiles.

Grown and Flown is not a two-woman effort. Every day we have the joy of working with talented, dedicated women who bring compassion, sensitivity, and their intellectual talents to this community and website. Susan Dabbar has been our partner in providing unparalleled college admissions expertise. Maureen Stiles (also a writer appearing in this book), Lisa Singelyn, Carolyn Brown, Dee Dee Becker, and Helene Wingens help moderate the Grown and Flown Parents Group, passing the baton between us 24/7, every day of the year. Allison Lancaster was the very first person to bravely jump into this work with us, and she makes every day easier. Lauren Lodder works her magic in letting the world meet our wonderful writers, and she is a joy to work with. Melissa Milsten has walked us through the book publicity process and quickly became someone whose insight and judgment we value immensely. We are grateful to them all.

Theresa Kilman was responsible for every photograph that appeared on Grown and Flown for years. Without her talent the site would have been a dreary place.

The Grown and Flown Parents Group, as of this writing 110,000 strong, has shown us how a community knit together by a common interest lifts its members up with support and care. The group has truly become the heartbeat of Grown and Flown, as parents who would otherwise be strangers share their encouragement, insight, and guidance. If we could say thank you to each and every member, we would. So much of our inspiration came from Janet Ross's first email to us, and we are so happy to see how her family has begun to heal and thrive.

Grown and Flown could not be the site or the community it has become without Helene Wingens's care in every single thing we do. As managing editor, she sets the editorial tone for Grown and Flown and works with all of our writers. In fact, she is herself one of our very best writers. Yet she contributes even much more as our partner, confidante, and friend.

Molly Friedrich led us to publication with perseverance and her vast experience kept us on track all along the way. Nancy Trypuc saw a book in Grown and Flown long before we did, and we will always be grateful for her vision and encouragement. Sarah Murphy has guided us through the writing process, showing patience with us as writers and attention to every word we produced. You hope your editor will be knowledgeable and insightful, and Sarah has been both. But you are truly lucky writers if she is also a teacher, mentor, and advocate. We cannot thank her enough.

When we are newly married or just starting our families, it is easy to feel as though we could not love our partners or babies any more than we do right then. But this life has taught me one of its most profound lessons. As Mark and I shared the decades and our boys became teens and then young men, I learned that we only come to know and love our families better. My heart bursts with gratitude to Sam, Tommy, and Harry for giving me the gift of being their mother. It has been a joy beyond anything I could have imagined. And nothing I have done in my life would have been possible without the endless encouragement of my husband. He is the most optimistic, caring, and joyful person I have ever known, and it has truly been a gift to share this life with him.

From our earliest days as rookie parents, exhausted with little kids, to standing shoulder to shoulder while our eldest and then youngest received their college diplomas, there has never been a single moment when I did not feel loved and supported by you, Mel. I cannot imagine a more patient, generous, and caring husband and father. Walker and Annie, you inspire me, challenge me in all good ways, and I am so grateful to you both for giving me the role in life I cherish most—that of your mother. Mom, at ninety-two, you have been the most amazing mother to Carrie and me, and, as Walker reminds me, "Granny set the bar high" as a grandmother and mother. I aspire to be like you, a living testament to the central theme of this book, "Parenting never ends."

Twenty-Seven Pages to Bookmark in *Grown and Flown*

Grown and Flown Discussion Questions

1. What has changed the most about how teens and parents relate since you were growing up? What has stayed the same?
2. Many students struggle with school-life balance. What are some ways you have helped your teen find balance?
3. To check or not to check: Where do you fall in the debate over grade portals?
4. How have technology and social media affected how you connect and stay connected with your teen?
5. Depression and anxiety have soared among young adults in recent years. How has mental health impacted your teen? How have you approached these conversations with them? What resources have you found to be helpful?
6. How have you approached talking to your teen about love and sex? Do you find that the current social and cultural conversations provide a helpful context for these conversations?
7. "Coming to terms with the fact that our kids are doing just fine, even if they are not given the accolades of a standout, can sometimes be a greater challenge for a parent than for their teen" (page 159). How do you manage your expectations for your teen, academic or otherwise?
8. What are some of the biggest challenges you've faced in staying close with your teen as they grow older and leave home? Where have you had the most success?
9. What are your feelings on location-based tracking apps? Do you consider this a helpful tool or an invasion of privacy? Does your teen feel differently?
10. "While we teach our kids respect for expertise and authority, it is also important for them to understand that no one knows their body and mind better than they do" (page 91). How have you taught your teen to advocate for their own health?

11. "Letting go of our kids has become an almost contentious issue. On one side of the philosophical spectrum are parents who argue that clinging to your teens is a selfish act that impedes their progress toward adulthood. On the other side are parents who argue that we cannot love our kids too much" (page 240). What are your thoughts on how much to stay close to our teens and how much to let go?

12. A four-year college is not the only option post-graduation. What other opportunities have you considered with your teen? How do you feel about those possibilities? How do they feel?

13. "Sadly, college admissions is viewed by many as the ultimate report card on parenting: a single, defining letter grade given at the end of eighteen long years of loving effort" (page 197). How has social pressure surrounding college admissions affected you as a parent? Does your teen have a different perspective? Do you think those cultural pressures and expectations are shifting?

14. "We asked hundreds of parents how they best dealt with their teens going off to college. The number one response was focusing on how happy their kid was in their new environment. The second most popular way to adapt was to focus on the kids who were still living at home" (pages 288–289). How do you think you will deal or how did you deal with your teen going off to college? What would you recommend to other parents going through the same thing?

15. "Students are likelier to have a successful sojourn on campus when they involve themselves in the life of the college—academically, socially, athletically, or in any other constructive manner" (page 324). What are some ways your teen has been able to engage and thrive in college?